NO SUBSTITUTE FOR SUNDAYS

BRETT FAVRE

AND HIS YEAR IN THE HUDDLE
WITH THE NEW YORK JETS

STEVE SERBY

WILEY

John Wiley & Sons, Inc.

Published by John Wiley & Sons, Inc., Hoboken, New Jersey
Published simultaneously in Canada

Library of Congress Cataloging-in-Publication Data:

Serby, Steve.
    No Substitute for Sundays: Brett Favre and His Year in the Huddle with the New York Jets / Steve Serby.
      p. cm.
    Includes index.
    ISBN 978-0-470-46494-6 (cloth)
      1. Favre, Brett.   2. Football players—United States.   3. Quarterbacks (Football)—United States.   I. Title.
GV939.F29S47 2009
796.332092—dc22
[B]

          2009014011

Printed in the United States of America

10 9 8 7 6 5 4 3 2 1

Contents

Opening Rant

By Joe Benigno

It's New Year's Eve, New Year's Day, '64 to '65. The Orange Bowl, between Alabama and Texas. Namath is the quarterback. Ernie Koy, Pete Lammons, Jim Hudson, and George Sauer are all on this Texas team that's playing Namath and Alabama.

My father's telling me about this kid from Alabama. I'm eleven years old.

I'm already big into sports: "I want you to watch this kid from Alabama, he's got bad knees, he's terrific, though. His name is Joe Namath. I want you to watch this game, watch this kid."

Alabama loses 21–17. The game ends with Namath on a fourth-and-goal at the 1-yard line trying a quarterback sneak to win the game and being stopped on the goal line. But from that point on, I loved this guy. He was cool. He had the white shoes. It was obvious his knees were still not 100 percent. The fact that he had been suspended from school for drinking, I kinda thought that was pretty cool. And just the fact that my father was so adamant that "you gotta see this guy play, he's gonna be a big star in the NFL."

And, as things turn out, where does he wind up signing a contract?

Coming to New York to play for the Jets! The two guys I liked the most at that point, before Namath came into my life, were Y. A. Tittle and Jim Taylor. But here he is, in New York, this is my guy, I'm ready. And little did I know the kind of heartbreak I was gonna have from that point on, but that's how I became a Jets fan.

My father had passed away in September of '67; my uncle Charlie took me to a Jets-Broncos game. December of '67 Steve Tensi was the quarterback for the Broncos and Denver beat the Jets 33–24. I did not go to a Jets game in '68. But my uncle and I drove to Philly, 'cause the game was blacked out in New York, to watch the AFL Championship game against the Raiders. It was at some motel that they were having a deal right outside Philly. What I remember most about that game is that Namath throws the interception to George Atkinson that sets up the go-ahead Raiders touchdown at 23–20. And the fact that it took Namath three plays to take the lead after that touchdown. The out to Sauer, the 52-yard bomb to Maynard down the sideline—but when you see replays of it today, I don't know if he actually held on to the ball or not, but nevertheless—52-yard bomb down the sideline to Maynard, and then the touchdown pass to Maynard. And then, of course, Ralph Baker recovered the lateral to Charlie Smith from Lamonica that sealed the win. And being ecstatic. I'm going nuts.

My uncle's telling me on the way back that there's no way they're beating this Colts team, the Colts are gonna kill 'em, look what they just did to Cleveland, they beat 'em 34–0, fuggeddaboudit, you're not winning this game. Be happy today, because two weeks from now you're not gonna be too happy.

I'm a sophomore in high school, and everybody in school is against the Jets in this game. Everybody. "No way they're winning the game, no way." I must have had fifty different bets on the game. All even money! I wasn't even getting the eighteen points. That's how sure I was they were winning this freakin' game. The total was about $200. I had no idea how I was coming up with the money if I lost.

We were living with my grandmother Anna at that time. It was my mother actually watching the game with me, my uncle, her brother, and that was it. I'm a wreck because it's my team with a chance to win, and I'm a wreck, thinking, how am I gonna pay off this money if I don't win this game? How can I possibly ask my mother, after my father had been a big gambler, and was part of the reason he died at a young age, how am I gonna tell my mother, "Mom I need $200 to pay off all these gambling debts I have because I bet on this game?" She had no idea. No clue.

When we had that drive to take the lead 7–0 and Snell goes in for the touchdown, at that point we're up 7–0 at halftime, and you had the big interception already in the end zone off of Mitchell's shoulder pads by Beverley, and then the pick by Jim Hudson right before halftime with the fleaflicker, at that point I'm saying, "You know what? We are gonna win this game." I felt real good at halftime.

I remember at halftime having to get up and go outside—it was January, it was cold—but having to walk around a little bit 'cause I was just flipping out.

The second half comes, 10–0, 13–0, Unitas comes in the game, we get the last interception from Beverley—I'll never forget the interception by Sample and he gets the ball and he taps it on Willie Richardson's head at the goal line. I got a little nervous when Unitas came in. A little nervous. Ultimately, Namath's running off the field with No. 1, and I'm walking around on air. I'm flying around. 'Cause everybody has told me how this isn't happening. I barely slept. I was just watching anything I could watch about it. And was just salivating at the thought of going to school the next day, and walking around like the king of the world. And I did.

When I went into school the next day, I had guys just throwing money at me. They didn't even want to talk to me. Ten dollars? Here's your ten dollars. One guy, who I had a $20 bet with, you know what he does, the bastard? He gives me a bag—what the fuck is this?—$20 in pennies he gave me! Twenty bucks in pennies! I even had bets on how many times Bubba Smith was gonna sack Namath. I said he wouldn't sack him twice. I think he sacked him once.

I thought this was the beginning of a tremendous run.

And remember something too: this is also the beginning of seeing the Mets and the Knicks win within the next year and a half.

The Jets were back in the playoffs the next year against the Chiefs, and I was at that game. I remember begging my mother—this guy had tickets, his family had two tickets, he couldn't go 'cause it was a Saturday. I said, "Look, I want those tickets, how much?" He told me, "I'll charge you sixty apiece." They probably were cheaper than that. I went to my mother and told her I don't want anything for Christmas. I want to go to this freakin' playoff game next Saturday. She says, "Okay," gives me the money, and I bought the tickets.

Brutally cold, and we're playing this great Chiefs team, one of the most underrated Chiefs teams of all time. But, I'll never forget, we're down 6–3, first-and-goal on the 1 . . . two runs by Matt Snell, they stop him. Third-and-goal from the 1, Namath tries a bootleg in, and Buck Buchanan just *blasts* him. Turner kicks a field goal, tied the game at 6–6. And then two plays later Dawson hits Otis Taylor for about 50 yards down the middle against the great Cornell Gordon. And that sets up the touchdown to I believe it was Gloucester Richardson that put 'em ahead 13–6. Fifty seconds to go and the Jets are gonna get the ball again down a touchdown, with good field position at about midfield, and Mike Battle, who all he ever did in his life as a Jet was eat glass and hurdle a guy in the Giants exhibition game when they beat 'em 37–14, fumbling the punt with 53 seconds to go and the Chiefs recovering, and realizing that we lost.

I was devastated. My friend and I took the subway back to the Port Authority to take the bus back to Jersey, and I'll never forget this guy who was just ossified walking next to us, and his friends are propping him up and basically carrying him to the subway. They're telling this guy, "No, no, we lost, we didn't win the game," he's so wrecked he didn't know what the hell happened. "We're out, we lost." I went home and probably cried for a good hour.

When Namath retired, I felt as if Camelot was over.

Lou Holtz—to this day I hate the guy. Hate him. Gutless. Couldn't coach in the NFL, had no business being in the NFL. We moved out to Columbus, 'cause I was married to my first wife at this point, for me to look for a job out there because I had relatives out there. We actually went to Opening Day of '76 against the Browns in Cleveland. We lost 34–17. You knew they weren't a good team, and then I always hated Lou Holtz 'cause he crapped out, he didn't even finish the season. He quits after the next-to-last game of the year.

I was all pumped up again in '81. I'd waited twelve freakin' years to be in the playoffs again, and going to that game, the playoff game against the Bills, and just being freakin' devastated as I walked out of that place. Devastated. Bruce Harper, who every time I see him I remind him, opening kickoff, fumbling it, and Charles Romes is still running with the fuckin' ball. (In '96, I met Bruce for the first time in Miami the Saturday night before a Dolphins game. First thing I say to him: "Bruce, I love ya. But you fumbled that freakin' opening kickoff. I'm waitin' twelve years, Bruce, twelve years I'm waitin' for a damn playoff game. We finally get one, you fumble, opening kickoff, you fumble, Charles Romes is still running." He looks at me, and he says, "Hello to you too." The people we were with explained to him what kind of Jets fan I am and all: "You gotta understand Joe, he's a huge Jet fan.")

It was very hard to deal with no football on Sunday during the strike in '82. We tried to make up for it by playing tackle football on Sunday. I was hoping for a home playoff game, then they don't even show up for that last game against the Chiefs that would have given them a home playoff game, and now we gotta go on the road. Killed the Bengals, the defending AFC champions. Now the next weekend of course they're playing the Raiders on Saturday in the divisional playoff. Well, my wife, that weekend, we were supposed to go up to Great Barrington, Massachusetts, to see the in-laws, which we used to do periodically. So I told her, "I'm not going."

"What do you mean you're not going?"

"I'm not going."

Because I had never seen the Jets win a game up there. Ever. This is too big a game. I'm not goin' because we're gonna lose if we go. And she thinks I'm out of my mind.

We were in the car—this is no lie—in the car, packed up, all right? We get in the car, we're driving, I said, "You know what? I'm not goin'. I don't give a shit what you want to do—I am not going." I got about a mile from the house. I said, "I'm not going, 'cause I know they're gonna lose this game if we go." She goes, "You're out of your mind." I said, "If you want to go, you go. I'm not going." She didn't go. She watched the whole game with me. And the Jets won, of course. Lance Mehl with those two late interceptions to save it after Freeman fumbled it.

My uncle called me and said, "If we win next week, we're all set, we're gonna go to Pasadena and go to the Super Bowl."

Before the game, I had a little ritual I used to go through for road games. For about an hour before the game, I'd go in my room and just put my music on and get myself psyched up. Stones, that kind of stuff. Stuff to get me pumped up. I'd always play "Gimme Shelter." My mother and stepfather coming over to the house, they wanted to watch the game with us, couldn't do it. My stepfather said, "I'm not staying here with him, I can't watch the game with him, he's gonna make me crazy."

I was devastated again by this game. I was also having an affair with a married woman at the time. And that had broken up somewhere in the playoff run, I think before the Raiders game. She couldn't do it anymore because her husband was getting wind of it, and I was married too. So it was a very difficult time 'cause I was going through the Jets disaster and then the fact that I was losing this girlfriend, which I wasn't happy about. It was a tough month and a half after that, recovering. My uncle called me after the game to console me. He said, "You still want to go?" He went. I didn't.

Still, I thought next year was going to be our year. And then I remember, I'm working one day—of course we didn't have talk radio at that time—and one of the guys I'm working with, we're setting up a store 'cause I'm working for White Rose at this point—asks if I heard the news that Walt Michaels had been fired and they hired Joe Walton to be the head coach. I thought Walton was gonna be fine, because Todd's best years were when he was the offensive coordinator.

Drafting O'Brien over Marino in '83 . . . ugh. Set the franchise back ten years. Maybe. I loved Marino at Pitt. Loved him. And I knew he was gonna be a big-time quarterback. There was no doubt in my mind. I had no clue who O'Brien was. Never heard of the guy. And remember calling Sportsphone to find out about the draft, and finding out, "Who did we take? Who is this guy from Cal-Davis? And Marino went afterward to the Dolphins?" And being just totally pissed off. Totally pissed.

But in '86, I was very happy with O'Brien. We started 10–1, and I had visions of a Jets-Giants Super Bowl. I had a very memorable week that year—greatest sports week of my life. I went to the Monday night game, where they beat the Broncos, who were undefeated coming into that game, and we kicked their ass. The following night, I was at Fenway for game 3 of the World Series; my then brother-in-law had season tickets for the Red Sox. Lenny Dykstra leads off with a home run off Oil Can Boyd, we win that game, come back down 2–1. The following Saturday, I'm at the Buckner game at Shea, and the next day, I'm at the Jets-Saints game, where Al Toon has a huge game, kills the Saints, but was also the last game of Lance Mehl's career, he tore his knee up on the artificial turf. And that was the beginning of things going bad now in '86 for the Jets. It becomes like a domino effect. Mehl's out, Klecko's out, Gastineau tears up his knee. And then we go to that freakin' Monday night game in Miami. What a fuckin' disaster. And I've always hated the Dolphins, but after we got the shit beat out of us 45–3 . . . I hated Shula 'cause he didn't put the tarp on the field (the Mud Bowl). He was gonna do whatever he had to do to make sure we didn't win that game. And he still had a hard-on for the Jets for beating him in Super Bowl III. Shula and Marino, I hated 'em.

We stagger into the playoffs—Pat Ryan with the quarterback draw on fourth down, Kevin MacArthur with the big interception right after halftime, runs it in for a touchdown, we kill the Chiefs. Now I'm pumped again. We can beat the Browns the next week in Cleveland.

I have my Jets jersey on, I am pumped for this game. And I'll never forget, when McNeil runs in for the touchdown to make it 20–10 with about five minutes to go, I am like, "We're goin' to Denver for the championship." I figured the Broncos were gonna beat the Patriots the next day, we're gonna be playing Denver. I am ready. We can beat them too. We beat 'em already earlier in the year, and we can beat 'em again. I am pumped.

And when Gastineau hit Bernie Kosar, roughing the passer, I could see it coming. I said, "Don't tell me this is gonna happen to me again. Don't tell me." It was so bad—this is true—I actually, while we were in the first overtime, I actually walked out of the house. I told my friends, "I can't take it, I gotta get outta here. I can't take it." And I'm getting out of the house to go into the car, I was gonna go to a bar 'cause I knew they were gonna lose the game. I said, "I can't watch, I can't deal with it anymore." It's obvious to me, 'cause remember Ryan started that game and got hurt, and O'Brien had to come in, and it was obvious to me that Joe Walton was not gonna let O'Brien do anything to try to win this game. He wasn't throwing the ball, he was being so goddamn conservative I couldn't take it, I'm going freakin' wild.

As Moseley is lining up for what looked to be the game-winning field goal in the first overtime, I get up, I tell my wife, "Look, I can't deal with this, I'm leaving. I'm leaving. I'm going to a fuckin' bar, I can't believe they blew this game, I'm outta here." I'm walking out the door, she runs out and yells, "He missed it, he missed it, come on back, he missed it!" I'm like, "What? It's like a twenty-yard field goal."

"No, he missed it."

So I come back in. I said, "Okay. Maybe the gods are gonna smile on me and we're gonna finally pull this fuckin' game out." Well, we know how it ended. I have to say, without a doubt, the worst loss in the history of the franchise. The Mud Bowl they lost 14–0, they couldn't do anything offensively the whole day. This game they had a 10-fucking-point lead with five minutes to go! How could they blow this game?

I hated Leon Hess. I thought he was the biggest problem why it had been twenty years without a Super Bowl. I thought he was a horrible owner, didn't know what he was doing. We're playing at Giants Stadium, what is this? This is not our home stadium. What is the deal here?

I wasn't upset when they hired Coslet, but I hated him. I thought he was almost as bad as Walton—too conservative, you know, the king (of course Paul Hackett's now the all-time king for this) of it's third-and-5-and-we-throw-a-4-yard pass. That summed up Bruce Coslet.

I didn't have a problem with Pete Carroll either. I thought he got a raw deal after only one year. I thought he got screwed by Leon, who didn't know what the hell he was doing.

The Fake Spike—ugh. I was at the game with my daughter Samantha.

I still blame Boomer for that game. We're up 24 to freakin' 6 in that game, and we're driving again for the clinching touchdown, and he throws a piss pass that Troy Vincent intercepts. Turned the whole game around. I'd seen so many collapses over the years, it became predictable. You *knew* when they were gonna blow a game, I don't care how big the lead was. You knew.

I actually didn't have a big problem with Kotite 'cause I thought he had done a pretty good job in Philadelphia. First game, in Miami, 52–14, I was like, "You gotta be kiddin' me." The worst moment of the year, though, I thought, was the Sam Mills shovel pass with Bubby Brister. That was the highlight of the lowlight of the year. Even after 3–13, I was willing to give him more than one year. I wasn't going nuts yet.

I liked us drafting Keyshawn Johnson. I thought he was gonna be a big-time star, and we needed some identity. I had no problem with O'Donnell, because we needed a quarterback. I knew we were dead on Opening Day of the next season with O'Donnell getting killed in Denver and realizing that we suck. I said, "We gotta get a new coach in here." I wanted a defensive guy in there who had had a history of winning. He could have been a first-time coach. I remember mentioning Joe Greene as a possibility. I liked Barry Alvarez.

I was ecstatic about Parcells. I remember doing a show one night where I was actually fighting with the callers that we were giving up a number one pick or how many picks we gave up to New England. I said, "What are you, crazy? We're getting one of the best coaches there is." And I would say, "And let's take a look at the history of our picks over the years. We're not gonna give up a couple of number ones, a number one, and a number two to get maybe the best coach there is? C'mon."

When Parcells was finally in place, I was certain we were going to the Bowl, finally.

The last game of the '97 season was when it all started coming crashing down for me with Bill. Because I will never forgive him because he was not gonna let Neil O'Donnell be a hero that day.

First of all, what the hell was Ray Lucas doing in the game? This is the question I ask now these years later: if Bill wasn't trying to stick it to O'Donnell in that game, then how come he couldn't wait to put Ray Lucas into that game when he'd never thrown a pass in his NFL career? But then two years later, when Rick Mirer was the quarterback when Vinny went down in '99, why did it take Bill six games to go to freakin' Ray Lucas that year? Somebody give me the answer to that. Is that a fair point to make?

I was in San Francisco for the Garrison Hearst game at the start of the '98 season. I felt good about Glenn Foley, but we didn't win, so I had shades of Browning Nagle in my head. I was thrilled when Vinny took over after Foley got hurt in the Ravens game, and was pissed off that Bill was going back to Foley for that Rams game that they wound up losing. When they signed Vinny, I was against him completely, 'cause I thought he was terrible, all he'd do was throw interceptions, what'd he do in Tampa? But after he won his two starts when Foley was out, I said, "Maybe we got something going here." And I'm saying to myself, "Why is Bill going back to Foley for this game against the Rams, okay?" It didn't make sense to me. Of course, little did I know that Bill was really setting Foley up for the kill in that game, which he did, because Curtis Martin didn't even dress for that game and he didn't even go.

With Vinny in there, we lose only one other game, in Indianapolis, where we always lost, and I'm thinking Super Bowl. I was at the Jacksonville playoff game with my present wife, Terri, and my two daughters, in tickets given to me by Belichick, by the way. Belichick used to listen to my show when he was up in New England with Parcells. I used to go out to Hofstra to see Belichick, and he would talk to me all the time, which pissed off the beat writers, since the Emperor (Parcells) would not let his assistants talk to the media.

I was going to the Super Bowl if we beat the Broncos. I watched that one with my wife. I needed her there. I said, "You gotta be with me for this game." Forget the 10–0 lead we had; my memories of that game are how all of Bill's guys killed me in that game: Byars, Curtis, Dave Meggett. That's the thing that pisses me off the most about that freakin' game. That it was all Bill's Boys. You know, Keith Byars never fumbles, fumbles in this game. Curtis Martin never fumbles, fumbles in this game. Dave Meggett . . . w-what are you doin', not covering the fuckin' kickoff, what's that? What is *that*? So I was already pissed at Bill to begin with, for what happened with the O'Donnell disaster the year before, and now I was even more pissed at the fuckin' guy.

I was very pissed off, because I'm waiting sixteen years to get back in this position again from 1982, I'm all pumped up, I got Parcells as my coach, I figure here we are, we're finally gonna get it done, and we blow it again. And it's all his guys that kill me in this game. I was aggravated. But I reconciled in my mind that Denver was better. I really felt that the Broncos were the better team, they had won the Super Bowl the year before, and I was very excited for the prospect of the following year. And that's how I walked away from that game— stupidly, because I'm an asshole, because I should know better, but because I felt pretty much the same way I felt after the championship game loss to the Dolphins in '82.

I was in the press box for the start of the '99 season. My recollections of that game are, first of all, being pissed off at Curtis Martin for fumbling the ball that wound up tearing Vinny's Achilles'. Vinny goes out of the game—I knew right away he was done for the year, there was no doubt, done for the year. And Parcells pisses me off *again*, because he's gotta show that he's always right, it's always about Bill. Tom Tupa comes in the game, throws two touchdown passes to Keyshawn. *Two!* We got the lead. But Bill has gotta put fuckin' Rick Mirer in the game, excuse my expression, to start the fourth quarter. What are you doin'? And of course he gave the spiel after they blew the game: "Oh well, I didn't want my punter to get hurt." C'mon. C'mon. *C'mon!* The guy was playing terrific, he threw two touchdown passes to Keyshawn. And as it turned out, if we win that game, we would have made the playoffs. I was ticked about Vinny, but I was even more pissed because we still shoulda won the football game. And I was mad at Bill, because why did he put Mirer in the game? And then Mirer threw a big interception that led to the go-ahead, game-winning field goal, whatever it was.

When Bill stepped down, I wasn't that upset. I wanted Bill out now, because I felt that we had underachieved under him, I felt that we should have made the playoffs in '99 and we didn't because of him because he didn't have a backup quarterback for Testaverde. First of all, I was pissed because he blackballed Glenn Foley, and if we would have had Glenn Foley as the backup quarterback that year with Vinny, maybe we wouldn't have been in the same situation we wound up being in. So I had a lot of problems with Parcells, and I wasn't upset that he was out. Don't let the door hit you in the ass on the way out.

I didn't know how good a coach Belichick was gonna be. I still have memories of Cleveland in my mind. Great defensive coordinator, I don't know how good a head coach he is.

I had gotten up, I had not turned the radio on or anything yet, and a friend calls me up and says, "Joe, what happened?"

"Whaddya mean what happened?"

"Belichick resigned."

"What? Whaddya mean resigned?"

So immediately I go to the radio, put it on, and find out HC of the NYJ (head coach of the New York Jets) . . . what the fuck is goin' on here?

So my immediate reaction was, I remember calling (Belichick aide) Berj the next day and saying, "What the fuck's goin' on?"

"Ah, I can't really talk now, in the next few days, you'll see what's going on."

And I remember saying to myself, "This guy left because of fuckin' Bill." He didn't want any part of Bill Parcells.

I wound up hating Al Groh. I blame Al Groh for them not making the playoffs that year. I totally blame him because I think he had a foot out the door before the season was over. I don't buy that, all of a sudden, after they lost that disastrous game, the Sunday, Bloody Sunday Christmas Eve game to the Ravens that cost them the playoff spot, I don't buy that he all of a sudden got a phone call from the athletic director of Virginia and decided to take the job. I say that three weeks before that, when they were 9–4 and then choked the last three games away, I say that he was already gone before the season was over.

So I'm totally pissed off, brutally pissed off after that game. Go to my sister's house, 'cause it's Christmas Eve, to visit. I said, "Ter, I gotta get out, I gotta go see my sister, I'm just totally disgusted." Go there, my brother-in-law's—and I don't drink scotch—and he says, "I got some nice scotch for ya, take this, you'll feel better." So I drink one scotch, drink another one, before you know it I had about three scotches. Get in the car, leave there, go to my grandmother's house. By the time I get to my grandmother's house, I am wasted. Wasted! To make a long story short, my cousin has to drive me home; I could not drive home. Christmas Eve. I walk into the house, I am devastated by this loss, I am trashing everybody. I'm trashing Parcells—how could you do it, how could you trade Keyshawn? I was pissed about the Keyshawn trade, ugh, totally pissed about that. I was pissed at Groh, I was pissed at Parcells, I was pissed at Francesa, I was cursing him out. I was just so pissed. And my wife is like, "Joe, Joe," she thought I was gonna have a heart attack. I was totally out of it, to the point that I wind up puking on the floor. My wife has to undress me and put me in the fuckin' bed. And *then*, somehow, I made the mistake of mentioning to Bernard McGirk what happened that night. So it got onto the Imus show, and it became like a whole controversy with me and Francesa set up by Imus, that it got into the papers because Raissman wound up calling me, asking me, "What's going on with you and Mike? There's a feud, there's this, there's that, what's up?" So a whole controversy was created after that game by Imus because I went home and got smashed 'cause I was so aggravated that they blew that game.

When Herm Edwards was hired, again, okay, fine, a new guy, you're giving him a shot, let me see what he is.

I love Chad. But I don't think they can get to the Super Bowl with Paul Hackett as the coordinator. He's horrible. I sit there and call the plays. I know exactly what he's gonna do.

And I said to Herman on the air, on my show, "Coach, you have seventy-six thousand fans every week at the Meadowlands who would be better offensive coordinators than Paul Hackett." He laughs. He goes, "Joe, you're killin' me."

When Chad broke his wrist in the preseason game against the Giants, I was coming back from Arizona that Saturday night. Did not know that he got hurt until I got off the plane, called in to the station, and Harris Allen, who was doing the updates, told me that Pennington got hurt. I thought he was bullshitting me. That was my reaction. This is the Jets, this is the team I root for.

I am convinced that as long as I am alive, I will never see the Jets in the Super Bowl again.

Benigno thought Pennington—or Clemens—would be his 2008 quarterback when his telephone rang one morning, at 12:30 a.m. It was his buddy Ox from Montvale, New Jersey, a caller to the show.

"We got Favre!" Ox said.

"You're kiddin'," Benigno said.

Ox wasn't kidding.

"It was an upgrade over Chad," Benigno would remember thinking toward the end of the 2007 season. "Maybe we can make some kind of run. Why not? I'll take a shot with Favre for one year."

Preface: Of Lombardi and Legacy

America's fascination with Brett Favre reached epidemic proportions over the offseason.

For those captivated by the NFL's Last Gunslinger, Favre will forever be their Everyman quarterback. For those aghast at his melodramatic sagas of the past two offseasons, he had become Everyman for Himself, a selfish, disingenuous diva toying with the emotions of the football public, threatening to breach a critical trust.

Favre's roller-coaster odyssey, from Green Bay to New York and now—following surgery in May by renowned orthopedist Dr. James Andrew to repair his tattered shoulder—to the Minnesota Vikings has revealed him to be the NFL's Tortured Prince. When he quit the Jets and then began scheming his way back to join an archrival that would have had many Packers fans howling Benedict Brett, Favre's image came under attack:

Hall of Fame Vikings quarterback Fran Tarkenton on Favre's infamous waffling on 790 the Zone in Atlanta: "I think it's despicable. What he put the Packers through last year was not good. Here's an organization that was loyal to him for seventeen, eighteen years, provided stability of organization, provided players. It just wasn't about Brett Favre. In this day and time, we have glorified the Brett Favres of the world so much, they think it's about them. He goes to New York and bombs. He's thirty-nine years old. How would you like Ray Nitschke in his last year [playing for] the Vikings, or I retire, and go play for the Packers? I kind of hope it happens, so he can fail."

Rodney Harrison, who retired from the Patriots and joined NBC, on the *Dan Patrick Show:* "From the players I've talked to, a lot of them seem to think Brett Favre is pretty selfish. Each and every offseason bringing so much attention to himself. It's just really a disappointment to hear that time and time again. If you've been in the league thirteen, fourteen, fifteen years or so, you know if you want to play. The circus shouldn't have to go on for three to four years. It's just a disappointment. Then the media, they're just so caught up and in love with Brett Favre. It's ridiculous because a lot of guys are doing good, positive things in the National Football League and those things keep getting overlooked."

Favre didn't help his cause with Packers fans when he appeared on HBO's *Joe Buck Live* in June and said, "I don't know what to tell them. Vince Lombardi went to the Washington Redskins, and his name's on the trophy. We give that trophy out every year. I don't hear too many people going, 'That damn traitor, he went to Washington.'"

Lombardi had five years left on his Green Bay contract when he left the front office to coach the Redskins, which gave him the ownership interest he had sought from the Packers. Favre might have been better served to read page 460 of David Maraniss's *When Pride Still Mattered:* "Word of Lombardi's departure curdled like sour milk in some parts of America's Dairyland. For all the recognition of what he had brought to Wisconsin, there was an underlying feeling of being jilted. Fans who once saw Lombardi as a symbol of loyalty and discipline now whispered that he was as greedy as anyone else. It was impossible for him to leave without appearing hypocritical. He had railed against Jim Taylor and any player who dared play out his option, he had tried to stop Bill Austin from leaving for another assistant coaching position, he had blasted the players union for splitting player from coach and putting money before team, and now he was breaking a contract, abandoning a struggling team, drawn away by nothing nobler than the scent of more power and money."

"It is true that our hero has treated us rather shabbily at the end. Vince Lombardi has gone off, without asking us about it, and made himself a deal in a foreign land to the east. He has cast us aside, rather roughly at that," wrote Glenn Miller, sports editor of the *Wisconsin State Journal*. "It is probably true that our former idol has been crafty, calculating, even a little deceitful with us."

I asked Vince Lombardi Jr., whether his father might have left the Packers for a division rival such as the Vikings, Bears, or Lions. "I think it would have been a much, much, much tougher call," he said. "It would have taken a lot more thought than going to the Redskins. It certainly would have been a factor. For Brett, it seems to be a factor the other way. It would have been a bigger factor for my dad."

Indeed, exacting revenge on Packers general manager (GM) Ted Thompson, who slammed the door on the Favre Era and traded him to the Jets on August 7, 2008, had been at or near the top of Favre's motivations. His job was handed to Aaron Rodgers, his backup. Lombardi, a victim of burnout, had relinquished the Packers coaching reins a year before leaving for the Redskins to Phil Bengston, his trusted defensive aide.

"I think there were some people who were upset, sure," Lombardi Jr. said. "I don't think it was on a par with people being bent out of shape over Brett."

Asked why that might be, Lombardi Jr. said, "I don't think my dad jacked anybody around. He didn't do a 'maybe-I-will, maybe-I-won't' kind of a thing."

Favre is hardly the first icon who has flip-flopped on retirement (remember Muhammad Ali, Michael Jordan, and Roger Clemens). The money is always a factor, but for Favre, there was no substitute for Sundays.

"He's got every right to do it," Lombardi Jr. said. It's his career, his life, his legacy. The Vikings viewed Favre as the final piece of the puzzle. Of course, so did the 2008 Jets. Favre's meltdown—the deterioration of his arm, the reckless interceptions down the stretch—cost the Jets the playoffs and their head coach, Eric Mangini, after the quarterback they discarded, Dolphin Chad Pennington, marched into Giants Stadium and left as AFC East champion.

This book chronicles Favre's exhilarating and unfulfilling stand as Broadway Brett. It will expose as myth the notion that Favre was an island on the Jets. It will reveal how his teammates saw one Favre at the end—a debilitated shell of his former self—while the club's power brokers apparently saw a different Favre.

The Jets bent over backward to accommodate Favre. But while the swamps of New Jersey are not Times Square, they are not Green Bay or Hattiesburg, Mississippi, either. Minnesota offered Favre a smaller pond for a big fish, a dimmer media spotlight, and an offense he knew like the back of his hand. Favre's friendship with Jets owner Woody Johnson and GM Mike Tannenbaum enabled him to seamlessly secure his release once Mark Sanchez was drafted to become the next franchise quarterback and, hopefully, the next Joe Namath. The Jets never begrudged him scratching his itch elsewhere.

Conflicted as always, Favre agonized over whether to unretire for a second time, and on July 28, 2009, he said good-bye. Again.

"It was the hardest decision I've ever made," Favre told ESPN's Ed Werder. "I didn't feel like physically I could play at a level that was acceptable. I would like to thank everyone, including the Packers, Jets and Vikings—but, most importantly, the fans."

It was the right call. It lasted all of twenty-one days.

"I found out after the surgery that I still have a tear in my rotator cuff," Favre said at his latest introductory press conference. "That scared me. I didn't want to say, 'You know, what if?'"

He should have stayed scared. He will be forty years old by the time he shows up in purple at Lambeau Field on November 1. No quarterback that age has won a Super Bowl; John Elway (at age thirty-eight) is the oldest quarterback to win one, back in 1999, after which he promptly retired.

Time heals all wounds, and one day, when Mike Holmgren, Favre's old Packers coach, is presenting him at the Football Hall of Fame in Canton, the cheeseheads who worshipped him for bringing Titletown back to Green Bay will more readily forgive and forget his sleeping with the enemy.

"If he goes to Minnesota and goes to the Super Bowl, how is he tarnishing his legacy?" asked Patriots tight end Chris Baker, a Jet last season. "I don't think he's concerned about his legacy if he's going to the rival team. . . . He's worried about playing for what he wants to play for, and whatever happens, happens."

It was suggested that Favre would be tarnishing his image with Packers fans.

"They'll get over it," Baker said. "If you, like, truly idolize this guy and everything, if they love him for putting Green Bay back on the map, I think they'll get over it."

Just not right away.

"I think if you're a true Packer fan, you understand," Favre said. "Will it be different? Sure it will. Is it odd, the way it's unfolded? Absolutely. But if you're a true fan, you say, 'You know what? He chose to continue playin', they chose to go in a different direction. It's part of the business. He has to play somewhere if he wants to play.'"

Favre swears that revenge is not his motive. "If it was about revenge, I would have signed on the dotted line the first day, and said, 'We'll worry about the arm, we'll worry about everything else later,'" Favre said. "But it wasn't about that. . . . I'm in it for the right reason, and if people can't understand that, I'm sorry."

Perhaps Favre will defy the odds and have the last laugh. Or perhaps this book will offer a primer on what the Minnesota Vikings and NFL fans should expect from the old gunslinger.

This much is certain: no matter what you think of him, you will watch him.

"There's no substitute for playin' on Sundays," Favre said.

ENTER THE MAN

Joe Namath was my favorite football player in the '60s and early '70s, not so much because he was an antihero at a time when the Vietnam War divided America, but because he could do two things I couldn't: throw long touchdown passes and date beautiful women. The Jets signed Namath out of the University of Alabama on January 2, 1965. By July 19, he was on the cover of *Sports Illustrated*, the lights of Broadway shining in the background. "When Joe Namath walks into a room," Jets owner Sonny Werblin said in the article, "you know he's there. When any other high-priced rookie walks in, he's just a nice-looking young man. It's like Babe Ruth and Lou Gehrig or Mickey Mantle and Roger Maris."

It was Werblin, with his appreciation for show business flair, who stunned the Establishment NFL's St. Louis Cardinals by landing Namath with a $427,000 contract and a Lincoln Continental. On January 12, 1969, Namath led the AFL Jets to a Super Bowl III upset over the NFL Baltimore Colts, who had been 19-point favorites. I was in college then, wearing white shoes in the dead of winter, and

purple tie-dyed jeans, hoping that some bombshell coed might con-
fuse me for Broadway Joe. Here is how the October 16, 1972, *Time*
magazine chronicled the effect Namath had made:

> Sonny Werblin, the Jets' high-rolling owner, got Joe with what
> was until then the biggest salary-cum-bonus offer ever given to
> a football rookie. Namath quickly won the starting assignment
> from Regular Mike Taliaferro and the man who had beaten him
> for the Heisman Trophy, Notre Dame's John Huarte. Before
> Joe, the Jets might as well have been the Pottstown Firebirds
> for all anyone cared about them; their only fans were grumpy
> football buffs who could not afford to pay scalpers' prices for
> scarce New York Giant tickets. Werblin knew what he was
> about; in fact, he was positively prescient. "I don't know how
> to define star quality," he said, "but Joe Namath has it. Few
> do. If we knew what makes it, we would have had 100 Marilyn
> Monroes. But it's something Joe will always have. When he
> walks into a room, it changes." Werblin added in extravagant
> understatement: "Joe likes excitement. He's single and young
> and doesn't have to be at work until noon. You can't ask a man
> like that to sit at home and read a book."

Woody Johnson recently recalled Namath's undeniable *it* factor.
"Almost day one, his personality showed up," the Jets owner said. "I
think the people in New York identified with him immediately. It's
one of those things that it's very hard when you go back and try to
explain what it is about the person that really sets him off and sets
him different. You can't really put your finger on it. We're talking
about Brett Favre—it's the same thing. Even our current quarterback, the one we just drafted [Mark Sanchez], for some reason he's
captured the attention. . . . I don't think it's anything you can put
your finger on. It's not his looks, it's not the fact he's a quarterback
from USC or any of that—it's something else we're talking about."
Namath's final season with the Jets was 1976. By then, his rav-
aged knees had plotted their final acts of betrayal, and he was
forced to ride into the sunset in 1977 with Carroll Rosenbloom's
Los Angeles Rams.

As the 2008 Jets prepared to open their training camp, it marked thirty-two years since they had seen a star of Broadway Joe's magnitude.

Brett Favre wasn't exactly a household name as the 1991 NFL Draft neared. He could throw the ball, all right, but Southern Mississippi was not what anyone would call a football factory. The marquee quarterbacks that year were San Diego State's Dan McGwire, brother of tainted home-run champion Mark McGwire, and USC's Todd Marinovich. McGwire (Seahawks) and Marinovich (Raiders) were the only quarterbacks selected in the first round.

Bruce Coslet had taken over for Joe Walton in 1990 as Jets head coach, and he wanted his own quarterback to groom and eventually replace incumbent Ken O'Brien, who had endured too many beatings behind a series of porous offensive lines. Favre happened to be the target of general manager (GM) Dick Steinberg and right-hand man Ron Wolf when the second round of the 1991 NFL Draft began. They were forced to put on the bravest of faces after the Falcons, with the thirty-third pick, beat the Jets to Favre, whose name was mistakenly pronounced "favor" when the NFL's Don Weiss read his name off the card handed him at draft headquarters. Steinberg and Wolf, with the thirty-fourth pick, settled for Louisville's Browning Nagle, who could throw a ball through a brick wall but proved incapable of learning Coslet's offense.

Maybe the young Favre wouldn't have made it big in New York, because he clashed with Falcons head coach Jerry Glanville and partied and drank his way out of Atlanta after one season on the bench. By this time, there was a new GM in Green Bay who wanted to find out for himself whether Favre could grow up and become a professional quarterback. His name was Ron Wolf. Wolf parted with a first-round draft choice—a bold move questioned by many.

Under the nurturing and guidance of head coach Mike Holmgren, Favre eventually transformed Green Bay into Titletown, U.S.A., once again. If Bart Starr, Vince Lombardi's legendary quarterback, was ice, then Favre was fire. He looked forward to football Sundays the way a little boy looks forward to Christmas mornings. He led the league in the unconventional on the field and in human frailties—most notably an addiction to the painkiller Vicodin—off it. It only added to his charm. Life's vicissitudes would knock him down, and he would always get up, defiant as ever.

But over the last several years, the game had begun to wear on him mentally, as it does for most athletes in the twilight of their careers. The firing of Mike Sherman and the hiring of a new coach, Mike McCarthy, meant Favre would have to master a new offensive system in 2006. The Packers had slipped into mediocrity, and some fans and some in the media began wondering aloud that maybe it was time for Favre to go. Another season would end without a berth in the playoffs, and inevitably send Favre back home to Hattiesburg, Mississippi, pondering retirement.

Favre wanted Packers GM Ted Thompson to consider Steve Mariucci, his old quarterbacks coach, to replace Sherman. His pleas for Thompson to get him help in free agency fell on deaf ears. The possibility that he would be trapped inside a web of rebuilding was distasteful to him. Finally, in April, Favre announced that he would be returning. The Packers, recognizing that it would be folly to turn the team over to novice Aaron Rodgers, welcomed him back with open arms.

The same song and dance unfolded following the 2006 season. The Raiders were shopping disgruntled wide receiver Randy Moss. The Packers and the Patriots were the only suitors. Bill Belichick stole Moss for a fourth-round pick. Favre was livid.

"I know what we could have signed him for," he told Memphis television station WMC-TV at his annual charity golf tournament in Mississippi. "We could have gotten him for less money than New England did. He wanted to play in Green Bay for the amount of money we could have paid him. It [was] well worth the risk.

"The last thing I want to do is start anything," Favre added. "But I think he would have been a great addition. You throw Randy Moss, you throw Donald Driver, and you throw Greg Jennings on the field at the same time, and go three–wide receiver set, I think it's pretty intimidating. And we lost out on that, and it's a shame because I know we could have had him."

Then came the 2007 season.

• • •

No one expected much from the Packers. The Bears, who had lost Super Bowl XLI to Peyton Manning and the Colts, were considered the class of the division. McCarthy, before the season started, had implored Favre to improve his declining completion percentage. In week 2 against the Giants at Giants Stadium, the first evidence that Favre had reinvented himself was there for all to see. He completed his first 14 passes of the second half, threw three touchdown passes, and led the Packers to a 35–13 victory. He passed John Elway as the winningest quarterback in NFL history (149) and was awarded the game ball.

Much to Favre's glee, Jennings had emerged as a vertical threat, and running back Ryan Grant, released by the Giants, was a revelation. Favre broke Dan Marino's record for touchdown passes with a 16-yard slant to Jennings in the first quarter against the Vikings, his 421st, and a congratulatory message from Marino was played on the Metrodome scoreboard.

The Packers finished 13–3. Favre frolicked in the snow and led the Packers to a 42–20 playoff victory over the Seahawks at Lambeau Field. One step from the Super Bowl, in minus-twenty-three windchill temperatures, Favre was outplayed by Eli Manning, and walked off the famed frozen tundra a 23–20 overtime loser.

What appeared to be Favre's last Lambeau Field pass had been the Corey Webster interception in overtime that propelled the Giants to Super Bowl XLII. Cheeseheads held their breath—an annual rite of winter in and around Green Bay—most hoping that Favre would decide to return for another season. "I'm not going to rush to make any quick decision, but I think probably it'll be much quicker than it has been in the past—and people will probably appreciate that," Favre said. "But I'm just going to try to enjoy this season we had as much as I can and try to block this game out. It's going to be very hard. I'm not going to let this game sway my decision one way or another."

But Thompson and McCarthy had decided that it was time for the franchise to move on with Rodgers, who had been Favre's backup from the time he was drafted out of California in the first round in 2005. They had grown weary of Favre's constant waffling on whether he wanted to retire or play. The bottom line, however, was they convinced themselves that it was highly doubtful that Favre, who would be thirty-nine years old in October, could repeat his 2007 magic. Common sense tells us that if they truly believed in Favre, they would have simply told him, "Take as long as you like to make up your mind, the door will always be open for you to return." Instead, they pressed Favre for an answer.

And that answer, given in March, was a sobbing farewell, to Green Bay, to the Packers, to the NFL, to the game he loved. Favre told ESPN's Chris Mortensen:

> I know I can still play, but it's like I told my wife, I'm just tired mentally. I'm just tired. If I felt like coming back—and [wife] Deanna and I talked about this—the only way for me to be successful would be to win a Super Bowl. To go to the Super Bowl and lose, would almost be worse than anything else. Anything less than a Super Bowl win would be unsuccessful. . . . And honestly, the odds of that, they're tough. Those are big shoes for me to fill, and I guess it was a challenge I wasn't up for.

Lawrence Taylor retired from the Giants following the 1993 season because he had lost the will to hit. Phil Simms, on the other hand, was a salary cap victim that spring and pondered signing on with the Bill Belichick Browns—they never struck a deal—because he felt he had more to give.

So, it turned out, did Favre.

The truth of the matter is, Favre first began musing about retirement six years earlier. Here he is in a September 9, 2002, *Sports Illustrated* article: "I think about retirement a heck of a lot more than I used to. I miss home. I know it's nuts, but [Coach] Mike Sherman told us today he was giving us Saturday and Sunday off this week, and the guys were all excited. All I could think was 'I wish I could be on my lawn mower back home.'"

But Favre had played at such a high level in 2007. Former Raiders coach John Madden used to say he never returned to the sidelines because he found that television could replace the void. Bill Parcells, on the other hand, could never replace his addiction to football, to Sundays at 1. He tried television, but it wasn't the same rush, not even close; he craved the competition inside the arena. He quit the Giants and came back; he quit the Jets and came back; he quit the Cowboys and came back.

And sure enough, the whispers started that Favre was having second thoughts about his retirement. At first, he denied there was anything to them. The Packers checked back with him. Their nightmare scenario was Favre changing his mind after they had already pulled the plug on the Favre Era. An April *Los Angeles Times* story indicated that Favre was indeed getting ready to unretire.

And he sure was.

In a three-part interview aired July 14–16, he decided to tell his side of the story to Greta Van Susteren of Fox. He confirmed that he felt pressured to make a decision about retirement at a time too close to the end of the season when he is normally emotionally drained and burned out.

"I'm guilty of one thing," Favre said, "and that's retiring early."

It left the Packers with two choices: accommodate Favre, or stand their ground. They had already tailored their offense to Rodgers, and had drafted Louisville quarterback Brian Brohm in the second round.

John Unitas didn't finish his career in Baltimore; Joe Montana left his heart in San Francisco to play two last years in Kansas City; Namath hobbled off to Los Angeles for one final swan song. So even the great ones don't always get to leave on their own terms. Not everyone gets to play with one team his entire career and go out with back-to-back Super Bowl championships, as John Elway did.

The Packers decided there would be no turning back for them. Rodgers was their story and they were sticking to it.

The Packers wound up offering Favre a $20–$25 million personal services marketing deal if he would stay out of their hair and retire. For a short time—hours more than days—Favre considered it. But he was no mercenary; he was a proud gladiator overwhelmed by his raging competitive juices. Finally, he told the Packers thanks but no thanks. He wanted to play, and he wanted his old job back with the

Pack. He would report to Packers camp. If the Packers wouldn't have him, his desire was to play for the Vikings or the Bears, so he could exact a swift revenge inside the NFC North. Hell hath no fury like a cheesehead scorned—just imagine how Packers Nation would have reacted if Favre led the Vikings to the NFC North title, and perhaps beyond. Before flying from Mississippi to Green Bay, where Favre hoped to force a resolution, he told ESPN, "My intentions have been to play, and with Green Bay. They say no, so I still want to play in this division for obvious reasons, which I made clear to management. If they won't let me play in Green Bay, let me play against you. That's where I am."

The moment of truth was here. Favre had finally been reinstated by NFL commissioner Roger Goodell. He flew into Austin Straubel Airport in Green Bay, even as McCarthy and Thompson were promising nothing more than a backup role behind Rodgers. But all parties knew that the presence of Favre in training camp would cause division within the ranks and be nothing short of a Hall of Fame distraction, a Barnum & Favre Circus. Who was going to blink first? Favre met with McCarthy late into the night, for five and a half hours, as the media waited fruitlessly inside the Packers facility. No verdict was forthcoming. But behind closed doors, McCarthy concluded that the open wounds on both sides were irreparable.

Favre's Packer days were over.

The Jets watched the Favre-Packers impasse with more than a passing curiosity. GM Mike Tannenbaum had been given the green light to open owner Woody Johnson's wallet to the tune of over $140 million over the off-season. The offensive line was an Achilles' heel? Here come Alan Faneca and Damien Woody. Nose tackle was an Achilles' heel? Meet 360-pound Kris Jenkins. Pass rush was a priority? Calvin Pace to the rescue.

One problem—who plays quarterback?

Jets head coach Eric Mangini had announced an open competition between Kellen Clemens, who had finished the 2007 season, and Chad Pennington, who had started it. Neither was an inspiring choice: young Clemens offered little evidence that he was ready for the job, and Pennington's lack of arm strength limited the Jets offense and hardly struck fear into the hearts of defensive coordinators.

There were other considerations: Manning and the Giants had just won Super Bowl XLII and ruined the Patriots' bid for a perfect season in a stirring upset for the ages. The Jets had forever been the second team in town, but now they were a distant second. Following their 10–6 season in 2006 in which the rookie coach was hailed as Mangenius and Pennington, forced to swallow a prohibitive pay cut to stay with the team, fashioned an unlikely personal comeback to notch a surprise playoff berth, the wheels came off and the Jets plummeted to 4–12. Management's ill-advised decision not to pay left guard Pete Kendall money he felt was promised to him resulted in his trade to the Redskins. It sabotaged the offensive line, as well as free agent plum Thomas Jones's chances for a significant season. An icon such as Favre would play very well in the New York tabloids and give the Jets a back-page presence.

Then there were the controversial personal seat licenses (PSLs)— season-ticket holders were about to learn that the cost of being a fan at the new 82,500-seat stadium the Jets will be sharing with the Giants starting in 2010 would be going from expensive to prohibitive and outrageous. Fans with seats in the lower bowl and mezzanine end zones would have to pay from $4,000 to $20,000. Premium seating that will feature climate-controlled lounges would go for as much as $25,000 per seat. While Giants fans in the upper bowl will pay from $1,000 to $5,000 for PSLs, the Jets opted to leave twenty-seven thousand seats in the entire upper level PSL-free.

The Jets and the Giants each hoped to make an estimated $170 million from PSLs; the stadium cost an estimated $1.7 billion.

Signing a popular, legendary quarterback such as Favre would, for those Jets fans immune to the hard-hitting recession, make the prospect of anteing up for the dreaded PSLs slightly more palatable, even though it was highly unlikely that Favre would still be playing when the new stadium opened. It was a move, therefore, that would be a no-brainer both from a football and a business sense.

Woody Johnson had this to say about Favre: "He was always a player that everybody talked about, everybody knew about, including me. He epitomized what is great about NFL football." Because? "Because he played every game . . . he was a competitor . . . you could see his players rallied around him, and he led the team; the quarterback is supposed to be the leader of the team. When you were playing the Green Bay Packers, they were never out of a game, because he could always bring them back."

In the summer of 1991, after graduating from the University of Massachusetts, Tannenbaum volunteered to work for the Pittsfield Mets of the New York Penn League. The following February, Packers GM Ron Wolf traded for Favre.

"How can a smart guy like Ron Wolf give up a first-round draft pick for a guy not playing?" Tannenbaum wondered.

It wasn't long before Tannenbaum, like every other football fan in America, fell in love with Favre's passion, competitiveness, daring, and golden right arm.

The Favre speculation had begun heating up almost immediately after the fortieth and final training camp opened at Hofstra. Favre had already confirmed rumors that he indeed had an itch to return to the Packers. The Packers had been encouraged by Goodell to seek out trade partners. Mangini was asked whether he was interested in adding any veteran quarterbacks to his roster. "I'm really happy with the quarterbacks we have on our roster," he said.

It was either a lie, the truth at the time, or a misdirection play.

ESPN.com was soon reporting that the Jets had received permission to talk to Favre about a possible trade that would make him Broadway Brett. Tannenbaum, indeed, had received a call in his office from Thompson on July 17.

"What did you have in mind, Ted?" Tannenbaum asked.

"I've never been through this before," Thompson said.

"Neither have I," Tannenbaum said.

Tannenbaum later recalled: "He [Thompson] said he had no idea what was gonna happen but we should just stay in touch."

Tannenbaum broached the topic with Johnson and Mangini, and all fully understood that landing Favre was a long shot. "I made a passing comment to both Woody and Eric, but it was just that, like, 'Hey guys,' as oftentimes another club called, just to kinda kick the tires," Tannenbaum recalled.

But Tannenbaum didn't merely want to kick the tires; he wanted to look under the hood, just in case, and the owner was all ears. "If we're truly committed to getting better, which we are, we owe it to ourselves to monitor the situation," Tannenbaum said.

Out of professional courtesy, Tannenbaum addressed the fluid nature of the situation in private with both Pennington and Clemens. "He just let me know exactly what the situation was," Pennington said. "[Tannenbaum said] they received a call. Other than that, my whole focus is on this camp and winning the starting quarterback job. As a player, you never react until it's actually done."

Said Tannenbaum, "I don't try to address every rumor every day with every player, but I did feel that, given the high profile of the Brett Favre name, that this was a unique situation and to be proactive and talk to the players first. Out of respect to the players, I wanted to give them the heads-up and hear it from me."

Tannenbaum told Pennington that Favre was a rare player, and he owed it to the team to check out any and all possibilities. "I don't think he liked it, but he certainly understood," Tannenbaum said.

On July 26, Tannenbaum telephoned Favre rep Bus Cook. "Look," the agent told Tannenbaum, "I don't really know what's gonna happen here either. It's a fluid situation."

Tannenbaum pressed on anyway. He began a player-by-player comparison of the Jets' and Packers' rosters and impressed upon Cook that the Jets would be able to protect Favre with four first-round draft choices on their offensive line.

"Hey, look, I know he may retire, but I think we've got a great story to tell," Tannenbaum told Cook. "He'd like it here."

There would be three or four more conversations between the general managers during the preliminary stages when the Packers debated their Favre crisis internally. "By the seventh day," said Tannenbaum, "I think we had our second conversation and got the sense that, 'You know what? I think they're gonna really consider trading him.'" The calendar had just turned to August. "I kinda really started thinking back to June of '98 with [Vinny] Testaverde. Is this one of those unexpected opportunities?"

Team Tannenbaum shifted into Brett Favre overdrive. "We watched tape on him; we put together a booklet on Brett . . . New York Jet history of points scored over the last ten years . . . the success rate of points scored and playoff correlation," Tannenbaum said. "We made a few calls to people that knew Brett—just try to be prepared."

But Broadway Brett was hardly on the tip of Favre's Cajun tongue. For sixteen years, he had been quarterback of the Green Bay Packers. Suddenly he was ready for a seventeenth.

F-Day—Favre Day—was drawing near.

"No one was walking around the building saying, 'Oh gosh, we're gonna get Brett Favre,'" Tannenbaum said.

Nevertheless, after practice four or five days before F-Day, a critical meeting took place around a table in Tannenbaum's office involving Johnson, Mangini, and offensive coordinator Brian Schottenheimer. The essence of the powwow: could Favre be successful in an unfamiliar offense? "Eric and Brian felt they could tweak things where he could be successful," Tannenbaum said. "Mike McCarthy and Brian are very, very close friends. That relationship helped things from the standpoint we knew what we were getting, what Brett liked and didn't like. That football discussion was really important in terms of me feeling good."

Favre's arrival would mean less sleep for Schottenheimer, but he didn't care. "It was something I was looking forward to," Schottenheimer said.

Schottenheimer saw everything he expected to see while reviewing cut-ups of Favre's 2007 season. "It was a no-brainer when you looked at the film," he said.

Now it was a Monday night in the first week of August—three nights before the preseason opener in Cleveland—and Tannenbaum, in his office at Weeb Ewbank Hall, was on the telephone giving Favre, at home in Hattiesburg, the sales pitch of a lifetime. It lasted twenty minutes.

Tannenbaum: "Look, you won't be practicing in Times Square. The only time you'll see a big building, Brett, is when you want to see one, I promise you. It's not what you think it is. In terms of where we're gonna be is rural New Jersey. There are a lot of good people here . . . we have four first-round picks on the offensive line. . . . You can make your own judgment, I think Green Bay has good skill players, but so do we. I feel like we have a good team . . . you give us an opportunity to make it better. You don't know me, I don't know you, but from everything I understand about you, we have a lot of things in common in terms of how we see building teams, and people, and things like that."

Did Favre, a notorious hunter, have any specific concern at that point? "I think the area, the media, the traffic," Tannenbaum recalled.

Finally, Favre told Tannenbaum, "We'll talk soon."

Indeed, in a November 1997 *Playboy* magazine interview, Favre had expressed reservations about playing in New York.

Playboy: When Atlanta drafted you in 1991, the Jets were poised to take you on the next pick. Would you have liked being Broadway Brett?

Favre: I didn't want to be. You can own New York if you do great, but if you screw up the media and fans will disown you. Atlanta was closer to home. I was relieved to hear, "Atlanta takes Favre with the 33rd pick."

Johnson, no stranger to hunting himself, delivered his pitch the next day from his Manhattan office. Johnson was a supporter of President Bush, and in 1998, he impressed pro-Bush business leaders in Texas by showing up for a bird-hunting trip with a powerful elephant gun he had used to hunt game in Africa. And it just so happened that Johnson had an invaluable bargaining chip in his hip pocket—his six hundred–acre farm compound in Bedminster Township, some ten minutes from Jets headquarters. A veritable Hattiesburg North.

"There's a lot of rural qualities in New Jersey that people just don't know about, or in New York," Johnson would say. "They just don't think it's here."

For Favre, Johnson's compound would indeed serve as Hattiesburg North. It was the perfect escape on Mondays or Tuesdays, the players' day off, and was welcome to all Jets. "He did bow and muskets," Johnson would recall about Favre. "He liked to go by himself. It's great for bird watching—we've had bear there, there's coyotes, all kinds of wildlife . . . turkey . . . deer."

Mangini's pitch came later that night, after 8 p.m., in Tannenbaum's office. "It was really funny," Tannenbaum remembered. "Eric had done a lot of work on hunting . . . he had all sorts of statistics about the state of New Jersey and hunting. He was like a chamber of commerce guy. He had like a script ready. He just ripped it out of his shorts pocket." Tannenbaum was fairly certain that Mangini didn't know the difference between a buck and a lamb. "And here he is, enumerating all these seasons, and licenses, and what you can kill, and where you can kill 'em. He was really on his game." Mangini talked about the team he would be coaching, of course. "We have a lot of good people in the locker room," he told Favre. "We have a lot of people that really care about football. You'll be very comfortable in our locker room."

His pitch lasted an hour. Tannenbaum chimed in with a second pitch that lasted another thirty minutes.

It only helped change the course of NFL, Jets, and Packers history.

It was a two-horse race, but speculation was mounting that the Packers were on the verge of trading Favre to the Bucs. Tampa Bay head coach Jon Gruden, a notorious collector of quarterbacks, wasn't enthralled with incumbent starter Jeff Garcia.

Grant Goetsch, vice president of Wisconsin Aviation, was the pilot on the Wednesday noon flight that took Favre, his wife, and agent from Green Bay back to Hattiesburg-Laurel Regional Airport. "He didn't want to really go to the Jets. . . . The comment was made that he wasn't as interested in the Jets. . . . It was a somber trip," Goetsch told the *Watertown Daily Times*.

The Jets were boarding for their Wednesday Delta charter to Cleveland. "I was standing right outside the gate; I'm like ten feet away from getting on this plane," Tannenbaum said. That's where he answered a cloak-and-dagger call informing him that Favre was leaving Green Bay and flying home to Mississippi. "But Tampa Bay is breathing down his neck," the man said. "If you fly to Cleveland, he could very well be a Buc."

The caller was an anonymous NFL source. "He said Tampa Bay's really trying to put pressure on Green Bay to get a trade done," Tannenbaum recalled. "If you're out of pocket for two hours, this thing could be over."

Tannenbaum knew he had to rush back to Weeb Ewbank Hall and had Casey Lane of the club's operations staff take him there. If worse came to worst, he would fly to Cleveland the next day. "I'll kill myself [if], because I'm on a team charter, we lost out on this trade," he thought. "I told [director of security Steve] Yarnell to tell Eric I wasn't going."

Meghan Gilmore, the Jets media relations coordinator, noticed the empty seat in the first-class cabin. "I had an inkling of what was happening," she said, "because Mike wouldn't miss a plane unless something very important was going on . . . but to know that it was Brett was a shock."

Tannenbaum's office quickly transformed into a beehive of activity. "We had this great ten-page document on all things Brett," Tannenbaum said. "Age of successful quarterbacks . . . his game-by-game breakdown . . . his breakdown by months . . . we had it all flushed out."

Senior director of media relations Bruce Speight, getting ready for the CBS production meeting on the second floor of the Cleveland downtown Marriott, received an e-mail from Tannenbaum at 7:19 p.m.: "I need you to be ready at a moment's notice—be ready."

Speight hadn't noticed Tannenbaum's empty seat on the plane. He thought the general manager was in his hotel suite.

Speight e-mailed back, "Where do you want me positioned?"

Tannenbaum's return e-mail: "I don't know. You there, I'm here."

Speight e-mailed back, "I will come over and wait outside your suite."

Tannenbaum's return e-mail: "Bruce, I'm in Long Island, I didn't get on the plane."

It hit Speight like a Favre fastball between the eyes. "Whoa," he said to himself, "this thing is serious!"

Speight instructed director of media relations David Tratner to skip the production meeting and head to his room to begin working on a press release and alerted senior manager of public and media relations Jared Winley and Gilmore that something might be going down.

There was also the problematic matter of getting Pennington to the airport for the last flight to New York, if need be, at 8:40 p.m. Tannenbaum sent Speight this e-mail at 7:27: "Be on standby—I'll keep you posted," followed by a list of flight time departures from Cleveland to New York.

Speight e-mailed back at 7:29: "To confirm, you want me to pull Chad and get him to the airport."

Tannenbaum's 7:30 e-mail read, "If and when it's necessary be ready; nothing yet, however."

At 8:30 p.m., Speight and his PR staff met in Tratner's room to brainstorm. "Let's plan as if this press conference is going to happen," Speight told them, "because if it doesn't happen, we're fine." So many questions—Could they hold a Brett Favre press conference at the hotel? How much time would the media need to get there? How would they get a big enough Jets backdrop from New York to Cleveland?—so little time, perhaps. At least Tratner had a draft of the press release ready. "If we had to pull the trigger, we could," Speight recalled.

At 10:20, Speight returned to his room. His wife, Angelique, is from Cleveland and was on the trip with their two daughters, Bailey (age nine) and Braedyn (age six). She had been watching the news.

"Babe," she asked him, "is this going to happen? Everybody's talking about it."

"I don't know," Speight said. "He just told me to be ready."

Winley had retired to his room, and gotten into bed. "I remember going back to my room thinking, 'This is not gonna happen,'" he recalled.

The drama had ratcheted up considerably back inside Weeb Ewbank Hall, an ebb and flow of highs and lows that had Tannenbaum and his minions on pins and needles. At one point, Tannenbaum was getting word that Brett the Jet might very well be nothing more than a pipe dream, and he sagged. He called his wife, Michelle.

"It's over," he told her.

She consoled him and said, "Okay, go get a good night's sleep."

Tannenbaum, however, stubbornly forged ahead, seemingly against all odds. It ain't over till it's over. "A couple of hours later, I'm still trying to keep this thing alive," he recalled. "I finally got [Favre's agent] Bus Cook on the phone."

Cook told him, "Right now he feels more comfortable going with Tampa Bay."

"I wanted to know why," Tannenbaum recalled. "He wouldn't tell me why."

But Tannenbaum, negotiations concluded, had an important ally on his side: the Green Bay Packers. "Green Bay wants to wait as long as possible," Tannenbaum recalled. "They prefer to trade him to us." Perfectly logical: the Jets are in the AFC. The Bucs, like the Packers, are in the NFC. "The reason we're still alive is because they want him to come to New York," Tannenbaum added.

Tannenbaum was not about to consummate any blockbuster trade, however, if there was a good chance that Favre would be averse to coming to New York. But Team Favre favored Tampa Bay.

"They have one more vote," Tannenbaum recalled. "They vote for Tampa Bay."

Cook called Tannenbaum back. "Mike," he said, "he does *not* not like you guys. He feels more comfortable in Tampa because of the offense and Jon Gruden."

Cook was noncommittal on the notion of Jet Favre. "I'm not saying he's not coming; I'm not saying he is," the agent said.

It was ten o'clock when Tannenbaum initiated a three-way conversation with Johnson, who was in his Manhattan apartment, and Mangini, in Cleveland. It lasted half an hour. "Look, guys," Tannenbaum said, "what do you want to do here? We could trade for him—I think he's gonna come; he's preferring Tampa Bay over us. We could take a calculated risk—but what happens if he doesn't show up? Do I think he may come? Yeah, I think he may come. I can't promise you that."

Johnson was satisfied that the Jets had done everything in their power to make it happen. "I do remember Eric saying he felt he had a good conversation with Brett and he felt Brett would come as well," Tannenbaum recalled.

Speight was getting restless. He e-mailed Tannenbaum at 10:39: "Your wingman is still on high alert. Any update?"

Seconds later, Tannenbaum e-mailed back: "Hang in there my man."

Tannenbaum, the trade papers on his desk, called Thompson. It was nearing eleven o'clock. "Ted," he said, "we're gonna do it."

"Sign those trade papers right now," Thompson said.

Brett Favre was a Jet. But only if he wanted to be a Jet.

At 11:07, Tannenbaum e-mailed Speight: "We need to speak ASAP."

Speight had closed his eyes; his BlackBerry was next to him in bed. "For whatever reason, it didn't vibrate," he recalled.

At 11:10, his hotel room telephone rang. It was Tannenbaum. "We're still in this thing," he told Speight.

Speight called Tratner. "Let's get back together," he said.

Tannenbaum called Cook. "I got some interesting news for you," he began. "We just traded for a guy named Brett Favre."

Cook was flabbergasted. "You did what? I can't believe you just did that!"

Tannenbaum told him, "We just had to have Brett."

Cook said, "Okay, I'll call you back."

Recalled Tannenbaum, "I'm thinking, 'Oh boy, it's not exactly what I wanted to hear.' I'm walking back and forth in my office: 'Come on, come on, call!' He called back six minutes later. At the time, it felt like six hours."

With Speight, Tratner, Winley, and Gilmore stirring restlessly back in Tratner's room, Speight received another e-mail from Tannenbaum. It was 11:26. It said, "Just be ready to go guys."

Then, at 11:28, Tannenbaum sent out another e-mail to Speight and cc'd Johnson, Mangini, and executive vice president for business operations Matt Higgins: "We have signed trade papers; the agent knows, no reaction from the player yet."

Speight's cell phone rang. It was Tannenbaum. Speight retreated to the privacy of Tratner's bathroom.

"Don't say anything to anybody," Tannenbaum began. "We traded for him, but I haven't talked to him yet. We can't announce anything until I talk to him."

Winley figured it had to be Tannenbaum on the other end. "All I can remember thinking in my head was when [Mets manager] Willie Randolph got fired," Winley said. "All I remember is the visiting team's [the Angels] backdrop at the press conference. I didn't want that to be us. I didn't want a Cleveland Browns backdrop while we're introducing Brett Favre."

Speight emerged from the bathroom.

"What's up?" Tratner asked.

"Mike just gave me an update, but nothing's final yet," Speight said.

Senior director of operations Clay Hampton was mentored by his father, Bill, who started as equipment manager under Weeb Ewbank the year the Jets moved to Shea Stadium (1964) from the Polo Grounds, and stayed thirty-seven years before his retirement. While he was a student at Nassau Community College, the younger Hampton would shuttle the replacement players during the 1987 NFL strike to and from the Long Island Marriott to Weeb Ewbank Hall in a van. He started full-time when Coslet arrived and credits Parcells with teaching him invaluable life lessons about accountability and professionalism.

One day, the Jets were inside the practice bubble when the newly installed coach-to-quarterback communication system went awry.

"Clay!" Parcells roared.

"I'm standing there holding the [first-down] sticks on the other side," Hampton recalled.

"Get your ass over here! What the f—— is wrong with this thing?"

"I don't know, Coach. . . . It's a league-wide problem."

"We're not league-wide! We're the Jets! I want this thing fixed by tomorrow! I don't want to hear this crap!"

Hampton contacted Harvey Shuart, who had installed the system, at Control Dynamics in Philadelphia. "Look, this is Coach Parcells," he said over the telephone. "He wants it fixed. I can't tell him no."

Shuart was there the next day to fix it.

Hampton had flown into Cleveland, as he always does, a day before as the advance man. Now it was 11:30 p.m., half an hour after bed check, when his cell phone rang. It was assistant GM Scott Cohen.

"We could have something going on here," Cohen said. "Just make sure you have your phone on."

Favre learned that he had been traded to the Jets while watching ESPN. "I was laying down with my 9-year-old and was gonna take her to her first day of school the next morning," he told the *Orlando Sentinel* after the season had ended. "I had last say, more or less, but the trigger had been pulled. No matter what Tampa was giving up versus the Jets, I still had final say. I could have said, 'No.' But without coming to me, the Packers just went and made the trade, just agreed to it. Mike Tannenbaum and I have become good friends. He knew that by making that trade there was a chance I could turn it down, but when the trade was made and it was public news without my knowledge, how could I change my mind? There had been enough dirt kicked around up to that point. And it was a tough, tough decision. When that was done for me, without my consent, I was like, 'I'm not going to make things any worse.' And I think that's exactly what the Packers were banking on."

At 11:46, Speight received this e-mail from Tannenbaum: "No word from the Favre camp."

Until Cook called Tannenbaum, and asked, "Okay, what's gonna happen now?"

Tannenbaum: "I'll feel a lot better if I can talk to Brett, even if it's for thirty seconds."

Cook put Tannenbaum on hold and put Favre's wife, Deanna, on the phone.

"Hey, Mike," she said.

Tannenbaum was tickled that he could hear happiness and relief in her voice. "Hey, Deanna," he said, "we're gonna make this work. We couldn't be more excited. It's gonna work out."

Then he asked, "Can I speak to Brett?"

Brett the Jet, that is.

"I think you're gonna be really happy here," Tannenbaum told his new quarterback. "Do you have any concerns?"

"Yeah," Favre said, "what's the dress code on away games?"

"It's usually coat and tie," Tannenbaum said.

"I like to wear camouflage on away games," Favre said.

Tannenbaum was still in make-a-deal mode. "If you can wear camouflage," he said, "are you a Jet?"

"Well, can I wear camouflage?" Favre asked.

"He said yes and I said yes," Tannenbaum recalled.

Favre said yes for two reasons: He had more to give to the game he loves. And he burned to stick it to Thompson for not letting him play for the Vikings and trading him instead to what he considered a veritable football Siberia.

At 12:14 a.m., Tannenbaum sent this joyous e-mail to Speight, and cc'd Johnson, Mangini, and Higgins: "I have great F——G NEWS! CALL ME! GREAT NEWS!!!!!!!!!!!"

There were eleven exclamation points at the end of it.

From his Manhattan apartment, Johnson called Tannenbaum. "I remember the tone of his voice," Johnson recalled. "He was about as keyed up as I've heard him. Mike is normally steady as you go. I was pretty excited as well because I knew that at that point, that year's football would be entirely different."

It was still all so hard to believe. "This is an amazing turn of events," Johnson said, looking back ten months later. "It was off-and-on going for weeks—we don't have him, we do have him, we don't have him, we do have him."

Johnson and Tannenbaum then set up a conference call with their new quarterback.

"I'm happy to be a Jet," Favre said, "and I'll play hard. I can't wait to meet you."

Hampton was in the hotel lobby when Tannenbaum called him, seeking Pennington's room number. But Pennington was on his hotel room telephone when Hampton tried to reach him. "My first reason for contacting him was to try to set up his meeting with Eric," Hampton recalled. So Hampton called vice president of security Yarnell in his hotel room. Yarnell, with Hampton standing alongside him, knocked on Pennington's door, and Pennington answered. He had already been informed by Mangini that the Jets had traded for Favre. "Okay, I'm gonna go up there," Pennington said. "I'm finishing up in here."

Schottenheimer and receiver Laveranues Coles went to Pennington's room for a last heart-to-heart, a poignant good-bye but not au revoir. So did backup quarterbacks Clemens and Brett Ratliff.

Tratner grew up a Jets fan in Oceanside, Long Island, when the New York Sack Exchange was the rage. "Wow," he remembered thinking. "The Jets are getting Brett Favre!"

It was 12:36 a.m. when Tratner sent out the release. "It was surreal," he said.

The release read:

August 7, 2008—The New York Jets have acquired QB Brett Favre from the Green Bay Packers. The announcement was made by Jets General Manager Mike Tannenbaum.

"I am looking forward to seeing Brett Favre in a New York Jets uniform," said Jets Chairman & CEO Woody Johnson. "He represents a significant addition to this franchise, and reflects our commitment to putting the best possible product on the field. Mike Tannenbaum and his football administration staff did a great job of navigating this complex process. I am excited about welcoming Brett, Deanna and their family to the Jets organization."

From her Hofstra dormitory room, intern Christie Upton had called fellow intern Matt Hintz. "Did you see it on ESPN?" she asked.

He had. "We really didn't know what to expect exactly," Upton recalled. "So I remember I changed into a suit real quick."

She met Hintz, clad in his suit and tie, in the hallway of their dormitory. Upton drove them to Weeb Ewbank Hall to record the 1 a.m. Tannenbaum conference call and transcribe it.

At 12:53, Tannenbaum e-mailed Speight: "R we ready to go guys?"

Ready.

"We just felt like this was an opportunity for us to go get someone of Brett's stature and what he's accomplished," Tannenbaum told the media. "Woody, Eric, and I felt that it was in the best interest of the team. When the opportunity presented itself, we felt it was the right move for us to make and we went ahead and did it."

The Jets did it by offering a conditional fourth-round draft choice that would improve to a third-round selection if Favre participated in 50 percent of the plays in 2008. If Favre was on the field for 70 percent of the plays and the Jets made the playoffs, the pick would become a second-round selection. If he played in 80 percent and the Jets made it to the Super Bowl, the Packers would receive a first-round pick. If the Jets traded Favre to the Vikings, they would have to give the Packers three first-round picks. No chance there.

The trade didn't shock Pennington, because any Rhodes Scholar could have read the handwriting on the wall.

"What does that mean for me?" Pennington asked Mangini.

"We're gonna let you become a free agent."

"Why did you want to let me go?"

"We feel like Brett gives us the opportunity to push the ball down the field more and gives us more down-the-field opportunities."

Pennington made no attempt to plead his case. He knew that it was time for him to move on. The conversation would last almost an hour. "Most of it was not about football," Pennington recalled. "It was just about life in general, and what true success is all about."

By that Friday, Pennington had signed a two-year, $11.5 million deal with the Dolphins.

In Green Bay, the Packers released a joint statement from Thompson and Packers president Mark Murphy: "Brett has had a long and storied career in Green Bay, and the Packers owe him a tremendous debt of gratitude for everything he accomplished on the field and for the impact he made in the state. It is with some sadness that we make this announcement, but also with the desire for certainty that will allow us to move the team and organization forward in the most positive way possible."

Hampton had more work to do. It was 1 a.m. "Once we knew the whole thing was gonna occur, it was getting Chad home," Hampton said. "Mike called me and asked me to arrange a private jet for him to get home."

The resourceful Hampton called a man named Bill Harpole, who had worked for the Denver Broncos. "He knew somebody that did charter business out of the Buffalo airport," Hampton said. The company, Prior Aviation, had the private jet ferried over to Cleveland Hopkins.

At 2:25, Speight and his staff edited the transcript of the Tannenbaum conference call.

At 2:46, Speight received an e-mail from assistant GM Cohen: "Any idea what time you would do a press conference with Favre at the stadium? He will get there around 5:30."

At approximately 3 a.m., Hintz and Upton headed over to the soccer field to cut down and roll up the Jets' ten-foot-wide green banner that had served as the backdrop for training camp on-field interviews. "Meghan called us and asked to get the banner because it had to go out to Cleveland for the press conference the next day," Upton said.

"We had to hop the fence first because we didn't have a key to get in the gates," Hintz said. "Had to go get a couple chairs too as well."

Upton held up the light from her cell phone as Hintz, standing on a chair in his suit, snipped off the zip ties one by one with a pair of scissors. The banner spent the night in a media relations office inside Weeb Ewbank Hall.

"That night, probably around eleven-thirty, twelve o'clock, I had booked a car to take her to Mr. Johnson's office in the city," Gilmore said.

At 3:15, Tratner spoke with CBS producer Steve Scheer regarding network requests before and during its telecast.

At 3:22, Speight sent an e-mail to senior director of operations Hampton, asking him to reserve a meeting room at the hotel for a press conference, if the stadium wasn't an option.

Tratner sent out the Tannenbaum transcript at 3:39 a.m.

Tannenbaum had left his office at 2:30 and got to his Roslyn, Long Island, home at 3 a.m. and was up an hour later. "Let's go," he said to his wife. "We're going to Mississippi."

"What do I wear?" Michelle Tannenbaum asked.

"Well, this could be a national story, so . . . ," Tannenbaum told her.

So what did she wear?

"I think she wore a pants suit," Tannenbaum recalled.

What did he wear?

"I wore a blue golf shirt and a blue sport coat."

The Tannenbaums met director of player development Dave Szott at Republic Airport in Farmingdale, Long Island, at 5 a.m. Michelle Tannenbaum was giddy.

"Michelle, what are you doing?" her husband asked.

"I've never been on a private plane before."

"Would you act like you've been there before?" Tannenbaum pleaded.

"I haven't!" she said.

Speight went to bed at 4:15 and was up two hours later. There already was an e-mail from *USA Today*'s Jarrett Bell, one from *Mike & Mike*, and one sent to Tratner from Jay Beberman of Bloomberg Radio at 5:57: "Do you have anyone from the business side who can give us five minutes this morning to discuss Brett Favre? Looking for the sales and marketing angle."

At 8:15, Speight received word that Amy Palcic, then the Browns communications director, had arranged for a press conference to be held in a room at the stadium adjacent to the visiting locker room.

At 8:19, he received this e-mail from Dave Hutchinson of the *Newark Star-Ledger*: "Any way we can get Chad on a conference call?"

• • •

It would be a two-hour flight to Hattiesburg for the Tannenbaums and Szott. Tannenbaum looked over at Michelle, who had a huge grin on her face.

"This sure beats JetBlue," she said.

Tannenbaum slept the whole way. When they landed, before heading over to Cook's office in their limo, the Jets general manager began texting Favre. "And I find out what kind of dip he wanted," Tannenbaum recalled. "He said, 'Copenhagen.' I said, 'Okay.' And then I said, 'The other thing is, after everything we went through, when we meet, I don't want a handshake, I want a hug.'"

Cook drove Tannenbaum in his car to Favre's house; the limo took Michelle and Szott there. Tannenbaum gave Favre—clad in camouflage shorts, a T-shirt, and a hat—the Copenhagen. Now they were getting ready to leave for the first day of the rest of Favre's life.

"Hey, Mike, I just killed this deer, you wanna go see it?" Favre asked.

"Heck no!" Tannenbaum said. "I want to get on the plane and get rollin' here. We got a lot to do."

Pennington and Hampton left the Cleveland Marriott at 9 a.m. An eight- to ten-seat jet with two pilots was waiting for them.

"Thanks for everything," Pennington told Hampton.

"No no no, I'm going with you," Hampton told him. Recalled Hampton, "He didn't say anything, but I could tell he appreciated it."

Hampton has seen plenty of players, their dreams snuffed out, come and go, and now here was one of the true gentlemen of the game, suffering his own cruel fate. "It was kinda awkward," Hampton said.

It was a one-hour flight. During the first part, Pennington reminisced about his Jets career. "We just started talking about all the things that had been accomplished when Chad was here," Hampton said. The conversation shifted away from football the last half of the flight. Pennington had two young sons; Hampton's boy Bryce had turned four in March. "Make sure you take time, especially when you have it, to be with your family," Hampton recalled Pennington telling him.

For a short period, the two fell silent, and Pennington was alone with his thoughts, peering out the window. Hampton wasn't sure whether the former quarterback of the Jets was pensive or just plain tired. But never did he sense devastation. "Through all the stuff he had gone through, something like that, it certainly wasn't gonna rattle him at all."

They landed at Republic Airport in Farmingdale. Lane drove up on the tarmac and picked them up. It was a twenty-minute ride to Weeb Ewbank Hall. Pennington went in to see Ari Nissim, the director of football administration. Then he made the rounds, saying good-bye to some of the same people in the building to whom he would send Omaha Steaks every Christmas. "He had to go to his dorm room to get whatever he had over there; he didn't have much," Hampton said. "I think he came back one last time, and then he got in his pickup truck and drove home" to Melville, Long Island.

At 9:44 a.m., Speight sent out an advisory: the press conference was scheduled for 6 p.m. But then he fielded a call from Tannenbaum from Mississippi that felt like a blow to the solar plexus. "I don't know if we're gonna make six o'clock," Tannenbaum said.

"I was thinking, 'I'm the PR guy that called the press conference for the biggest story of the year so far, and it may not happen," Speight recalled.

As they're getting out of the limo at the Hattiesburg airport, Tannenbaum noticed a bunch of cameras. "Brett, put this on," he said.

It was a Jets hat.

Favre's wife, Deanna, said to him, "You're gonna break a lot of hearts when you get out of this car."

"And he gets out of the car with the Jets hat," Tannenbaum recalled.

Back at Hofstra, meanwhile, the banner had been folded and taped in the locker room, and at around 9 a.m., Upton placed it in a Town Car that drove her to Johnson's 30 Rock Manhattan office. "The driver couldn't help me in with it because he had to stay with the car," Upton said, "so I was walking through the lobby with this huge banner, and kinda shoved it into the elevator. At one point so it wouldn't crease, I had one of the security guards grab the other end so I wouldn't have to fold it in half or anything."

Upton had called Johnson's assistant Laura to let her know that she was ten minutes away. "I dropped it off with the woman at the front desk, because she knew it was coming, they were expecting it," Upton recalled.

The backdrop was given to executive vice president for business operations Higgins, who would take it to Teterboro Airport to join Johnson, Favre, and Tannenbaum on the trip to Cleveland.

Higgins also brought the jersey Favre would hold up at the press conference, compliments of Daisy Johnson, the Jets owner's youngest daughter from his first marriage, who was a marketing intern with the club. "She actually made the first Brett Favre jersey, and she brought it to Woody's office," Higgins said.

Michelle, Deanna, and Szott sat in the back of the plane. "I'm sitting next to Brett, and halfway through the flight my adrenaline runs out," Tannenbaum said. "He's talking to me and I could not keep my eyes open. I'm sitting about a foot away from him."

Tannenbaum was not happy with Tannenbaum. "Boy, I'm really embarrassing the team right now," he thought. "'Mike, way to go, just traded for a freakin' Hall of Fame quarterback—way to represent the organization here.' I'm getting really angry with myself."

Fortunately for him, Favre wasn't getting angry with him. "Am I boring?" he wanted to know.

"I was very apologetic," Tannenbaum recalled.

While Tannenbaum nodded off, a restless Favre was kept awake by the magnitude of it all—the off-the-charts expectations, the New York media, having to learn a new offense on the fly—and it hit him now like a ton of cheeseheads. "Oh no!" he thought. "What am I doing? I'm making a big mistake."

Favre would confide months later to *Sports Illustrated*'s Peter King that Deanna quickly straightened him out. "Hey, whether you're here one year, two years, or five weeks, whatever," she told him, "you've got to be committed."

"He was excited," Szott said, "but I remember a couple of times he said, 'I hope it works out, but you know what? Maybe it won't.'"

Szott told Favre that he admired him for meeting such a huge challenge head-on. "I commend you," Szott told him on the flight, "that you're willing to take this on at this point in your career." Szott was also impressed with the support Deanna Favre offered her husband. "I saw that at every level with her," Szott said.

CNBC, the business channel, went as far as interrupting its programming to show a live shot of Favre and Tannenbaum landing in Morristown, New Jersey. "And now I understand what it's like when the president goes someplace," Tannenbaum said. "It was . . . crazy."

Tannenbaum, Johnson, Szott, and Favre flew from there to the owner's farm. On the way, Favre received a brief aerial tour of the club's spacious new $75 million Atlantic Health Jets Training Center in Florham Park, New Jersey.

"We just drive around the farm and try to get Brett in his comfort zone," Tannenbaum said.

Mission accomplished. This wasn't Times Square after all. "I could just see that he was getting more relaxed," Tannenbaum said. "It wasn't what he thought New Jersey would be."

From there, they took a helicopter to Teterboro Airport to head to Cleveland. But first Higgins called Speight on his cell: Mayor Bloomberg had invited Favre to city hall the next day. "We feel it's right to accept the mayor's invitation," Higgins told Speight.

Higgins broached the subject with Favre on the flight. "This is the mayor of New York; I know you probably don't want to do this, and normally we wouldn't," Higgins told him, "but it is the mayor, and he's been good to the Jets, very supportive of us, and he wants to welcome you."

Higgins recalled: "We said our approach is gonna be for twenty-four hours; we're gonna do the things that you would expect you would do when something like this happens—Brett Favre coming to New York is a big deal—and then we're gonna shut it down entirely."

Favre understood. "That makes a lot of sense," he said.

It was between 4 and 4:30 p.m. when Speight telephoned a contact from the mayor's office to go over the logistics.

Hampton had intended to fly back to Cleveland out of LaGuardia Airport. But Yarnell arranged for him to meet Johnson and his travel group at Teterboro to fly with them on the owner's private jet instead. Lane drove Hampton to Teterboro. Hampton was already on the jet when Johnson and Favre walked on. Hampton had met Favre once at an NFL function, and Favre knew his older brother Bill.

"Do you need anything special in your dorm room?" Hampton asked.

"Just give me a bed and a pillow, and I'm fine," Favre said.

He was adamant about his wardrobe, however. "He said he would not wear a tie, and he would take the fine," Johnson recalled. "He's not wearing a tie, not wearing a sport jacket, period, end of discussion, fine me, do whatever you want, I'm not wearing it."

Higgins asked Favre how he viewed any marketing aspect. "All I want to do is play football," Favre told him.

Speight and Jets director of stadium security Robert Mastroddi were waiting at Cleveland Hopkins International Airport. "I remember a helicopter circling waiting to get a shot of the airplane landing and Favre getting off the plane," Speight said.

Speight shook Favre's hand, and the Jets contingent—Favre, Johnson, Tannenbaum, Higgins, and Speight—hopped into a van for the ten-minute ride to the stadium. "He was excited," Speight said. "He was smiling. I remember him and Mike joking."

They pulled up under the stadium where the buses drop off the visiting teams. The cameras followed Favre to the locker room. "When we were walking through the tunnel, it was like you were walking in with the president," Hampton said. Favre met some of his new teammates and coaches in the locker room. "Man, he's cool," Jerricho Cotchery said to Speight.

Favre walked up behind Nick Mangold, his new center, and introduced himself in vintage Favre fashion. "My hands are gonna be tickling your balls," Favre said, and Mangold laughed.

Favre met Mangini in the head coach's office and the two chatted privately for a short while. Johnson was in there with them when Schottenheimer walked in. "I could tell he was a little bit nervous," Schottenheimer said. Schottenheimer moved swiftly to put Favre at ease.

"Tell me a little bit about this digital system, how it works," Favre said to Schottenheimer.

"We have code words. . . . You and I can speak the same language," Schottenheimer told him. "There'll be a little translating going on, but this thing is flexible enough."

Added Schottenheimer: "We changed the code words and names of some of our plays to things he called in Green Bay. The hard part was getting everybody on the same page in terms of the adjustments."

Favre then shook hands with the rest of the media relations staff. One of the PR people, as part of the standard prep work prior to press sessions, lobbed this one at the owner: "Is this a marketing ploy?" At which point Favre, wearing his "I'm here to play football" look, said, "Geez, I hope not!" Tratner had what he figured was a likely question from the New York media for the most famous Jets quarterback since Namath. "I said, 'These guys are probably gonna look for some sort of guarantee,'" Tratner recalled. Kickoff was at 7:30. "I'll try to limit it to twenty minutes," Speight said.

A makeshift dais was set up in a packed room—150 media members—in the bowels of Cleveland Browns Stadium for the momentous press conference. "So as we were holding back a crowd so Brett could walk through, Jared was sprinting the banner down the tunnel so we could put it up on the wall before the press conference started," Gilmore said.

Winley recalled, "I met [Higgins] as he's coming off the van, and I take the backdrop from him and run it into the room where the press conference was at. I had it over my shoulder; I didn't know how much time was between him getting out of the van and him sitting in front of the media. We wanted to get it up immediately."

Winley, with the NFL Network's live cameras on him, helped Gilmore and a small army of assistants tape the banner that Hintz and Upton had retrieved from Hofstra. "We got it up in five minutes," Winley said. "[The press conference] didn't start for another ten or fifteen minutes."

Favre sat between Tannenbaum and Johnson. Favre held up his green Jets No. 4 jersey and cameras flashed. A beaming Johnson spoke first. "Sorry we're a little bit late here, and I want to apologize for the interview that I did the other day, where you asked me what was going on, I couldn't give you the answer. But now you can see there is an answer to what the questions were last week, and we got Brett Favre as a new member of the Jets. We went through this process for the same reason we've been running the team all along with Mike and Eric—to try and improve this team each and every year. And I just want to say that it was difficult with Chad, particularly, because Chad kinda came in the same time I did [2000]. And we owe Chad Pennington a big voice and . . . a lot of gratitude for the dedication and for his dogged, team-oriented, persistent . . . even in light of all of the adversity that we had in some years. That he was always in it, always a good teammate. So, thanks to Chad.

"But today we're here to talk about what we're doing going forward. So I'd like to toss it over to Mike, and he can describe what happened in the last twenty-four hours."

Tannenbaum is a bright (cum laude, Tulane Law School), pleasant man who learned his craft at the feet of Parcells. "I've worked very hard to develop multiple skill sets," he said. The biggest lesson he had learned from Parcells? "Drive the train. If you gotta run over the league office, if you gotta run over the media, if you gotta run over the other thirty-one teams . . . just drive the train, do what you think is in the best interest of your organization every single day."

When he was promoted to replace Terry Bradway not long after landing Mangini, Tannenbaum had informed the media that he would try to help them do their jobs. Mangini, who was schooled under both Parcells and Belichick, had said the same thing at his introductory press conference.

What that turned out to mean was the Jets Wonder Boys would be eager to regale anyone and everyone with tales about their respective battles of the bulge and budding fatherhood, but once the subject turned to the football team, you didn't get much more than name, rank, serial number.

"Thanks, Woody," Tannenbaum began. "I don't have too much more to add since the last time we spoke. I don't think I've gone to sleep since that time. It is a bittersweet moment . . . we have released Chad; I have spoken to him, Eric's spoken to him, Mr. Johnson's spoken to him, and again, just on the record, I have all the respect in the world for Chad for what he's done on the field as well as off the field. He's a good player, he's a great person, and he's done a lot of great things for our organization, and I wish him nothing but the best. And fundamentally, the decision was made between Eric, myself, and Mr. Johnson from a standpoint that, when this opportunity presented itself, we felt we were getting good play at the quarterback position, we felt this was an opportunity to improve upon that, and that's why we went ahead and made the decision. We did a voluminous amount of research on not only Brett as a player but also as a person, and making sure that we thought he can fit in in the locker room, and we were extremely comfortable not just [with] what he did on the field but as importantly what he is off the field and what he stands for, so, we're happy, we're excited, we're really glad that he's a member of this team and I think Brett, I can say this, on his behalf—that I think we're all looking forward to getting past this stuff and going out there and playing some football."

The cameras kept flashing. It was Favre's turn.

"Yeah, thank you, Mike, Mr. Johnson. The last twenty-four hours have been crazy. Really, the last two weeks, three weeks, this whole off-season has been bizarre . . . whatever you want to call it. But it is what it is. I'm a member of the Jets; I'm excited about the opportunity." He turned to Tannenbaum and smiled. "No one works as hard as this man right here. I was told by numerous people to at least talk to Mike over the last month, and as I told him today, I said, 'The only reason.' . . . And I wouldn't talk to him up until maybe a little longer than twenty-four hours ago. Because I knew I would be convinced once I talked to him."

• • •

It was time for Favre to walk onto the field. Gilmore was in the entourage that accompanied him. "It's very rare to be in an opposing team's stadium and they actually cheer for your player to come on the field," Gilmore said.

Favre wore khaki shorts, a white cap, and a white Jets T-shirt on the sideline. He wore a headset and carried a play sheet. CBS never took its eye off him. There's Favre tossing the ball. There's Favre cutting up with teammates. There's Favre chatting up Kellen Clemens and Brett Ratliff. Following a lightning delay, equipment assistant Cortez Robinson became the first Jet to catch a Brett Favre pass. "I just happened to have a couple of footballs, and he kinda signaled," Robinson said. Favre had made a throwing signal with his right hand. "Didn't expect the ball to come that fast," Robinson said. They stood fifteen yards apart. Their catch lasted ten minutes. "Actually had a bruise on my [right] thumb after I was done; the guys were giving me crap, but it was fun," Robinson said.

It could have been worse, actually. "Oh, I wasn't throwin' it that hard," Favre told Robinson. "Trust me—you woulda felt it if I was throwin' it hard."

To Robinson's credit, he didn't drop a single throw. And he didn't even wear gloves. "I didn't want to embarrass myself in front of Cleveland Browns fans, and television," he said.

Never in his wildest imagination could he have envisioned catching passes from Brett Favre. "Growing up in Minnesota, I was not a Packers fan at all, and he was like the face of the Packers so . . . I didn't really like the guy," Robinson said. "But from the first time I met him, and playing catch with him and everything, my mind changed, and he was just like this unbelievable guy and great personality."

During the game, Palcic asked Winley for a favor. "[Browns quarterback] Derek Anderson's a big Brett Favre fan," she said. "He wants to know if he can meet him at some point." Winley said, "I'll see what I can do." He quickly learned that this was more the rule than the exception after games. "Some random players from other teams would be standing around him trying to say hello to him," he recalled.

The game was over now. Tannenbaum, Johnson, Higgins, and Favre flew to New York on the owner's private jet and stayed the night in Manhattan.

"I thought to myself, 'There is nothing to prove,'" Favre said. "'Go in there, have fun, do everything you can do. You don't have to show anybody anything.'"

"The whole way back he was talking football—he was talking plays and he was talking strategies, what he had done at Green Bay basically play-wise," Johnson recalled. "Was he dying to be a Jet and to play for the New York Jets? I didn't get that feeling. He would say, 'I'm older, I'm not the player I was ten years ago'—all the stuff that anybody would know. But he was trying to paint, maybe, a more realistic picture of . . . but on the other hand, 'I'm still Brett Favre. I've still got a gun.' He didn't say that. What my read was, he wasn't overselling . . . which makes it more intriguing. Maybe that's why the public focuses on this guy."

There was no rest for the weary that next day, Friday. Favre was escorted to city hall by Johnson and Tannenbaum to meet Mayor Michael Bloomberg. "Time will tell, but I don't want to say, 'Be patient,'" Favre said. "I have to get a lot done in a short amount of time. They wouldn't have signed me if they didn't think I could do that."

"The legendary No. 4 has now become Jet Favre," Mayor Bloomberg said, "and we're delighted to welcome him to city hall." He presented Favre with a large "Broadway" street sign, several cheesecakes from Brooklyn's legendary Junior's, and a MetroCard with $4 fare on it. "If you had picked a number higher, you would've gotten more money on your MetroCard," Bloomberg cracked. The mayor also gave the quarterback a copy of his book and an empty key ring. "You win the Super Bowl and I promise you will get a key," he said.

Favre would reveal weeks later that Tannenbaum had hoped to get a two-year commitment from him. "I said, 'Mike, let me give you the best year I can possibly give you and let's go from there,'" Favre recalled.

Unlike Namath before Super Bowl III, Favre would make no guarantees, either about the 2008 season or beyond, that day at city hall.

"Let's enjoy this year," he said. "The future is now. I don't have seven-teen more years to play, I don't think. I want to give the New York Jets and the people of this city the best year possible. Believe me."

Everyone *wanted* to believe him.

After the meeting with the mayor was over, Johnson arrranged for a helicopter to take Favre from lower Manhattan to Hofstra.

Now, back at Hofstra, it was time to force-feed Favre. "We laid out the passes from all of the previous seven installations and went through them one by one," Schottenheimer said. "Do you like this? Do you not like this? What do you think about this?" Favre would ask: "Why do you call it this? Why do you call it that?" Or he would say: "Yeah, I'll try that." Or: "No, I haven't had a lot of success with that." Or: "Look, I'll try anything once."

One specific play installed for Favre was called Fox Z X & Y Hook. "It's a West Coast staple—he can throw it with his eyes closed," Schottenheimer said. The outside receiver weak runs a twelve-yard curl route out of a pro set—two backs, one tight end. The tight end runs about an eight-yard curl route. The Z receiver runs a deep post. The fullback runs to the left, the halfback to the right. "If the safety sits down on the tight end, you have a chance to throw the ball over the top," Schottenheimer said.

Favre Fever was rampant. Over the first twelve hours since the signing was announced, more Favre jerseys had sold than any other Jets jersey for the entire year to that point. A record thirty-eight hundred Reebok Favre jerseys sold within the first twenty-four hours. A day after the trade, StubHub brokered more than $1 million in Jets ticket sales. The Jets soared onto the front pages of the tabloids. Even former New York mayor Ed Koch, eighty-four years young, sounded swept away. "For an old man, he's doing pretty good," Koch was quoted as saying in the *Los Angeles Times*. "Because he's past his prime, he's made old men all over the city feel good. In that way, he's really helped us. There are a lot of old men in this city—of which I'm one."

Gilmore's computer nearly exploded. "I had hundreds of e-mails; I couldn't get to them all for a week or so," she said. "It was at the point where the interns were checking Bruce's voice mail because it kept getting full faster than he could check it."

By now, Schottenheimer had spoken with McCarthy, who happened to be one of the groomsmen at Schottenheimer's wedding. "You're really gonna love the guy," McCarthy told Schottenheimer.

THE FIRST DRAW

Preseason

To better understand what Favre meant to Jets Nation, you have to review the litany of quarterbacks who, to be kind, could not carry the torch from Namath and light a fire under the franchise.

Richard Todd was the first quarterback of the post–Namath Era. He came from Alabama, same as Namath. Unfortunately, that was where the similarities ended. The Jets made Todd the sixth pick of the 1976 draft, and Walt Michaels, the new head coach in 1977, anointed him the starter. Todd could throw a football, but he simply did not have the temperament for the New York market. During one game at Shea Stadium, the Jets' home until they moved into Giants Stadium in 1984, Todd flipped the bird to the boobirds. In an attempt to make light of his low popularity, he showed up one day at practice with the words BOO TODD etched on the back of his jersey.

He went as far as assaulting yours truly. Here's what happened:

I had written a column under a headline that read: WITH TODD AT HELM, JETS WILL NEVER WIN SUPER BOWL. For Todd, tired of reading my campaign to unseat him with backup quarterback Matt Robinson, this was the last straw. For six weeks or so, aware that he was livid, I had limited one-on-one contact with him. Finally, on November 4, 1981, a Wednesday before a game in Baltimore, I attempted to make peace in the locker room before practice. Except Todd wasn't in the mood. We wound up engaging in an expletive-filled exchange, and as I stood maybe ten yards from his locker, my notebook at my side, a sense of impending doom came over me. Something told me an attack was imminent. And here he came, charging at me, grabbing

my neck with his right hand and smashing my head into the top of a locker across from his that belonged to a wide receiver named Bobby Jones. I slumped to the bottom of the locker, and the next thing I remember is defensive end Mark Gastineau standing over me, telling me it appeared that my nose had been broken. Thankfully, it wasn't, but I was shaken up, driven to a nearby hospital for examination, and removed from the beat for two weeks. That Sunday I was home listening to Bob Costas (pro-Serby) and Bob Trumpy (pro-Todd) debate Serby versus Todd on television during a Jets blowout fashioned by Todd. We shook hands before the season ended.

Todd piloted the Jets to the playoffs that year, and again the next, but it ended horrifically for him in the infamous Mud Bowl in Miami, when he threw five interceptions, no fewer than three to linebacker A. J. Duhe, in a devastating 14–0 loss that turned out to be the last game of the Michaels Era. Todd lasted one more season before Walton, the man who succeeded Michaels, traded him away to the Saints.

The new golden boy was Ken O'Brien.

The Jets owned the twenty-fourth pick in the first round of the 1983 draft. Four quarterbacks had already gone off the board by the time it was their turn to pick—Elway (Colts), Todd Blackledge (Chiefs), Jim Kelly (Bills), and Tony Eason (Patriots). Walton, getting ready for his rookie season on the sidelines, had been the offensive coordinator the day Todd sank in the mud. He craved a new quarterback, one he could mold. When the Jets were on the clock, Dan Marino from the University of Pittsburgh was still available. The Jets, concerned about unsubstantiated drug rumors about Marino, as well as how well he would be able to master Walton's offense, passed. Instead, they shocked the football world and Jets draftniks with the selection of O'Brien, a relatively unknown quarterback from California-Davis.

Jets player personnel director Mike Hickey was certain he had scored a coup with O'Brien, who was tall, dark, handsome, and bright. Several years ago, then Dolphins coach Don Shula was asked what his reaction was when the Jets left Marino for him. Shula beamed and said, "Yay!"

O'Brien had his moments, just not nearly as many as Marino, a first-ballot Hall of Famer who did not win a Super Bowl but was

Namath South nevertheless. O'Brien, behind a sieve of an offensive line, was eventually beaten to a pulp, and when Walton was finally fired by owner Leon Hess, new coach Bruce Coslet was soon looking for his own quarterback.

Hess had hired Steinberg, the football executive the Jets had been lacking during the Walton years, as general manager. Before the 1991 draft, remember, Steinberg and Wolf targeted a Southern Mississippi gunslinger named Brett Favre. But the Atlanta Falcons traded ahead of them to draft Favre. The Jets settled for Browning Nagle, who owned a Browning rifle for a right arm but little else required to play quarterback in the NFL. Coslet, considered an offensive guru with the Bengals, tried to force-feed Nagle, but before long it became obvious to him that it would never work.

Enter Boomer Esiason.

Esiason was, at the very least, a big name who brought some credibility with him. The 1988 NFL MVP had taken the Bengals to Super Bowl XXIII, only to lose to Joe Montana's last-minute heroics. Coslet had been his offensive coordinator in the late '80s. Esiason grew up in East Islip, Long Island, and his proud father, Norman, would watch the Jets practice from an easy chair overlooking what must have been his own personal field of dreams. Esiason was a media darling, glib and colorful and insightful, and a natural leader. There was one problem: he was thirty-two years old, and a shell of his former MVP self. Actually, there were two problems: his offensive line gave him no chance. So Esiason couldn't save his old Cincinnati friend.

Hess turned to new head coach Rich Kotite, a dese-and-dose guy and former overachieving tight end from Staten Island who lived out a dream playing for the Giants in 1967 and again from '69 to '72. Kotite had enjoyed a modicum of success with the Eagles (36–28, one playoff victory) but was hardly an inspiring choice, considering his 1994 Eagles had lost their last seven games. Following a 3–13 season on the Jets sideline, Hess, eager for his favorite-son head coach to succeed, apparently at all costs, opened his checkbook for team president Steve Gutman to pursue Steelers quarterback Neil O'Donnell.

O'Donnell had taken the Steelers to Super Bowl XXX, even though skeptics claimed that the Steelers had taken O'Donnell there.

He threw two interceptions to cornerback Larry Brown in a 27–17 loss to the Cowboys, but he was considered a significant upgrade over Esiason. The Jets were offering a blockbuster five-year, $25 million free agent contract; the Steelers offered $1.25 million a year less, but the comfort of home and a quality team and coach (Bill Cowher) as well. That O'Donnell was as conflicted as he was—he deliberated long and hard—should have set off alarm bells. Finally, with agent Leigh Steinberg pushing for a presence in the New York market, O'Donnell toasted with a cranberry and vodka at his New Jersey home and went for the big bucks.

It proved to be a disaster.

O'Donnell came across as an introvert. He tore a calf muscle in warm-ups before one game just as he was preparing to return from a shoulder separation. He lacked strong leadership skills . . . he was an Invisible Man during the rehabilitation process. He was the anti–Phil Simms. Kotite was mercifully gone after a 1–15 nightmare.

The new Jets coach in 1997 was Bill Parcells, who maneuvered his way out of Robert Kraft's New England into the waiting arms of Hess, who was eighty-three years old and desperate for a savior. Parcells walked into an immediate controversy when wide receiver Keyshawn Johnson, the first overall pick of the 1996 draft, referred to O'Donnell as a "stiff puppet" and receiver Wayne Chrebet as a mascot in his book *Just Give Me the Damn Ball*.

Parcells put out the fire but became infatuated with backup quarterback Glenn Foley, a firebrand with freckles and a gunslinger's mentality. Foley got his feet wet as Instant Offense off the bench, and Parcells rode him and O'Donnell to a 9–6 record heading into the season finale against the Barry Sanders Lions at the Silverdome. A win and the Jets were in the playoffs. A loss and they were out. Parcells invited disaster by inserting inexperienced backup quarterback Ray Lucas to throw one pass and halfback Leon Johnson to throw another. Both were intercepted. Bottom line: if he had complete faith in his quarterback, he never would have taken the ball out of O'Donnell's hands.

The O'Donnell Era was over. Foley was going to get his shot. But Parcells wasn't certain Foley could handle the burdens of the job, so he signed Vinny Testaverde as insurance in the off-season. Unlike Foley, Testaverde was as big and strong as a redwood, with an arm that could make every throw. Unlike Foley, Testaverde had been through the wars. In fact, playing for Belichick in Cleveland, he had beaten Parcells's Patriots in a 1994 playoff game.

Foley proved too brittle. He suffered a rib injury, and then, fearing that his once-in-a-lifetime opportunity was in severe jeopardy, that the skids were being greased for him, blurted his disenchantment to the media, a no-no in Parcells's world. Testaverde started, and won, and soon the job was his. Parcells and offensive coordinator Dan Henning kept the reins on Testaverde, who had a penchant for careless errors. Once they saw that he could manage the game, Foley became an afterthought.

The team responded to Testaverde, who developed a wondrous chemistry with Johnson as well as with Chrebet, and thereby opened up the running game for Curtis Martin. Testaverde, who grew up a Namath fan in Elmont, Long Island, became the hometown hero. He was thirty minutes from taking the Jets back to the Super Bowl, before Elway and the Broncos shattered the Mile High dream in Denver.

Parcells was confident that 1999 would be the year, finally. But on a picture-perfect Opening Day, under blue skies and warm, bright sunshine, Testaverde crumpled to the turf, his Achilles' ruptured, and the Jets season along with it.

Parcells quit as coach after the season but stayed on as general manager, and after designated successor Bill Belichick told the Jets to Take This Job and Shove It, he convinced new owner Woody Johnson to hire his longtime aide Al Groh to replace Belichick. Parcells, fearing that Keyshawn Johnson would stage a disruptive holdout, traded him to the Bucs, arming himself with four number one picks in the 2000 draft. One of those picks would be a quarterback out of Marshall named Chad Pennington.

Testaverde fashioned a gallant comeback in 2000 but cost the Jets a playoff berth on the last Sunday of the season in Baltimore when he threw three interceptions. Herm Edwards inherited Testaverde in 2001 when Groh bolted for the Virginia job. As Testaverde floundered out of the gate in 2002, Edwards gave the ball to Pennington, who had been learning how to be a professional from Testaverde for over two years. Pennington showed up as a wunderkind, a natural who was so accurate he invited comparisons to Montana. He was the toast of the town as he carried the Jets to an unexpected playoff berth.

But he couldn't escape the injury bug. Valiantly, he led the Jets to the brink of the 2004 AFC Championship game—with a torn right rotator cuff the club kept secret. Doug Brien's missed 43-yard field goal at the end of regulation against the Steelers at Hines Field cost the Jets a shot at the Patriots.

Pennington was never the same after the surgery. And yet, against all odds, he wrote that heartwarming Comeback Kid story in 2006 and helped Mangini to the playoffs. It turned out to be his last hurrah as a Jet. He sustained an ankle injury in the 2007 opener against the Patriots, further weakening the velocity on his ball. Defenses ganged up on Thomas Jones and Leon Washington with eight men in the box and dared Pennington to beat them, and he could not. The Jets were 1–7 when Mangini turned to Kellen Clemens.

Clemens had thrown only one pass in his rookie season. Mangini and Tannenbaum had drafted him in the second round in 2006, passing on first-rounders Vince Young (Titans), Matt Leinart (Cardinals), and Jay Cutler (Broncos). He was the new regime's Quarterback of the Future.

One problem: the future wasn't now.

Favre was now.

"If there's a guy who can change a team around and get a team to contend for a Super Bowl, it would be Brett," Dan Marino said.

"I thought the Jets were gonna be a playoff team this year with Chad Pennington at quarterback," Phil Simms said. "So you bring in Brett Favre, that's not gonna change my mind any. I think it's an extremely bold move by the Jets, and they've made a lot of bold moves this off-season, and when you do all this, you do it for a reason—you want immediate, immediate results."

Among NFL observers, it was a virtual landslide—Favre could still play at a high level.

"For [Favre] to get to the NFC Championship game and play the way he played—he broke all my records last year—he looked healthy, he's got a lot of football left in him," Marino said.

"I thought he played one of the better seasons of his whole career last year," Simms said. "I thought he was steady for the whole year . . . at times it was great . . . and very few down moments."

Simms was nearing the end of his career when Favre was beginning his. "The first time I ever saw him play," Simms said, "I knew that his ability to throw the ball was something special. He's not the most nimble, but his arm flexibility and his ability to throw from every single angle— low, high, off-balance, running to his right, running to his left—is what gives him a dimension very few quarterbacks in history have had."

Marino was asked for one Favre memory. "Him playing that Monday night game [against the Raiders] after his dad passed away really showed his character and what kind of mental toughness the guy has and the kind of football player he is and how much he loves the game," he said. Marino felt that Favre had a chance to recharge his batteries with a new team. "To me it's sad he can't finish his career in Green Bay, it really is. In some ways, it could be a very positive thing for him. He's gonna be challenged more than he ever would have been challenged going back to Green Bay."

Yes, he would be. Marino, who tormented Jets fans for seventeen years, threw them a bone. "You gotta be excited having one of the great quarterbacks of all time playing on your franchise," he said. "The passion he has is gonna be fun to watch as a fan."

Former Jets Pro Bowl defensive lineman Joe Klecko seconded that emotion. "I think it's fantastic for the Jets," he said. "It gives them a better chance to win. He's a playmaker. He throws one of the best deep balls out there, and if it's one thing the New York Jets have been wanting to do for a while, it's get the ball down the field."

Fireman Ed Anzalone was on vacation in Wildwood, New Jersey, the night the Favre news broke. He had gone to bed at 11:30 p.m.

"About a quarter to six in the morning, my phone started ringing," he said.

His buddy Randy Lee, another Jets fanatic who can be found by parking lot 16 H before games, told him, "Turn on ESPN."

"He's got a big army truck—it's the best tailgate in the place," Fireman Ed said.

Fireman Ed's heart skipped a beat or three. "I *knew* it was Favre," he said. "I *knew* it." He turned on ESPN.

J-E-T-S JETS JETS JETS!

"I went nuts," he said.

He had become part of Jets lore back in the early '90s from section 133, making sure Jets fans young and old, male and female, went nuts for their team at Giants Stadium. "I hated the lower tier," Fireman Ed explained. "It was dying. [ESPN's] Chris Berman named me Fireman Ed."

One of New York's Bravest, from Ladder 28, a.k.a. the Harlem Hilton, he would sit atop his mountainous big brother Frank's shoulders, clad in his Bruce Harper 42 jersey, hold his green-and-white fire hat to the heavens, and lead a raucous chant of J-E-T-S JETS JETS JETS whenever the urge hit him. "The Jet chant is one of a kind," Fireman Ed says. "There's no other chant in all of sports that does what we do. Let's face the facts."

He attended his first Jets game in 1976, at Shea, when he was sixteen. He sat in the rain during the infamous Mud Bowl in Miami. He was in Denver for the 1998 AFC Championship game when the Jets blew that 10–0 lead.

"I did not win a world championship with Joe Namath," Fireman Ed said. "Getting Favre was as big as anything I've experienced as a Jet fan."

Fireman Ed had missed the 2007 season with knee and neck injuries suffered fighting a fire. At the home opener, he was back in his Harper 42 jersey atop the shoulders of his friend Bruce, who three years ago had replaced his retired brother Frank. Fireman Ed had never heard Giants Stadium louder than the days the Jets beat the Jaguars 34–24 in the 1998 playoffs and crushed the Colts 41–0 in the 2002 playoffs. It was loud again the day Favre showed up.

"I love this guy," Fireman Ed said. "I wish we woulda had him long ago. If we have him for one year, it'll be the best one year for me as a Jet fan. I just pray to God he stays healthy and he doesn't get hurt. If he stays healthy for sixteen games, we're gonna have a legitimate shot at a world championship."

Fireman Ed would honor Favre by wearing a 4 navy-and-gold Titans jersey when the Jets played the Cardinals. "This guy was born to be a quarterback," he said. "If you wanted your kid to be a quarterback, you would mold him after Brett Favre. . . . [John] Elway was a maniac too."

A maniac? "A maniac is a guy that you know there's nothing gonna stop him," Fireman Ed said. "It doesn't matter how many times you hit me, I'm gonna keep comin'. When I grew up in College Point [Queens], that's who I hung out with—they were all maniacs. They weren't guys who picked on anybody, they were tough guys. If [bleep] happened, bring it on, let's go! I didn't grow up with wimps. You had to survive. We grew up in the street. We played ball from seven in the morning till eleven at night."

It pained Fireman Ed to no end watching the Giants win a third Super Bowl championship in 2007. "I just wish we could get a little magic," he said. "The Giants keep getting this little magic. How about the Jets having a little magic? What's wrong with that? Same Old Jets—you guys like to write that nonsense. Can we get a turn? Is it all right if we get a turn? How 'bout us? Can we get a shot?"

Two days after the Jets-Browns game, Favre joined his teammates on the field, in uniform, for the first time. It was a bright, warm, sunny Saturday at Hofstra, two weeks before the Jets would say good-bye to old Weeb Ewbank Hall, for their spanking new facility. Long Island fans of the club would miss the short drive to training camp, but Jets fans who were certain that the building named for their only Super Bowl head coach was inhabited by ghosts were undoubtedly shouting good riddance. Normally, there are approximately thirty media credentials issued; on this day there were over a hundred. Said Gilmore, "We had to hire an outside company [Metrovision Production Group] to come in and help us run all the wiring to do the outside podium, and we had to rent platforms so all the cameras would have space . . . we had to make special arrangements with Hofstra so all the trucks could get down the access road."

Hofstra Public Safety bolstered security. According to Jets director of security Steve Yarnell, there were three times the number of Hofstra Public Safety and three times the number of Jets security that day.

Mangini, easing off on his players, had scheduled only one practice, at 1:30 p.m., instead of the dreaded two-a-days, one at 8:45, the other at 3:30 p.m. The packed bleachers, the fans, young and old, male and female, who lined the fences, told you that Favre was more than the new quarterback of the Jets. He was a rock star. Local and national television reporters flooded the place. Was this a Jets practice or a Springsteen concert? "It felt like a game," Tratner said. Bob Parente, the Jets ticket manager, looked around at the mob and said, "I don't have the real number, but they're saying it's just under ten thousand."

The real number was later announced as 10,500.

Tratner remembers *Sports Illustrated* senior writer Paul Zimmerman, the Jets beat writer for the *New York Post* during the Namath years, telling him, "Yeah, this is good. But when Namath would come out, *Playboy* and *Vanity Fair* and *Vogue* and the *Village Voice*—those are the people that covered Namath."

A roar erupted when Favre, wearing a red 4 jersey, took the field as—you guessed it—Springsteen's "Glory Days" blared from the speakers. Favre smiled sheepishly and waved his left hand to his new fan base. Enterprising fans who had been captivated by Foley—who also wore No. 4—taped a homemade AVRE over OLEY on the back of their old jerseys. A young man named Rob Meyer was going to buy season tickets behind the end zone from a friend of a friend for $1,000; when Favre became a Jet, they suddenly cost $1,500. Meyer bought them anyway. "Worth it, I think," he said.

A middle-aged man named Bill Manning, an original Titans season–ticket holder, wore a Namath 12 jersey. His eleven-year-old daughter Alexandra wore one of those green AVRE jerseys. "Decided to save money for the personal seat licenses by doing it this way," Manning joked. He was asked why he was so excited about Favre. "I'm looking forward to seeing the ball being passed downfield— something that we've been lacking for the past couple of years."

Joe Houghton was a Favre fan long before this day. "He loves to play the game," he said. "You see it on his face—when he's out there, he's like a little kid out there. You don't see that with athletes anymore."

There were even more than a few cheesehead sightings in the bleachers, those gold foam hats made to resemble a large piece of Swiss cheese that have long been the rage of Packer fans. P. J. Merante, mimicking Fireman Ed Anzalone, led a J-E-T-S, JETS JETS JETS chant atop the shoulders of a friend. "I can't take his spot," Merante said. "Just keeping the crowd excited here . . . keepin' 'em into it." *He* sure was into it. "Brett Favre's the Truth!" he said.

For the receivers, tracking Favre's ball was a new experience. "His passes are weird—like they whistle," Chris Baker said.

Every time Favre completed a pass, even if it was a 5-yard slant over the middle, the crowd cheered. "They'd do bag drills, people are cheering; handing the ball off, people are cheering," Winley said. "The first deep throw to Jerricho Cotchery was a pass I've never seen before. The tempo of the pass . . . the height of the pass . . . the accuracy of the pass, Jerricho not having to break his stride to get it. I remember saying, 'Wow! This guy's different.'"

The Jets owner recalled feeling the exact same way. "Unbelievable gun . . . great spiral, right on. It's all good. It's what you want to see in a quarterback," Johnson said.

Favre stood under the outdoor media tent, and the media hung on his every word. "I hope at the end of the season, I really do, that I feel like I made the right decision," he said. "I hope the Jets fans and the people throughout the NFL world feel like I made the right decision. At this point, I think it was the right decision. I'd love to win the Super Bowl, I would have loved to have gone and won it last year. I could say that for a lot of years. As I said yesterday and the day before, my intentions are to help this team win. I can't make any guarantees; I'm not going to make any guarantees. All I can say is I'll do my best, and hopefully that's enough. Whatever happens, happens."

He felt like a rookie again. It was all overwhelming to him at times—the crowd, the offense, the new teammates. "There were some times in practice today I was wondering if I made the right move," Favre said and smiled.

Still, he did better than he thought he would. "I didn't want to look too bad so I tried to put as much into it as I could, and I'll pay for it tomorrow, but I'll be okay."

Favre versus Pennington had to be asked.

"I think every time I've faced Chad, I've lost," Favre said. "He's played extremely well. I hope this time it is different. . . . I have nothing but the highest regard for Chad. Extremely bright guy. The knock on him was his arm wasn't that strong. So what? I can throw it through a wall, but I don't win every game I play in. It doesn't matter. He's very effective. I haven't heard one person say anything about him negatively. High-character guy, a lot of class. I'd just like to beat the guy for a change." Then he chuckled.

Speight was the communications assistant for the Carolina Panthers in 1996, and had stood on the sidelines when Favre and the Packers beat them 30–13 in the NFC Championship game at Lambeau. In an effort to pump up his defense, Speight had bellowed, "That Favre guy ain't nuthin'!"

Then linebacker Sam Mills intercepted Favre to set up the opening score. "I told you all Favre ain't nuthin'," Speight roared.

After Favre finished his press conference, Speight walked him back to the locker room. "I still can't stand you for '96," he told Favre. "I was with Carolina in '96; I didn't think you were all that. Then you threw the interception to Sam Mills and we scored—I *really* didn't think you were all that."

Favre stopped him right then and there. "You remember what happened after that, don't you?" he said and laughed. "We whipped that ass!"

Speight moved quickly to implement a New York media game plan for Favre and Cook. "Here in New York it's very competitive," he told them in separate conversations. "The biggest concern is getting scooped. If anybody reaches out to you, refer them to our department and we can handle all the requests." The Jets made an organizational decision to severely limit Favre's availability, which frustrated the New York media to no end. There was a one-on-one interview with ESPN Radio; one on WFAN; one with SNY, the Jets' television home; one with CBS's Marino; one with Steve Mariucci of the NFL Network; one with ESPN's Ed Werder; and one forty-five-minute session with the beat writers. "We were just trying to be fair with everybody," Speight said. "There was no way we were gonna be able to do one-on-ones with everybody, so where do you start, where do you stop?"

GQ wanted Favre for its cover. Regis Philbin wanted to come to practice to meet him. "Everybody said they knew him," Speight said.

The Jets moved swiftly to ease Favre's transition off the field as well. Szott's familiarity with the Morristown, New Jersey, area—he'd been born in Clifton and lived in the area for almost a decade—paid dividends. It enabled him to find the right school for nine-year-old Breleigh Favre, for instance. He also found the right rental house for the Favres near Morristown: a four-bedroom split-level designed and built by the architect who owned it. "It had a tremendous amount of detail—a lot of different paneling and molding," Szott said. "It was on probably six, seven acres. It had the right parameters Brett was looking for—to be private, have a lot of space, but not ostentatious." While her husband insisted on being treated as one of the guys, Deanna made an effort to be one of the gals. "She attended most of the other wives' functions," Szott said. "She acted like any other wife."

Favre's eagerness to show that he was one of the guys was evident the second day of practice when he and Mangold ran a penalty lap together following a fumbled exchange. The sight of Favre jogging in his red 4 jersey—red means stop, do not hit the quarterback—brought cheers from starstruck Jets fans. Favre could not recall if he had ever run a penalty lap. "It's not punishment," he said. "It's more of a team unity thing. I told Eric, day one, that unless I pass out, I am going to try to do everything that everyone else does.

"I'm no different, aside from being a little gray-headed and a little bit older."

His Hall of Fame right arm sure felt older five days into Brett the Jet. "My arm's kinda dragging a little bit today; it's not really sore but . . . fatigued," he said. "To be honest with ya, I'm surprised that—I don't want to say I feel good—that I've been able to make it through every practice so far. I think maybe this afternoon I'm gonna talk to Eric about it, limiting my throws a little bit. I didn't throw the ball very well this morning, underthrew some throws. No pain, but I'm thirty-eight years old. It's gotta be fatigued a little bit. My arm, for the most part, has felt great. Legs, a little bit fatigued. You've gotta figure I'm a little bit behind some of these guys."

He was starting the preseason game against the Redskins. "Believe me, the system's not easy, and I'm not gonna sit here and tell you I've got it down," Favre said. "I've got about just enough plays down to run those plays Saturday. And how it turns out, I have no idea. I hope it turns out well. Practice has been able to run, for the most part, smoothly. And that was my big concern, and I'm sure Eric and everyone involved . . . we bring Brett in, as a coach you're gonna say, 'We don't want to disrupt what we've been doing. We don't really want to stop and start over again. We want everything to run smoothly.' But that's easier said than done. But I'll say this: for the most part, we've been able to do that. We've had a few false starts, I've had to run a couple of laps. No big deal. You want it to run like it should, and I think for the most part we've done that. Now, they haven't thrown everything at me. But I could go into a game and I think I could manage a game okay."

The media were there in force. "We went from an average of about two hundred or something credentials to close to six hundred credentials," Gilmore said.

Favre was admittedly nervous and excited when he arrived for his first start at Giants Stadium. "Some feelings that I have not felt in a while," he would say. He would manage just fine, completing 4-of-5 passes for 48 yards, including a 4-yard touchdown pass to tight end Dustin Keller. "I feel like I'm a Jet," Favre said. "It sounds a little funny, but believe me, I feel comfortable here. It's still a bit awkward, but I don't know how else to tell you. I feel like I'm here for a reason. Like I told the guys, I feel like I'm here for one reason."

Favre immediately won over Keller when he insisted that the rookie keep the ball, and signed it for him. More importantly, he had to win over Laveranues Coles.

Pennington had had a special relationship with Coles, on the field and off. They had been part of the same 2000 draft class, Pennington the eighteenth overall pick and Coles a third-rounder. They immediately developed what was tantamount to telepathy. After Coles had left the Jets for a five-year, $35 million ($13 million signing bonus) free agent deal from Daniel Snyder and the Redskins following the 2003 season, Pennington had taken a $2 million pay cut to enable the Jets to trade Santana Moss to the Redskins to bring him back in 2005.

"How Laveranues runs a slant versus Jerricho or Chansi [Stuckey]—I don't know all the little ins and outs," Favre said. "To me the most important thing right now is getting to know those guys . . . what they run well, just talkin' to 'em. There's no way—and this goes back to playing with the guys in Green Bay—you never practice every route. But we knew each other fairly well. I knew what I threw best, I knew what those guys ran the best, and we kind of incorporated it into our system. And here—like I was telling Schotty [Brian Schottenheimer] and [quarterbacks coach Brian] Daboll last night—that I really want to just kinda watch some film of last year and see how Laveranues runs a deep corner route . . . and how Chris Baker runs a crossing route. Those type of things. And then, when I go out and throw, if it's a tight coverage or something, I got a feel for where they're gonna be."

Favre revealed that he had had a private chat with Coles just that morning. "I said, 'Look, I heard you're not talking to the media,'" Favre said. "I said, 'I understand you don't want to say anything good about me, that's okay.' He said, 'No, it's not that, it's not that.' And I obviously was joking with that." And Coles laughed. "But, I said, 'Look, I'm not here to take Chad's spot, or replace him, or whatever.' It is what it is. And I said this the other day: I don't think I've ever beaten Chad. Those two guys had a great rapport together. I said, 'Look, I'm not trying to replace him. I'm here to help you guys win. I hope you respect me for that,' and I said, 'I can't guarantee you that.' I would love to say I'd come in here and help this team not only get to the playoffs but get to a Super Bowl, and I think I should think that way. But I'm not gonna make any guarantees. . . . I'm not gonna come in and promise that I can throw him ninety balls. All I can promise is I'm gonna do everything I can to not only help him but help this team win. And I said, 'And whatever you had with Chad, may that continue.' I think he'll realize if he hadn't already that I'm an easygoing guy, easy to work with. If you drop a ball, so what? I throw bad passes. So we're in this thing together and I'd like for us to come out of it together."

To facilitate the getting-to-know-you process, Mangini would make sure that Favre and Coles were locker-room neighbors when the Jets moved to Florham Park five days before the September 7 opener. "I don't know Laveranues well enough for him to make any kind of judgment on me," Favre said. "What he probably knows about me other than the last four, five days is what he sees and hears on TV. Of course, I'm very familiar with Laveranues as a player. He and Jerricho both are a lot like the guys I've been throwing to in Green Bay—quick, I think deceptively powerful guys, hard to tackle, good in and out of space. . . . Are those the type of guys that you want to drop back, throw it deep into coverage? Probably not, but I think these guys are definitely in-space type of players. And we made a living on yards after the catch in Green Bay. And I'd much rather have it in their hands. Laveranues is the prime example. Throw him a five-yard pass and let him do what he does. Hey, if you can throw a thirty-yard pass and complete it, great. But throw him a five-yard pass, and if they tackle him right there, it's five yards, easy five yards. But I would think that they're gonna break most of those tackles—they're gonna get ten, they're gonna get fifteen, twenty . . . then every once in a while they're gonna bust it. I think our receiving group here, in general, is that type of player."

Moments later on the practice field, Cotchery said, "Everyone knows Laveranues and Chad were great friends; as far as the relationship part you never can disconnect from that. But the football part of it, I think Laveranues is excited about it and everybody on the team is excited about what we have this season and we're just looking forward to trying to have a great season."

It was hard not to like Favre. He's real. There's no pretense about him. What you see is what you get. Ignore the graying head and face fuzz—the little boy in him never left. He's one of the most down-to-earth superstars you will ever meet. It's no wonder ESPN's television posse covered him as if he were the football pope. He doesn't take himself too seriously. In Green Bay, he was notorious for his practical jokes. You couldn't help but like being around him, whether you were a teammate or a member of the media.

Favre had made a fast first impression on Cotchery. "He said two things: 'We're gonna score touchdowns and have fun,'" Cotchery said.

For an organization lacking the wow! factor, Favre sure gave it to the Jets. "If you had Michael Jordan on your team, does his fadeaway on the baseline, someone's gonna be talking about it, even if they're in practice," Cotchery said. "Some of the throws that he makes out here . . . it's kinda crazy. But we're happy. We're happy to have those throws out here."

Favre won his Super Bowl with Mike Holmgren, a fiery head coach who freely dispensed tough love. But Holmgren was an offensive genius, and he found a way to harness Favre's undisciplined side and make him a champion quarterback. Now Favre found himself a year older than his new head coach, who was much more ice than fire.

"Great guy," Favre said. "I'm sure everyone here knows how soft-spoken he is. But very structured. A little bit different than what I'm used to as far as how we practice, how your day's laid out for you. . . . I think he handles the players really well. You know the old saying, 'players' coach,' I don't know exactly what that means, but I think guys respect him, and know what he stands for. They complain a little bit, but they're gonna do that anyway. . . . I don't complain, but they do. . . . He's been fun to work with so far."

Favre isn't different from any other grizzled veteran; training camp is drudgery. The endless meetings and the film study are never what you envision when you are a boy with a dream. It is never about Monday through Saturday. It is about Sundays. Or Monday nights.

"I love to play," Favre said. "I know I need to study, I know I need to practice, I know how important it is, doesn't mean I have to like it. The question I have to ask myself, 'Am I willing to do that?' And the answer is yes. There's no substitute for Sundays, and I said that way back when. There's no way playing in an NFL football game and getting to do the things that I've been able to do, you can replace that; it's impossible. Up to this point I'm willing to do whatever it takes to continue doing that. It's harder, it's harder. . . . I felt thirty-eight today, I'm not gonna lie to you."

So here was an old dog trying to learn new tricks. Said Favre, "My wife told me last night, she said, 'Your worst enemy probably is your memory. That you've remembered every play you've ever run.' We call plays out here and I revert back to . . . 'cause a lot of the terminology is used in this offense, but it means something totally different. Scat here is a totally different protection—in fact, it's a max protection here where in Green Bay, you had five linemen, so any blitz at all, you had to throw hot. So as soon as I hear 'Scat,' I'm going, 'Blitz, I gotta get rid of it.' That's not the case. . . . I gotta be able to process it in a hurry. And there are so many other things—shifts and motions and things like that that are so much different. . . . I don't even want to say different . . . totally new. But the bottom line is football is football, and a curl's a curl, and a Go route's a Go route. An off-tackle handoff to the left is an off-tackle. . . . How we call it is different. I have to process this information very quickly, and the most important thing, and I told Eric this, and I know Schotty and I have had this conversation numerous times, is for any player, whoever that player may be, the only way you play well consistently is to react, and not think. The less you have to think, the more you can react and just play. . . . Now, if that's going into a game with thirty plays, so be it. Going in with a hundred plays, if I can process that, so be it. But the bottom line is we have to know—me in particular—what to do, and do it fast. So that's been the biggest challenge for me."

Mangini liked to test his players with pop quizzes, and Favre would not be immune to them. Mangini asked him to name teammates based on uniform numbers and list the Jets' core values (communicate, trust, focus, finish). His new teammates cheered when Favre came through in the clutch—it meant an hour less of meetings and no curfew that night. "I thought I had him," Mangini said. "I don't know how he pulled that one out. The room exploded."

Favre completed 9-of-12 passes for 96 yards in his one half against the Giants. He threw the ball with his customary authority, and titillated the crowd with a 49-yard rope to Cotchery that would have been a touchdown if an illegal formation penalty against Bubba Franks hadn't called it back. But the Jets didn't score. The operation was sabotaged by penalties and mental errors. And Favre had yet to play with Coles, who was still nursing his thigh injury. After the game, Favre and Mangini left the door open to him playing in the fourth and final preseason game in Philadelphia. The fourth game is traditionally reserved for the reserves fighting to make the roster. But the Jets offense was far from perfect. Mangini decided he'd rather be safe than sorry, and Favre did not play.

With five days left before the first day of the rest of his football life, Favre was voted offensive co-captain along with Faneca by his teammates. "I'm honored," he said. "I feel like I have to earn it."

Pennington, meanwhile, took about ten seconds to win the respect of his new teammates. Guard Justin Smiley: "I mean, he doesn't know any of us from the man on the moon right now, but he comes into the huddle and says, 'Give me your eyes.' We didn't break the huddle good one time and he was like, 'Nah, nah, nah. Next time, we've got to stand and break the huddle.'"

When you are in the twilight of your career, no matter how successful you have been, you are always on guard against Father Time tapping you on the shoulder. So it was with a little bit of fear and apprehension that Favre approached the start of the 2008 regular season. In times such as these, it is commonplace for the proud gladiators of any sport to grasp on to whatever motivational tool works for them. Back in March when he announced his premature retirement, remember, he had talked in Super-Bowl-or-bust terms. His tune had changed dramatically. He had lowered the bar.

"I understand that most people think the odds are against me, and that's fine," Favre said. "I'm not here to be a god. I'm not here to get trashed, either. I'm here to help this team win. I still think I can offer something to the game of football, to myself. That's all I can do. I hope it works out, believe me."

He just wasn't certain it would and expressed his anxieties to Mangini. "I said, 'What drives me is fear of failure, not being the best.' That goes for each season and each game. As much success as I've had in my career, I've never gone into the next game or the next season and said, 'Whew, I've been playing well, that will continue.' I've been around other players who have had a lot of success throughout their career. For the most part I get the same response from those guys, in that there's this fear of not being at the top of your game week in and week out. I'm not saying that's right or wrong. But I think the fear of someone taking your job or not playing up to a standard that you have set should drive you. You should never rest on what you've done in the past. For me, that's about as much pressure as I can put on myself.

"This is a whole different situation for me. That in itself does present some different challenges, but the bottom line is, I still believe I can play at a high level. But there's that fear that I won't."

The press room that Wednesday was packed, naturally. Speight was in charge of leading Mangini to his 10:20 a.m. press conference; Tratner picked up Favre in the quarterbacks' meeting room and walked him to his 10:35 press conference. "I tried to keep him between fifteen and twenty minutes," Tratner said. Favre had a conference call with the Miami media immediately afterward and then practice at 11:20. It's an unenviable tightrope walk between accommodating and alienating the insatiable New York media. Tratner surveyed the room. "I try to look in everybody's eyes and see if most people are pretty satisfied with what they heard," he said. With Favre, most everyone usually is. Tratner marveled at how Favre handled the questions. "I just remember thinking, 'This guy's good,'" he said.

THE WEIGHT OF OBLIGATION

At Miami • New England • At San Diego • Arizona

Speight and Tratner were standing outside Dolphin Stadium waiting for the team bus to arrive when Pennington drove in. They waved and he waved back. Pennington parked his car, got out, and shook hands and hugged each of them. "Good to see you," Speight said. "Good to see you all," Pennington said. Then he headed to his new home locker room, and Armageddon against Favre.

"That was kinda cool," Tratner said. "There was no better guy than him."

Pennington, a white towel draped around his neck, hugged Favre and gave him a pat on the back after the coin toss. It was 1:05 p.m. when Brett Favre joined his new teammates in the huddle, a historic moment of hope for one of professional sports' more hapless franchises. Giddy Jets fans who had been pinching themselves from the moment the news broke that Favre belonged to them soaked up the surreal sight of No. 4 surrounded by Coles and Cotchery and Ferguson and Mangold and the rest of the Boys of Bummer. The Jets, born in 1960 as the Titans, had won the one championship, back on January 12, 1969, when Namath backed up his pregame guarantee by directing that stunning 16–7 upset of the Baltimore Colts.

Now here stood Favre, forty years later. "Clay Hampton and Scott Cohen had come up with this idea about using a shade to cover the bench. . . . They had seen it in Jacksonville," Tannenbaum said. "And I was watching these guys hold this thing up as much as anything because I'm like, 'This is a really good idea, we're keeping our guys out of the sun.' It was attention to details like that that I was really proud of."

The temperature was eighty-eight degrees; the last game he had played, the NFC Championship game against the Giants in Green Bay, it was 120 degrees colder. Favre revealed to concerned teammates and coaches, "I'm trying to conserve energy."

He needed to beat Pennington badly. "It's not me versus Chad," he said.

But in so many ways it was.

Pennington had dreamed of winning a championship for the Jets, had talked about it every single season. It was a blow to his immense pride when the Jets, in essence, said to him that he was no longer the man for the job. As is his nature, he pooh-poohed any notion that this would be about revenge for him.

So here stood Favre, after all the Jets quarterbacks who followed Namath, and never were Namath.

Pennington, long on courage and toughness and perseverance, kept fighting off the demise of his Jets career, and when the 2008 training camp began he was even money to take back the starting job he had surrendered to Clemens. Clemens had been a second-round draft choice out of Oregon in the 2006 draft, the first of the Mangini-Tannenbaum regime. The Jets, remember, had passed on Leinart, Young, and Cutler to build their infrastructure with D'Brickashaw Ferguson and Mangold before pulling the trigger on Clemens. But when he got his chance, Clemens did little with it, and the Jets brain trust headed into the off-season lacking faith in either quarterback. The off-season game plan seemed to be to prop up the eventual winner of the Quarterback Derby with some $140 million worth of free agents who would help block, tackle, and rush the passer.

Sure, the Jets had closed the gap on the Patriots. But the Patriots still had Tom Brady, and the Jets did not.

And then another thunderbolt no one saw coming turned the 2008 NFL season upside down.

At 1:25 p.m., as Favre was toiling under the broiling Miami sun, Brady, up in Foxboro, was hit on the left knee by Chiefs safety Bernard Pollard and crumpled to the ground, clutching his knee and screaming in anguish. Here was the league MVP—a star who had thrown 50 touchdown passes in 2007, who had won three Super Bowl championships with Belichick, and who was dating supermodel Gisele Bündchen—in severe distress, being helped off the field by a pair of trainers. It cast a pall over the stadium, and soon over the entire league. Before the sun had even set, word had spread as far as Miami that Brady had torn his anterior cruciate ligament and was done for the season.

Before he would learn that the expectations had changed, that he would be looked upon even more as the Messiah, Favre had to get past Pennington and the pesky Dolphins, and prevail with his head swimming in the terminology of a new offense, with new teammates he barely knew. "I knew that this would be a battle," he would later say. "I wasn't nervous. . . . I just wanted to make sure I played well enough the whole four quarters to give us a chance to win. . . . I didn't want to lose the game for us, in other words." In the Saturday production meeting with CBS's Simms and Jim Nantz, Favre divulged that he had approximately 75 percent of the offense down. His first play from scrimmage was an innocent 5-yard completion to Coles, the kind of safe pass, actually, that Pennington was asked to throw all the time.

It wasn't long before Favre reminded the Jets brass, and Jets fans, why they craved him.

Favre, at his play-action best, looked to his left and launched one of those ICBMs that always struck fear into the hearts of defensive backs and landed in the hands of someone like Antonio Freeman, or Donald Driver, or, most recently, Greg Jennings. Cotchery, streaking down the left sideline ahead of the field, slowed down a bit to haul it in, and sprinted to the end zone with a 56-yard touchdown. Favre watched the triumphant end of the play from his knees and thrust both arms skyward. Jets 7, Dolphins 0.

"I thought I overthrew it, but I obviously didn't," Favre said. "That's the one thing I didn't want to do, first big-shot play we had, was just unleash one and throw it in the second deck. Not that I underestimated his speed, but he's a deceptive player. Greg Jennings was one of those guys that all of a sudden you go, 'Man, was that Greg Jennings again?' And Jerricho's that type of guy . . . he's always around the ball. The guy can make plays. He's got deceptive speed too. I hope he keeps deceiving people."

To old-timers, this was Namath to Don Maynard, four decades later. To shorter-suffering Jets fans, it marked the dawn of a new day in which their quarterback could threaten the entire field. Testaverde could make all the throws too, but his fame was fleeting. He was never the same after his Achilles' betrayed him. Here was the first evidence that Favre, three months shy of his thirty-ninth birthday, might still be forever young—at least at that precious moment in time. Cotchery was developing a growing chemistry with him and seemed to be threatening Coles as the go-to guy. "He throws a great deep ball," Cotchery said. "Coach has been telling us, 'Just run.'"

Left unsaid: with Pennington under center, Coach never told his receivers, "Just run."

Most of the great ones have Nolan Ryan arms. Namath—Elway—Marino—Terry Bradshaw. Montana was an exception. He did it with accuracy and poise and mastery of the intricacies of Bill Walsh's West Coast offense. Favre added a fearlessness that sometimes crossed over into recklessness and an improvisational genius that often enabled him to turn a bad play into an awe-inspiring wondrous play.

Now he faced a fourth-and-13 from the Miami 22-yard line. The Jets' placekicker, Mike Nugent, had suffered a thigh bruise on the kickoff preceding his missed 32-yard field goal, and Mangini, who rarely leaves any stone unturned, suddenly found himself auditioning would-be extra point kickers, led by Clemens, on the sidelines. Bad idea. "Obviously, Mike being hurt, obviously changed everything," Favre said.

So Mangini instructed Favre to go for it. "I'm thinking, 'Okay, you don't want to take a sack,'" Favre would say later. "This is one time where if you throw a pick, so be it. You gotta take a shot, more or less."

Coles and Stuckey ran crossing routes by the goal line. Favre bought himself a precious split second in the pocket with a nifty shoulder shrug and, with what looked like a flick of the wrist, lobbed the ball toward the middle of the field as he was hit. Call it a Hail Chansi. "Got a little pressure . . . tried to throw it to where someone was, just give someone a chance," Favre said.

Did he see Stuckey?

"I saw him," Favre said. "I didn't think we had a chance in hell of catching it."

That line would crack up everyone in the interview room.

Stuckey waited and waited for the ball to come down and then couldn't wait any longer and leaped for it and caught it, just inside the end zone. "That ball," Favre would say later, "was like a shotput. I can't believe it went as far as it did."

Stuckey, a seventh-round draft choice out of Clemson who had spent his rookie season on injured reserve, was all smiles later on as he talked about his first NFL touchdown catch. "He threw it up and it seemed like it took forever to come down, so I was just waiting to get hit but nobody really hit me and I was able to come down with it," he said.

Stuckey was asked what Favre's presence was like in the huddle.

"He's real loose, he's not real uptight, keeps everything calm in the huddle, everyone sees the confidence, we listen to him, he knows what's going on—it's confidence, and it's calm in the huddle."

The final was 20–14. Mangini almost blew the game, taking the ball out of Favre's hands and handing it to running back Thomas Jones on third-and-7 from the Jets 21. That led to Pennington getting the ball back with 1:43 left, and scaring the Jets to death before Darrelle Revis intercepted a floater for Ted Ginn Jr. in the right corner of the end zone with five seconds on the clock.

Wouldn't Favre have relished having the game in his hands at that moment? "No," he said. "There's no guarantees that works.

The way our offensive line was blocking, we should get the first down. There'll be times for that—we won the game, and that's the most important thing."

Favre took a knee and it was over.

Pennington was crushed. "Right here," he said, pointing at his chest. "In my heart. My pride is hurt. Losing is not fun. We put a lot of hard work into it. It's one thing to have the will to win but you have to have a heart to lose."

The protocol is for the opposing quarterbacks to shake hands near the middle of the field. But Favre's postgame interview was a bit to the right side of the 50 coming from the chaotic Jets sideline. "I was nervous about moving him around before the interview," Winley said. When Favre was finished, Winley told him, "I can't find Chad." And Favre said, "Okay." And found Pennington soon enough.

Favre's teammates loved playing with him. It was calamitous at times, Favre sometimes making do on his wing and a prayer, but fun every step of the way. If you can't have fun playing football with Brett

Favre, then you're in the wrong business. "A couple of times I just winged it, and I said, 'Hey guys, same play,'" Favre said.

He was clad in a green shirt, his nose reddened by the sun, when he met the media inside a cramped Dolphin Stadium interview room. "A win's a win," he said. "They never get old. All the stuff that goes along during the course of a game—big plays . . . bad plays . . . that's what it's all about, to walk off that field with the win."

Favre heaped praise on the Jets' fortified offensive line, which helped Jones to a 101-yard rushing day. "We ran the ball well, and even though it was early, it opened up the deep ball to Jerricho. We probably could have taken some more chances during the course of the game like that, the way we were running the ball. I'd be lying if I sat here and told you that I feel real confident in the passing offense right now, from my end, what I need to study. . . . They gave us a few protection problems today that really fall back on me . . . some of those guys came free. . . . I was more concerned about who was lining up where. . . . We overcame that; the guys around me overcame that."

Jones summed up what the arrival of Favre meant to him. "Now you don't have to worry about nine guys in the box all the time," he said.

The media fawned over Favre. "Brett, all the things you did in high school, you didn't kick?"

"Badly," Favre said and smiled. "Brian Daboll, the quarterback coach, asked me on the sidelines, 'Hey, can you kick?' It was right after Mike had attempted that kick and missed it and I said, 'I can't even kick that well.'" Laughter in the room. "We never talked about it again, so . . ."

He reiterated that he knew he made the right decision to come back and play. He was trying so hard to convince himself that it was true. "One time during the course of the game I looked up and they were flashing scores, and I saw Packers-Vikings tomorrow night, and it wasn't like, 'Wait a minute, I'm supposed to be there.' I'm a Jet, I'm one of fifty-three on this team, and I'm proud of it. Had a great career in Green Bay but that's over and done with. It's what I do this year. It was a good start . . . shaky, but it was a good start, it's a win, and you can never question a win, and it is what it is."

Imagine when Favre developed some chemistry with Coles, who finally broke his self-imposed silence after the game. "We got a ways to go," Favre said, "but we are close."

The NFL's Iron Horse—254 consecutive starts—had taken a licking and kept on ticking. "Right now I feel fine," Favre said. "I got nailed on the one where they threw the flag. Which I told [Dolphin Matt] Roth later, 'You nailed me.' He said, 'Oh, you gave me a great fake.' I looked right at him with no ball in my hand!" Laughter in the room again. "And I saw him coming, and he hit me anyway, but I guess they wanted to test me . . . knocked me silly there for about thirty seconds, but for the most part, I can overcome all that stuff. I mean, I'll probably be sore as heck tomorrow, but a win sure makes it easy."

Finally, someone mentioned Brady.

"Just found out; I heard about that," Favre said. "That's terrible. Terrible. I guess it's an ACL [anterior cruciate ligament] or something. They've always overcome injuries and things like that, but that's pretty difficult."

Johnson, an eternal optimist, thought back to 1999, when he was bidding for the team and Testaverde was lost for the season with that torn Achilles. "That," the owner said, "was a tragic loss for them."

Brady versus Favre in week 2 probably wouldn't have been a fair fight. Daboll and Schottenheimer were furiously force-feeding Favre the offense and tailoring it to his strengths. But now, Favre versus Matt Cassel didn't look much like a fair fight either.

"We never really came back to certain plays," Favre said. "That's gotta be tough on Schotty, calling plays. There's probably something he really wants to call, and he's like, 'I don't know if Brett feels comfortable with it.' So really in some ways I'm putting him in an awkward spot too 'cause he wants to be productive, but you want to be able to scheme and do things like that. . . . There's no substitute for playing and kinda getting a feel for where you are."

One reporter wanted to know about the play where Favre had scrambled for a first down. "Nifty" was the word the reporter used. Said Favre, "I fell on the ball and it kinda knocked the wind out of me. But I knew I couldn't lay down. So I got up; I didn't have rib pads on. Came back to the huddle and first thing I did was I looked to see if I got the first down which made the wind being knocked out a little bit better. I wouldn't call it nifty . . . successful."

Speight stood below Favre, who was standing on a podium, and to his right. "This is the last question," Speight announced.

The last question was whether Favre was disappointed he didn't get to try to close the game out.

"All right, thank you, Brett," Speight said, and off Favre went to the visiting locker room.

Tannenbaum, before boarding the team bus for the airport, stood in a tunnel outside the locker rooms and was asked about Brady. "We don't know much more than what you guys know, and we'll get more information when their injury report comes out on Wednesday, but they're a really good team, they got a really good staff, and they're still the Patriots," he said.

But without Brady, they were not the Patriots. Sure, they still had Moss and Wes Welker and defensive champions such as Mike Vrabel and Richard Seymour and Rodney Harrison and Vince Wilfork and Tedy Bruschi, and they still had Belichick. But next in line behind Brady was Cassel, who last started a game in 1999, when he quarterbacked Chatsworth High School in California. He had backed up Carson Palmer and Leinart at USC, and Brady for three years as a pro.

If ever there was a time for Jetribution, if ever there was a time for the balance of power in the AFC East to finally change, if ever there was an opportunity for the Jets to show the world they were now the team to beat, this was it, all right. The Pats had ruled the division since Jets linebacker Mo Lewis knocked Drew Bledsoe (internal bleeding) out of most of the 2001 season and Brady Wally Pipped him.

You have to understand that Jets Nation had a pathological hatred of Belichick dating back to 2000, when he read his hastily scribbled statement that, after one day on the job, he was stepping down as "H.C. of the NYJ" (head coach of the New York Jets). The Jets' president at the time, Steve Gutman, went as far as questioning Belichick's emotional state. "We should have some feelings of sorrow and regret for him and his family," Gutman said. "He obviously has some inner turmoil." But Belichick knew exactly what he was doing; he had gotten along famously with Kraft, who was waiting with a handsome long-term contract and was not averse to embarrassing Parcells, who had wiggled from his contract with Kraft after coaching the Patriots to Super Bowl XXXI, where he lost to Favre and the Packers. Belichick, too, was troubled by the prospect of working under Parcells, the Jets general manager, and his giant shadow. Belichick knew Parcells well enough to know that just because Parcells says he will never coach again, doesn't mean he will never coach again. The pending change in ownership—from Hess to Johnson—brought about more uncertainty for Belichick. So he bolted to New England, struck lightning in a bottle with Brady, tormented the Jets over and over and won his three Super Bowls, soured on Mangini so much that it pained him to shake his pupil's hand after games, became even more of a villain after Spygate, and now here he was, seemingly ripe for the picking at last.

The Jets predictably downplayed the Patriots' loss of Brady, but behind the scenes they were licking their chops. With outside linebacker Bryan Thomas coming off a two-sack opening game—he recorded two and a half sacks in 2007—and outside linebacker Calvin Pace looking like the real deal, compensating for number one pick Vernon Gholston, who looked lost, the Jets were intent on rattling young Cassel. But Belichick, who could probably insert Kraft at quarterback and find a way to keep the game close, had other ideas. Belichick and his offensive brain trust were devising a game plan that would keep Cassel out of harm's way.

"We're still the team to beat," Moss crowed on a national conference call.

Favre, one game into his Jets career, wasn't about to disagree. To be the champ, you have to beat the champ, and Favre had barely beaten the Dolphins. "I haven't heard that we're the team to beat," Favre said at his Wednesday press conference. "I think the Patriots are still the team to beat until proven otherwise. We won one game. We barely beat Miami. Miami played their hearts out. We did, too. We made a lot of mistakes. We found a way to win it. It came down to one play. Chad played great. We could easily be sitting here saying, 'What if, and what kind of chances do you feel you have now against the Patriots?' We're not the team to beat.

"This team was 4–12 last year. The Patriots have dominated. As I said earlier, they have dominated this division as well as this league for a long time. One game doesn't make us the team to beat. I sure hope people don't feel that way. Does it give us a chance? A better chance, maybe. I think anytime you're not facing Tom Brady, it gives you a better chance. I'm just giving him the respect he deserves. The guy has been outstanding, as good as anyone that has ever played the game. Matt Cassel played great the other day when he came in. They assume he will do that. Tom Brady is Tom Brady. So that does give us a better chance. Ultimately, it comes down to how we, offensively, handle their defense. That hasn't been very good in the past. We hope that changes. You still have to stop Randy Moss. You still have to stop Wes Welker. . . . They still have a lot of great play-ers. Bill Belichick is one of the best, if not the best coach in football right now.

"I don't see how people can say we're the team to beat. I think we have a better chance given the circumstances, but we still have a long way to go. We have to play better than we did the other day for us to not only beat New England but to get to where we want to be."

But expectations had surely changed with Brady out of the Jets' hair. "He has been the face of that team for quite a while," Favre said. "It will be different."

The end of Brady's consecutive games streak (128) only served to underscore the wonder of Favre's own streak. "If I had to look back and if you would have told me prior to the injury which one would have kept me out, a broken thumb on my throwing hand," Favre said, "I would have said there's no way I can play with a broken thumb." The year was 2003. "I played nine games with a splint on my thumb."

He was about to play this one with handcuffs on his brain and arm. "For me, this is a totally new offense," he said. "The concepts for the most part are the same. I'm still thinking when I leave the huddle, 'Are we lined up correctly?' I'm asking myself that. The play is coming in, you have eighteen seconds left before you have to snap it and we haven't even broke the huddle yet. Or a play is coming in and it's sort of confusing, we get cut off, and sometimes you just have to react, you have to make plays. You would much rather not have to do that on a consistent basis.

"There is no way we can win if we have to go for it on fourth-and-thirteen like we did last week or if you have to call 'same play' in the huddle and hope that we line up and run it correctly. You just can't win that way. We did the other day, but we have to be more efficient the way it's supposed to be done. That starts with me. At least we have one under our belt. We'll see where we go next."

Where they were going next was Belichick.

No coach puts his players in a better position to succeed than Belichick, because no coach prepares his team for every possible contingency like Belichick does. Look how he rallied the troops immediately after Spygate. Behind closed doors, he was at it again, appealing to the pride of his three-time champions in the face of all the doom-and-gloom naysayers who were calling for the beginning of the end of a dynasty. Even the oddsmakers had made the Jets a slight favorite.

"I think he's one hell of a coach," Favre said. "I'm not inventing the wheel here, the guy has been pretty good. He has always overcome adversity. Somehow, some way, he has always had his guys believe that they can overcome adversity. To say that this is the biggest adversity they have faced yet, I would say yes. When they lost [Drew] Bledsoe [September 23, 2001], I'm sure everyone thought, 'Whatever chances we had are over and done with.' Now, look what happened. Tom has been so great for that team. You always knew having him in the game that you were going to win and he was going to be so productive. That's like playing the Rams that year in the Super Bowl [XXXVI]. No one gave them a chance, including me. They won the game. The thing about Bill, don't ever bet against him. Like you said, I think he's a great schemer. Just a few times I've had success against his teams. There have been more times than not that they've had the upper hand on us or teams that I've quarter-backed. He'll find a way to get those guys to rally around Matt and

he's probably telling them, 'No one gives you a chance now.' They're still pretty darn good."

Favre and Mangini, meanwhile, seemed to enjoy a mutual respect. "He's very, very unassuming and mild-mannered," Favre said. "He never raises his voice, but he gets his point across. One of the first things I told him when I got here, I said, 'I'm amazed at how many guys practice here.' There are one or two guys maybe at the most who sit out of practice. Everyone practices. Do they moan and complain and grumble afterwards? Yes, we all do. But they all practice and practice a certain way. He addresses things in our team meeting every morning and pulls up film of things that we did well in the game or in practice. Also, he addresses things we didn't do as well. . . . The old saying, 'The player's coach,' whatever that may be, he'll come up to me, I've heard him talk to numerous guys, 'What can we do as far as meetings? How can we make practice a little more fun?' He's willing to give a little bit. What he asks in return, from what I see, guys are giving him. . . . The way he handles himself, he kind of relies on the team to police themselves. I was asking a question to one of the security guards the other day. I said, 'Do they give us wake-up calls when we're on the road?' I've never needed one, but most guys would sleep in if they could. The response to me was, 'No, they have to know themselves.' He asks a lot of you. He's willing to give. To me, that's the best way to do it. I know how to practice. I know what's expected of me. Am I going to be perfect? No. If I'm not sure what we're supposed to be doing, I'm going to find out somehow, some way. Really, that's the way we should all handle it. He's going to address things that he sees are not getting addressed by the players."

Someone wanted to know whether Mangini treated Favre with more respect because of his years in the NFL. "Just because I'm older means nothing," Favre said. "I don't think he has bent over backwards for me. I would never ask him to do that. I'm not going to come in and start asking for all these special favors. I'm here to help this team win and he knows where I stand on that."

Favre was treated to a standing ovation when he trotted out for the opening series. It was ninety degrees and humid for the 4:15 p.m. kickoff. There were many more No. 4 jerseys in the stands than there had been in preseason.

Flag girl Gina G., one of the twenty-two members of the Jets Flight Crew that was formed in 2007, noticed an unmistakable difference in the air at Favre's first regular-season home game as a Jet. "It was a different vibe in the stadium," she said. "Everybody was going crazy. The fans are always excited, but it just seemed to be at a different level."

New era.

Same Old Jets.

On third-and-4 at his 26, Favre found Cotchery for 20 yards. It was Cotchery's last catch of the day. Favre marched the Jets into field goal position, but Jay Feely, signed as Nugent's fill-in, missed a 31-yard field goal wide right. Bad omen.

Cassel (16-of-23, 165 yards), meanwhile, looked like the coolest guy in the room. The Jets were taking away Moss (2-for-22 receiving) so Cassel looked for his backs and Welker. He completed his first four passes for 61 yards and soon it was 3–0. "They kept it simple," Kerry Rhodes would say. "They didn't want him to lose the game."

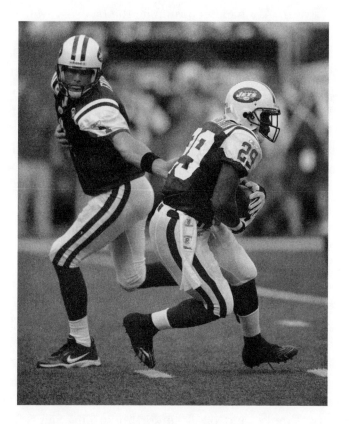

It was 6–0 early in the second quarter when Favre stepped up off a third-and-9 scramble and threw across his body to Coles for a 54-yard catch and run down the right sideline. Favre's chemistry with Coles (3-for-72 receiving) had improved, but where was Cotchery? "They mixed it up today," Favre said. "I'm sure if I look at the film tomorrow, I'm gonna see Jerricho open at times, gonna see LC open at times, Stuckey, and . . . whatever. . . . They didn't change dramatically, but they rotated in coverage a little bit and mixed it up, rolled to LC, rolled to Jerricho, depending on the situation in the game, and I thought they disguised well. Once again, I'll look at the film; there'll be times where he was open . . . maybe I didn't see him."

It wasn't long before Favre had it first-and-goal at the 3. Schottenheimer, from a power package that featured three tight ends and no wideouts, called a running play, Thomas Jones off right guard. It gained a yard. "We had been running the ball very well and liked our opportunity there," Mangini said. "We thought that was our best chance at that point."

Schottenheimer called another running play, Jones up the middle. It gained 1 yard. Then, much to the chagrin of a fan base that had seen this kind of play-not-to-win philosophy from Walton and, more recently, Edwards, Schottenheimer incomprehensibly called yet another running play, Jones off right guard. It lost 2 yards. Feely was summoned for the 21-yard field goal.

"Had we run it in on the first, second, or third play, it's a great call," Favre would say later in the interview room. "I don't second-guess Schotty's call one bit. Would I like to have thrown? I'd like to throw every play—but you're not gonna win that way. We have the offensive line to do it, we have the running backs to do it. And I know what Bill's saying over there—they have the defense to stop it. They stopped it today; there's no guarantee a pass will work. So, yes I would, but it has nothing to do with second-guessing the decision. I thought we could run it in as well."

Favre still had the whole second half to overcome Rangini. But on his first possession, he made the mistake that cost the game. On second-and-25 from his 24, he looked downfield for tight end Bubba Franks, and badly underthrew him. Safety Brandon

Meriweather intercepted, and soon it was 13–3, on its way to being 19–10.

"Maybe I got a little greedy; coulda dumped it in the flat," Favre said. "But I think if I'da made the throw I wanted to, there's no guarantee it woulda been caught, but it woulda been a much better opportunity. I just underthrew it. I saw the guy. Misjudged or . . . just made a bad throw. Like to tell ya something different, but it was a bad throw."

A bad throw the Patriots were waiting for him to make.

"He's the all-time leader in picks for a reason," Rodney Harrison said. "He's also a Hall of Famer. That's not to discredit him, but stats don't lie."

It was 16–3 when Favre (18-of-26, 181 yards, 1 TD, 1 INT) found a rhythm early in the fourth quarter. He was 6-of-6 for 51 yards on a drive that culminated with a 2-yard touchdown pass in the right corner of the end zone to Stuckey. This time, second-and-goal at the 2, Favre lined up out of the shotgun. It proved to be too little too late

because the Jets defense could not make the stand it needed to make against Cassel.

"It's a setback because I feel like this team is capable of winning every game, and I think that's the mind-set we have to have; I'm sure that's the mind-set the other locker room has," Favre said. He was wearing a white T-shirt, jeans, and flip-flops behind the podium. "Now, what do you do in a situation like this? Hope we rally together and find a way to overcome it. It's one game, and there's fourteen left. Who knows what's gonna happen, but nothing good'll happen if we don't do it together."

This was only Favre's second home opener outside of Green Bay, remember. "The expectations that I've always put on myself are the same," he said. "I expect to win, expect to play at a high level. This obviously was different for several reasons, but when we teed it up, kicked it off the first time, it was back to football, and I really thought we had a chance to win this game. I know you win some, you lose some, but . . . there were some bright things in this game. Home opener, we'll have seven more, hopefully a couple more after that. But it's not the start we wanted, that I wanted, but I think there's a lot of room for improvement. But this team can be pretty good."

Now someone asked, "After all of the choices that you've made to get to this point today, does this loss feel any different for you?"

"It hurts the same," Favre said. "I'd like to have come back and won every game, you don't have to dwell on the losses, or whatever, but . . . it's why I came back. It was fun out there today. No doubt it would have been a lot more fun had we won, but that's the way it goes. Once again, I enjoy these guys, I really do, it makes it easier. Enjoy working with 'em, enjoy competing with 'em. It's disappointing, but I know what I can do, and hopefully the rest of our team knows, and that's get better . . . , 'cause it can be as long or short as we want to make it. It's two games, we're 1–1, long ways to go, and . . . the more you lose, the longer it gets.

"And I'm not here to lose."

Finally, Speight, standing to Favre's left, announced, "One more question."

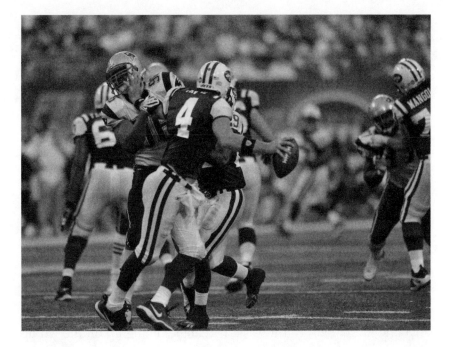

The question was whether Favre was okay with the offensive phi-losophy, which to this point was more conservative than Sarah Palin. "I'm fine with it," Favre said. "My job is to come here and run this offense. And believe me, regardless of the plays that were called, there were some opportunities—I looked at the pictures on the side-lines, and there were some opportunities for some big plays. And that falls back on me."

No one had the heart to mention that Rodgers had thrown for 328 yards and three touchdowns and led the 2–0 Packers to a 48–25 victory over the Lions. But since it was a one o'clock game, you can bet that Favre already knew.

Down the hall, Belichick uncharacteristically could not hide his glee. "I think this team was going to come down and do what we did today regardless of what anybody else thinks," he said defiantly. "That's just who they are and that's what they want to do. That's their job. I don't think it really matters what you think. That's what they're going to do regardless."

Mangini continued to take heat for the playcalling by the goal line. And Favre continued to defend his coach and offensive coordinator at his midweek press conference before the Monday night game in San Diego.

"It was frustrating that we didn't get the ball in, and hopefully these questions will subside at some point," Favre said. "I got the utmost confidence in our offensive line . . . would I have liked to have thrown it? Sure I would. But I would much rather get the ball in, whether it be running or throwing. Any quarterback who would sit up here in front of you right now and tell you that in that situation he didn't want to throw the ball would be lying. I feel very confident in Brian's playcalling ability. We made some off-season acquisitions as far as offensive line—of course, I'm one of those too. But we had chances to get the ball in on those three running plays, and for whatever reason, *we* didn't execute it. You give those guys credit across from us; that's what they're good at—their front seven is as good as anybody in football. But it was a bad angle, lining up on the wrong side, whatever it may be, that cost us not getting in. I'd like to tell you something different, but there's no guarantees throwing the ball would have worked. Do I like my chances? Absolutely. But I'm gonna say that no matter what. People can call it conservative or whatever. Had we run the ball in on one of those three, they're great calls."

Problem was, they didn't. Favre was asked whether he was disappointed that when the plays came in to the huddle, none of them were passes. "After the fact? Yeah," he said. "It's fun throwing touchdown passes, don't get me wrong. But I knew we were very capable of running the ball in. If I didn't think we could do it, I wouldn't rant and rant on the field, I would talk to Schotty about it."

Do you have the power to veto a play that comes in like that?

"No, not on the goal line, no," Favre said. "There's nothing to check to, no. But I felt very confident in his decision to run the ball. I didn't think it would take three times, to be totally honest with you. Historically, on the goal line, I've made a lot of plays. So I have a lot of confidence in what I do. But I have to be honest with you—I got a lot of confidence in our offensive line and our running backs; still do. If we got in that situation again, I think if we threw the ball we would score. But I think if we ran it we would score as well, I really do."

Have you felt restricted at all?

"No. We talk so much, aside from the typical meetings we've had, where we meet as a group," Favre said. "And I sit down with Schotty, and I sit down with Daboll and even with Eric at times, and they've all asked what I feel comfortable with. If there's something that we don't have in that I felt comfortable with in the past that we could put in, that fits into what we're trying to do, and we're trying to do that. I don't feel like the decisions that they've made with me in the room have changed when we're on the field. I feel confident that I can go to them at any point and ask for something, or install something that maybe we don't have in, and that it will get done. Just because I'm here, we don't change our offense. And I said this from day one—it's much easier for one to get on board with ten than vice versa. And it's been a great working relationship. Ultimately, we're judged by wins and losses, I know that, Schotty knows it, Eric knows it, on down the line. And how we get to that point is what we're trying to achieve right now. I didn't come here to lose . . . neither did Alan Faneca, Kris Jenkins, or the guys who have been here before. You could see, like, Shaun Ellis's frustration at the end of the game. I mean, that's ten years of frustration that he's had to go through, and we're trying to change that. Old and new. And I feel like the path that we're on right now is the right path. . . . Right now we're 1–1, we lost to a very good football team. Three plays in that game didn't make the difference. I had numerous opportunities during the course of the game on throws that I could have made that could have been the difference, that I missed. I underthrew Chris Baker on a corner route that was picked; it resulted in seven points, you can't do that. So you can point to a lot of plays. And I think we all need to take ownership in not only the wins but the losses, and that's the only way we're gonna get better. And I feel like the path we're on is the right path."

Favre started to feel confident enough in Cotchery and Coles to give them a jump ball from time to time and let his playmakers make plays. "I think the chemistry's gotten a lot better," he said. "I would hope that it would continue to get better—a lot like the chemistry I had with our guys in Green Bay the last couple of years. Of course Donald [Driver] and I have thrown the ball. . . . We had so much success together. But this group is more of a veteran group, has been around, knows the game, and so I would think the chemistry would come a little bit quicker. In my opinion, it has."

As for Pennington, it got worse before it would get better. In the fourth quarter of a 31–10 week 2 loss at Arizona, Pennington was yanked in favor of rookie Chad Henne, who looked impressive during garbage time. Had Pennington, 0–2, already lost his grip on the starting job? Were the Jets right about him? At his Monday press conference, Miami head coach Tony Sparano put an end to speculation that Henne would take the reins. The rookie coach wasn't ready to place his season in the hands of the rookie quarterback.

The talented Chargers had started 0–2, and were coming off a gut-wrenching 39–38 loss to the Broncos in which they felt jobbed when referee Ed Hochuli blew his whistle before a last-minute Cutler fumble that would have given them a hard-fought victory. So Favre and his receivers needed to brace themselves for an angry outfit and, very possibly, a shootout with Philip Rivers.

"Norv [Turner] may be saying this is a 'must win,'" Favre said. "I'm sure in the back of his mind they're all must-wins. I feel like we're in a must-win situation as well. At the end of the season when you look back, you can always say, 'That one game, or that one play, may have cost us a chance of the playoffs,' or whatever. It was heartbreaking the way they've lost . . . believe me, we'll see their best on Monday night, no doubt about it. So for us, we have to look at it as a must-win situation as well."

When you know you're playing a team with an offense like that, does that put more of an onus on you guys to match them?

"I think your mind-set should be not only this week but in every week. . . . I can never look at a drive as, 'Okay, guys, this is a drive we can afford to punt or go three-and-out,'" Favre said. "I just don't look at it that way, and that's the way I've always played my game. The way I've always looked at my game is regardless if it's a two-yard pass or a fifty-yard pass . . . whether the play's designed to go short, whether it's designed to go long . . . that we should score, or I should give us a chance to score on every single play. And no different on run plays . . . when I hand the ball off, I try to fake. I try to do whatever I can to deceive the defense so we can score or get a big play out of it. I think that's a mind-set that we all on offense should take. . . . When you have opportunities, however they may come, you gotta make the most of 'em."

Rodgers was certainly making the most of his. "Well, I'd said from day one, Aaron Rodgers would play well," Favre said. "Not once did I ever say, 'This guy can't play.' This is his fourth year, he's playing with a very talented football team, but he's got all the weapons, not only from a team standpoint, but himself. He's got a great arm, he's a real smart guy, he's played behind a pretty smart guy . . . maybe not as smart as him but . . . but he's seen me do it a certain way and he's gonna have his angles on how he wants to do things. But there's no reason that guy shouldn't succeed, none whatsoever. He's on a team that he can just dink and dunk it to whoever, he can throw it downfield—we saw that last year. So, along with the fact that the guys around him, the coaching staff . . . the team was 13–3 last year. He's inheriting a great football team, and I'm not taking anything away from him. The guy can play."

Favre's new team was 4–12 last year—but expectations were higher for the 2008 Jets than the 2008 Packers. Were they too high?

"I guess that remains to be seen," Favre said. "I like the fact that people expect a lot out of us, when maybe they didn't before. I think that's a good thing. Each individual in that locker room can look at it however they want to look at it. But I expect us to win. I think we have the nucleus in place; I think we have a very good coaching staff. Woody Johnson has done everything in his power to make it easy on us, and comfortable. Until they're dethroned, the Patriots are the team. And that's giving them all the respect they deserve. But we made some changes here this off-season that I think have bettered this team across the board, and that brings high expectations. But so what? And we had an opportunity to win that game the other day. So maybe what's happened here in the past plagued us some in that game, I don't know. I give them credit because they found ways not to lose a game, and we did. But if someone walks away from that game and says that we didn't have a chance, they're kidding themselves.

And we should feel like that every game we play—we should have a chance to win. Now we just gotta do it, we gotta win. So, if you want to call that high expectations—fine."

Over the weekend, Jay Glazer of FoxSports.com reported that the Jets were tailoring their offense for Favre.

"Well some of it doesn't hit my brain exactly the way I want it to," Favre said. "But, now, more so than in training camp when you start simplifying or game-planning where you just go in, 'Okay, this is how we want to attack Cover 2, this is how we want to attack man-to-man.' Then you kinda simplify and narrow down certain plays. But, what we have in, I feel like I've managed very well up to this point. I know there's a lot more we could put in, but I feel like what we have in, not only the last two weeks but what we're putting in this week, and probably in weeks to come, we can win every game with."

The Jets landed in San Diego Saturday night. Favre and the Jets would feel the tremors that were quaking Gillette Stadium the next day. Pennington completed 17-of-20 for 226 yards as the Dolphins stunned the Patriots 38–13 in a game that featured the debut of the wildcat—a direct snap to running back Ronnie Brown, who scored three touchdowns and threw for another to tight end Anthony Fasano. "We could have easily strolled up to New England and rolled our helmets out there because we were so disappointed in our performance against Arizona," Pennington said. "We didn't do that, and to me that was huge for us that these guys banded together and we came together and played well and won a football game; a game that no one expected us to win."

The Cowboys, meanwhile, brought Rodgers back down to earth in a 27–16 victory at Lambeau. Once again, the jury was out in Green Bay over whether its team had done the right thing.

For Favre, that had become a lesser concern. It was nearing time for him to give America one of his Monday night magic moments.

And that part of the world that wears green and white was clamoring for Mangini to open up the offense, to let Favre be Favre. Why else make the move to get him, for crying out loud—which many Jets fans were doing. The heat was on Mangini to take the shackles off.

The Jets were hoping to catch a break; LaDainian Tomlinson had been nursing a big toe injury that had him questionable. Everyone expected him to play, but the Chargers were getting backup Darren Sproles warmed up in the bullpen just in case. Sproles is a dangerous 5-foot-6 threat who can hide behind his blockers and break open a game at any time, but he is not LT. And outside linebacker Shawne Merriman, the Chargers' most fearsome pass rusher, was gone for the season with a knee injury.

But what was about to unfold was alarming to Jets Nation. The communication and chemistry between Favre and his receivers seemed nonexistent at times. The operation was helter-skelter, seemingly conflicted between two contrasting offensive philosophies as Mangini and Schottenheimer struggled to reach a middle ground with Favre.

The night started promisingly enough. Favre had himself a quick 7–0 lead, thanks to a 25-yard interception return by David Barrett. But the first hint of trouble came later in the first quarter when Favre, from the shotgun, looked for Thomas Jones in the left flat. But TJ kept zigging down the sideline while Favre expected him to zag, and he threw the ball underneath, where Antonio Cromartie was waiting. Luckily for Favre and the Jets, Cromartie dropped what would have been an easy touchdown. TJ lost a fumble on the next play anyway, and soon Favre trailed 10–7.

Favre, thanks to a bubble screen to Leon Washington and a bullet over the middle to Keller, drove to midfield, where, on the first play of the second quarter, he threw off his back foot for Coles in the left flat. Cromartie, who at 6-foot-2 is three inches taller than Coles, reached over the receiver's back, tipped the ball to himself, and raced 52 yards to pay dirt. "The one to LC, I think Antonio made a good play," Favre said. "It wasn't like he was wide open, but LC was in front of him. The one thing we knew going into this game, that Cromartie had great ball skills. He can pick it out from anywhere. So on that one, I tip my hat to him, made a good play. I thought the ball was incomplete, I actually didn't see him pick it." He didn't see Cromartie pick it because blitzing linebacker Matt Wilhelm was in his face. Cromartie: "Brett Favre tried to force it on a pivot route and

I had to make a play on the ball." The Chargers fully expected Favre to let them make more than a few plays on the ball. Indeed, Clinton Hart would drop a sure interception in the end zone, and Cromartie would drop one when he took his eyes off the ball. "Our biggest thing this past week was, 'Everybody get to the ball,' because there's gonna be a lot of tipped balls thrown, a lot of overthrown balls thrown because Brett Favre has a strong arm," Cromartie said.

Favre didn't have much time to feel sorry for himself, because the jitterbugging Washington, the Jets' most explosive player, returned the ensuing kickoff 94 yards, to the Chargers' 5-yard line. Now all of Jets Nation waited to see if Mangini and Schottenheimer would dare repeat the playcalling folly of the New England game.

On first-and-goal, here was Jones up the middle for a yard. You could probably have mistaken every Jets fan watching back in New York for John McEnroe. *You cannot be serious!* Were Mangini and Schottenheimer being stubborn?

The natives stopped being restless when they noticed Favre lined up in the shotgun on second down. And sure enough, Favre found Coles in the back of the end zone, and it was 17–14.

But here Mangini made a fatal mistake. He gave the green light for an onside kick, a low-percentage play used to change the momentum of a game. "We wanted to do it after a momentum-changing situation like a touchdown," Mangini said.

Except that Washington and Favre had just changed the momentum. The Jets defense, with Jenkins sidelined early with a back injury, was now softer against the run. The risk/reward, against a prolific offense like this one, was not in the Jets' favor. The Jets overloaded one side and Feely rolled one that Wallace Wright, a terrific special teamer, let slip off his fingertips. Chargers' ball. At Mangini's 44-yard line. Five plays later, Rivers hit Chris Chambers with a 27-yard touchdown pass and it was 24–14, and the Jets would never recover.

Mangini defended the call after the game, and again the following day after watching the tape. "In that situation I would definitely do it again if it was the same situation," he said.

Maybe he was dreaming that this was 1996, when Favre was leading the Packers to a Super Bowl championship and winning one of three consecutive MVP trophies. That Favre always had Holmgren's back.

But this was not that Favre.

Favre, third-and-9 from his 30, looked right for Cotchery, who broke inside underneath. Unfortunately, Favre threw the ball deep, to the sideline. Where safety Eric Weddle made a diving interception. And soon it was 31–14. "I thought Jerricho was actually gonna run up the boundary . . . but when I looked at the picture on the sideline, I had Chansi Stuckey wide open down the middle of the field and . . . that one falls on me," Favre said. "And I'm not saying Jerricho's wrong. That was a bad play on my part."

Washington positioned Favre at midfield with 3:06 left before the half with another stellar kickoff return. But Favre, third-and-9 from the Chargers' 32, was sacked out of field goal range by Shaun Phillips. Chargers defensive coordinator Ted Cottrell, who would be fired later in the season, was catching Favre off guard with the blitz.

"They did some things that disrupted us a little bit protection-wise," Favre said. "I thought their scheme was very good. They gave up some plays, but they also made some. I think tonight they played more attack than sitback based on what we'd seen in the past. I think they have two fine corners and they pressed 'em most of the time, and I think that's what they're best at, instead of playing off. They were able to get a pass rush with their different blitzes and things. Once again, we hadn't seen that. I thought we handled it okay, for the most part. It wasn't like we were totally surprised by it."

The gunslinger was going to have to empty his holster in the second half. He tried. But he clearly was nowhere close to being ready to carry his team. On the opening drive of the third quarter, Favre marched the Jets to the Chargers' 9, where he faced fourth-and-4. No shotgun this time.

Favre tried to hit Keller, who wound up in the back of the end zone. The ball wound up in and out of the hands of safety Hart just inside the end zone. "That's something that if we had to do over again, I wouldn't do the same thing," Favre said. "He may have ran a little bit deeper than I thought. Once again I'm not saying he's wrong, or I'm right, or whatever. We gotta get on the same page.

And I'm just talking about plays in general. We can go on down the line. I made numerous, numerous mistakes. Made some plays, but made too many mistakes."

The Chargers extended their lead to 38–14 and spent the rest of the night trading yards for minutes on the clock. Favre sustained an ankle injury early in that third quarter. Clemens played the last series. When it was time for the postgame sportsmanship, you could see Favre limping noticeably on his way across the field to shake hands with Rivers, then with LT. He looked every bit his thirty-eight years.

"We got beat," a somber Favre began in the interview room. "We made too many mistakes. Against a good offensive football team like that, they're gonna score points, they're gonna score points regardless and . . . we just made too many mistakes. And there's some bright spots, but . . . we gotta find a way to eliminate mistakes."

If Favre wanted to look at the glass as half full, he could have focused on the fourth quarter, when, from an empty formation (no backs), he threw touchdown passes to Stuckey and Keller. But the fact that his best work came during garbage time should have left him with a half-empty glass.

"I'd like to say that there is some silver lining in this game, and that's maybe we found something that we can go to bat with that is pretty productive. You see we can move up and down the field," Favre said. "And Eric said after the game this team has good character, very good character, but now we gotta find a way to use that to win ballgames, and I don't think anyone who watched that game tonight would question the effort, really, on either side of the field. But that only gets you so far. How we come together, if we do, or continue to do what we've been doing, you're ultimately judged by wins and losses, we all know that but, this team can be a very good football team. I really believe that. It's just a matter how quickly we can put it together."

He was speaking on a podium inside Qualcomm Stadium less than thirty minutes after the game. His ankle was wrapped with an Ace bandage.

Before long, it was time for Speight, who announced, "We'll do one more."

"Brett, did you get nicked up at all?"

"A little bit . . . rolled my [left] ankle up so . . . I probably looked like I was . . . been shot in the leg or something, but . . ."

"When did that happen?"

"Early third quarter. 'Course, as the game progressed . . . I'm sure it'll feel terrible tomorrow, but we just did some X-rays and I think they're okay—aside from old ankles."

He had thrown only 48 passes over the first two games. On this night, Favre (30-of-42, 271 yards) had thrown 42 times. "I feel better with the offense, I feel much better," he said. "I mean, there's no excuses from my end tonight, to say that I'm still learning the offense. I think I, as well as the rest of the offense, made some mistakes at times, whether it be protection issues . . . wrong read . . . throwing to the wrong guy . . . whatever. Those are things that are not a reflection at all of knowing the offense. That was just . . . you know, made bad plays."

By the time he had returned home from a sobering cross-country flight, Favre was fighting off demons that were telling him he had made a mortal mistake coming to New York. He underwent more tests, and Mangini was asked whether his quarterback's Iron Man streak—256 consecutive starts—was in danger Sunday against the Cardinals. "Brett usually plays," Mangini said, "and I would anticipate the same."

Favre was listed as questionable. "I would hope I would never go into a game and play to continue a streak even though I felt like I would hamper the team with this injury or a broken thumb or whatever," he said. "My philosophy has always been, if you feel like you can play and not hinder the team one bit, then at least try. Why not try? I think I owe that to not only my teammates but to myself. That's the way I've always looked at it."

Why not try? of course, has always personified Favre's mentality. "Anytime you bring in somebody new, there's a transition," Mangini said. "Favre had been in one system for a long time and the nice thing about that is that he had experienced a lot of different evolutions in

that system and there is tremendous carryover between the different family trees. They may be called different things, but they're
essentially the same. We're pretty flexible in terms of adapting to new
ideas, things that work, and we were able to incorporate a lot of those
elements that he liked, as well as translate some of the things that
we had into terms that he was more familiar with. I really thought
he moved the ball pretty effectively throughout the course of the
evening in the air. There were the turnovers, but as I say, when you
put the ball up in volume, you increase the odds of those things
happening."

So a growing sense of urgency gripped Favre and the Jets as they
began preparations for the Cardinals. The so-called experts who
had glanced at their schedule before the season had fully expected a
1–2 start. But this 1–2 start included a home loss to the Matt Cassel
Patriots. And the surprising 3–0 Bills had jumped out of the gate and
were sitting atop the division, with their next game in St. Louis against
the godawful Rams, one of the three worst teams in the league. In a
move that reeked of panic and desperation, embattled Rams coach
Scott Linehan announced that starting quarterback Marc Bulger was
being benched in favor of backup Trent Green, a forty-year-old jour-
neyman with a concussion-prone history.

The Cardinals were coming off a 24–17 road loss to the Redskins,
and stayed in Virginia afterward rather than return to Arizona to
diminish the evils of jet lag. Leinart had proven to be more Broadway
Joe off the field than on it, and lost the quarterback job to old hand
Kurt Warner.

Warner was a fantasy football player's delight: if you gave him
time, if you kept him upright and in one piece, he could air it out
with the best of them, even now, at thirty-seven. That made Larry
Fitzgerald and Anquan Boldin, arguably the best wide receiver tan-
dem in the NFL, all the more dangerous. In other words, Favre had
precious little time to steel himself for the daunting possibility of
another shootout.

The Jets had gotten back to New Jersey at around 8 a.m. Tuesday,
and when Favre met the media some twenty-seven hours later, the
ankle was still sore. He was limited in practice Wednesday. "I've been

down this road before, not only with an ankle injury, but with a lot of injuries," he said. "I respect Eric. He wants us to refer those questions to him. I understand that. I'm doing everything I can to get ready. How it will affect me during the course of the week or Sunday remains to be seen."

He admitted that it affected him in San Diego when he found himself throwing off his back foot. "The good thing is my mechanics were never good," Favre said. "You're saying that and I'm kind of laughing, thinking, 'You mean I actually threw off of a foot?' Normally I throw with both feet off the ground." Laughter. "There is a method to the madness to the way I throw or I wouldn't be here today. It affected me some. I thought in the second half I threw the ball pretty well. Now, we didn't really throw any deep balls. We really didn't throw any deep balls throughout the whole game. It remains to be seen how that would affect me with a deep ball. I'm not really concerned about it."

But what if he couldn't practice all week? He was asked the last time he played without any practice. "I don't know if I did last year or not," Favre said. "I can't remember. I missed the first three weeks of training camp, which is obviously different for me. Being that I need the work, today as well as any other day, mentally, has to be the most important thing. It's a short week. We're cramming a lot of stuff in. I'm not really concerned about the lack of or how much [I] practice."

His arm had never been the problem. "That's what I'm here for. No one wants to be injured. . . . I love to play. I didn't come here, first of all, to lose. I didn't come in here to get hurt and sit and watch. That's why I played every game. I could have sat out numerous games and no one would ever have questioned the fact that I was hurt. I wouldn't let it get that far."

There were people in baseball who thought that Cal Ripken was all about Cal Ripken when he refused to take a day off near the end of his Hall of Fame career. Favre may be damn proud of his streak, but no one ever thought that he played on strictly for the sake of extending it.

"I think the injuries that I've been faced with may keep the next guy out," he said. "For example, I go back to the broken thumb. Most guys would not even attempt to play with a broken thumb. Especially a quarterback, just because of what it might do, how bad they may look and how much it would hurt the team. I felt like I could play because I played the previous game with it, even though I didn't know. So I was willing to take that risk. In all those cases, I was willing to take that risk with the thought in mind that I wouldn't hurt the team. Who was going to argue if I said I was going to play, just because I had done it so many times? After the fact . . . 'Maybe we should have sat him.' I don't want that ever to come into play. I love to play, and that's what I'm here for. I feel like I can give this team a very good chance to win. Until I'm told otherwise, I'm going to do it."

Favre was aware of the Jets' tortured history, and the woe-is-us nature of long-suffering Jets fans. "I'm disappointed we're 1–2," he said. "I've been 1–2 before. I actually went 4–12 before. I've been in some early stretches during the course of a season, or through my career, where we didn't start off the way we had hoped. I like the way our guys have handled the last two weeks, even through the losses and the character they've shown. The bottom line is winning. How we get to that remains to be seen. Eric stressed this the other day before and after the game, I think it's so true, that once this team starts believing, all fifty-three guys start believing that it can be done, then it will be. When there's doubt creeping in from wherever, and you see flashes of how good we can be, as we have, then it's going to be the way it has been until we believe that 'Hey, we're pretty darn good, we're going to go out and we're not going to be beat.' We'll be much better off.

"There's no doubt from my end. I'll continue to do what I've done from day one, from the day I first stepped onto a field. If that's not good enough, then it's not good enough. It's been good enough up to this point. I've won way more games than I've lost. I don't anticipate that changing. I don't anticipate the way I prepare, the way I practice, and the way I carry myself as a teammate to change. I would hope that the rest of us do the same. I really believe we have the guys that will do that. It's just a matter of when we believe as one, which I totally agree, that we have that edge about us. As long as we do what we're supposed to do and play at a high level, we'll be fine."

Favre took solace in the view that the Jets were beating the Jets. "The little things, the self-inflicted wounds, you'll hear it from every team, you'll hear it from every coach, every professional team, whatever sport it is, they will kill you no matter how well you play," he said. "I'm here to tell you that that's the case for us. It's not a lack of effort. It's not a lack of the right game plan, wrong game plan, or whatever it is. You throw picks, you fumble, you have negative yardage, missed assignments, and it's going to beat you every time."

Those seemed to be the code words uttered in the meeting rooms: self-inflicted wounds. Because Mangini had already uttered them at his press conference. "He has a seventy percent completion rate," Mangini said. "That's a pretty high completion rate. He's throwing to multiple guys. Everybody got involved last game. I wouldn't say it's just a work in progress for those guys, it's a work in progress for us collectively. There's some things that we need to fix and get a lot better at as we move forward or otherwise it's going to be hard to execute the game-plan-specific things if you're not taking care of the self-inflicted wounds first."

But 70 percent completion rate or not, 1–2 was 1–2, and the questions about whether he was on the same page with his receivers continued to blitz Favre.

"My wife said when I got home that all the commentators kept talking about was, 'There's no way Brett can get this offense down in thirty days,'" Favre said. "You know, you have to let it go. We had enough ammo. I thought our game plan was a very good game plan. San Diego changed their defense completely for that game. I give them credit. They executed it well. We had plenty of opportunities. The bottom line is we gave them too many points, or gave them too many chances to score points from our end offensively. Make no mistake about it, their offense, you don't need to give them a short field. They're explosive. They're going to score thirty points on whoever they play. We don't need to give them fourteen. We're still trying to work some things out, sure. I don't think that had anything to do with that game the other night."

Of course it did. And now, after playing against Cassel and Rivers, quarterbacks who were born when Favre was in high school, the opposing quarterback this time would be a contemporary—the rejuvenated Warner. "He's a young guy," Favre joked, and everyone laughed. He remembered that Warner had been in training camp with him in 1994. That was before Warner, out of the Arena Football League, authored his rags-to-riches fairy-tale Super Bowl story with the Rams. "He was just a guy," Favre said. "Obviously, he's a lot different now. The guy has played phenomenal. I have a lot of respect for him. I didn't know much about him at the time. There are a lot of guys that come and go that just for whatever reason have never panned out. He's one of those guys that when he got the opportunity, he made the most of it. That's an understatement. I do remember, I don't know if Kurt remembers, when [Steve] Mariucci was our quarterback coach. He asked him to go in on a particular play. It was camp. He said, 'No, I'm not going in.' He wasn't ready. In fact, when Steve was here a couple weeks ago, we were doing an interview, laughing about that and how far he has come. He's not afraid to go in now."

• • •

Favre awakened to gray skies and showers on Sunday morning. There were a number of empty seats at Giants Stadium, in part because the Mets, tied for a wild-card playoff berth with the Milwaukee Brewers, were playing for their season in what would have been the last game at Shea Stadium in Flushing, Queens, if they lost and the Brewers beat the Cubs. Which was exactly what happened.

Favre's ankle was still bothering him. Not enough, of course, to keep him from starting his 257th consecutive game. Especially since Mangini and Schottenheimer had designed a game plan that any gunslinger would love.

But with the game 0–0, Favre, clad for the first time in one of those Titans throwback jerseys the club trots out every year now to honor its former namesakes, made the kind of amateurish throw you might expect from a rookie. Off-balance and looking left, he lofted a pass across his body, and it was intercepted by Chike Okeafor. Favre later explained that he thought he had a free play because of an off-sides penalty. Except no penalty was called.

"I thought it was a free play and I'm not gonna make excuses—how can you *think*, and still try to pull that off? You gotta know," he said.

But these were not the Same Old Bretts. Not on this day.

The final was Jets 56, Cardinals 35. Three times in his career Favre had thrown five touchdown passes. Never had he thrown six. Until now. The first three went to Coles. The next two went to Cotchery. The last one went to Keller. The last time a Jets quarterback had thrown six touchdown passes was 1972, in a 44–34 victory in Baltimore. The quarterback's name was Namath.

Coles was asked about his second touchdown catch, a 34-yarder down the left sideline midway through the second quarter after cornerback Eric Green crumpled to the turf nearby with a sprained right knee.

"I'm always in Brett's ear as soon as we leave the huddle, so if I ain't the first read, I make sure that he thinks I am," Coles said to laughter. "It's just one of them things where I know he's getting more comfortable with the offense and he's actually given me the go-ahead and talk to him when I'm coming out of the huddle and tell him what I have, and he's allowing me to say, 'Well, what do you think you can win on?' and I'm telling him, and he's giving me the freedom to run that route and he's trusting me to make those plays, so now that we've gotten to this point I think it's just something we need to build on."

From his press box perch, Tannenbaum was almost awed by the velocity on the ball. "One of the most amazing throws I'd ever seen," he said.

Favre said he didn't go out of his way to involve Coles early. "He's quietly just kinda snuck up the ladder with me, because he was injured, didn't really get a lot of time with him, and that's been well-documented," he said. "But I can't tell you how many people within this organization have told me week in and week out, 'You just throw the ball to LC and he'll make a play.' And I didn't go out there today and say, 'I'm just gonna throw it to LC.' I think the first touchdown he was like the second or third read . . . the guy's a playmaker, and our communication has been great, regardless of what people

may think. . . . I think it's a work in progress, but I think he's a heckuva player. You gotta find a way to get him the ball."

But it was what happened after Coles's third touchdown catch in the second quarter that cemented the bond between quarterback and receiver for all to see. "It's one of them things where he deserved it," Coles said. "I think our offense has taken a lot of criticism since we haven't been as explosive as people thought we were gonna be. And that was my third one of the day and it was my first time ever having, I believe, three touchdowns in one game. And I had the football in my hand. I think it meant a lot to me to actually go back and give a football to a legend and say, 'Look, thank you so much for everything you've done for me.'"

The Jets scored 34 points in the second quarter, a franchise record for most points in one quarter, and led 34–0. But then the defense, which had toyed with Warner, let its guard down, and all of a sudden it was 34–21. What did Favre tell his guys in the huddle when he got the ball back?

"We have a pretty experienced group of guys in that huddle, and on this team in general," Favre said. "And before I even got in the huddle, as I'm walking in, they were saying things that any coach would say, which you guys would say, what I would say: 'First and foremost let's get a first down; let's get some type of momentum.' Our defense obviously is struggling; that's an understatement. Their offense is explosive and at that time was very explosive. We can't think touchdown, we can't think twenty, thirty yards, we gotta think first down, and get a little breathing room. I just more or less reiterated that in the huddle, 'Guys, let's just get something going here.'"

Favre capped that critical drive with a 17-yard touchdown pass to Cotchery. "That type of play, that type of route, is one that I've always felt like I threw as well as any, a real skinny post . . . we got away from it last week, we put it in this week, and the one time we ran it in practice, I missed him again," he said.

This time he didn't miss him. "Jerricho runs outstanding routes; he's as patient as any receiver that I've ever thrown to."

"It's just a route we've been working extremely hard on," Cotchery said. "We've been trying to score on that for a while in practice." He chuckled. "We finally hit it. We ran it Friday, and Justin Miller was covering me and we didn't complete it."

In the fourth quarter, Mangini faced a fourth-and-1 at the Arizona 40. The Jets were leading 41–28 at the time. The same coach who had signed off on three Jones runs from the New England 3-yard line decided this was the right moment to go for it. Favre was asked if he had any input in the decision. "I'm always wanting to go for it," he said, "but I had no input. I think sometimes you gotta roll the dice, I really do. And sometimes they work, sometimes they don't—but

you won't know unless you try. . . . I felt good about the play; I was more worried about my execution, especially when I looked up and Jerricho was wide open, only thing I could think of was, 'Whatever you do, give him a catchable ball,' because he was wide open. But sometimes you gotta roll the dice. But to answer your question, no I didn't have . . . but I would have lobbied for it."

Favre's play-action fake helped sell a running play, and Cotchery knew he was in business when he saw the safety move closer to the line of scrimmage. Touchdown. "Before that play, me and Brett was talking, he was saying, 'If he's even close, just take him.' I was like, 'Well I already had that in mind.'"

In the locker room afterward, before he headed for the showers, Cotchery stopped Favre. "I thought he tied a career high or something like that," Cotchery said. "He was like, 'I've never thrown six.' That was like the end of the conversation. I'm scratching my head like, 'Really? He's never thrown six touchdowns before?' He played great. He was just dialing it up, telling everyone, 'Hey, get ready, the ball is coming.'"

Coles, his thigh much better, had lobbied the coaches during the week to get him the ball early, and they listened to him.

"Dealing with injuries . . . again, the big circus with Brett coming in town . . . it's been tough," he said. "I've taken it on the chin, I know there've been some things said about me, and me not being happy about him coming here . . . none of that was ever true. We've had great conversations from the time he walked through the door; I've done nothing but try to get on the same page with Brett since he's been here, and I'm sure he could tell you the same thing. I'm just excited about having the opportunity to play football with a legend. And I say that all the time that there's nothing I could do to enhance his career, but there's a lot he could do to enhance mine, with everything that he brings to the table.

"So anytime you have somebody that walks through the door like a Brett Favre, you have to be excited about it and just look forward to the opportunity that he's gonna give you."

Coles stepped off the podium in the interview room because Favre was ready. "Let the old man come on in," Coles said, and smiled as he walked past his quarterback. The following day, Coles revealed that he signed the ball he had given Favre. He had handed the ball from his first touchdown catch to a young fan wearing his 87 jersey. The ball from his second touchdown catch?

"Just keep it as a bragging piece that I could have later on that I can tell my kids that I caught a touchdown from Brett Favre," Coles said.

The first question for Favre, clad in a short-sleeved black shirt and a Titans cap, was about tying Namath's club record.

"Well, I'm proud of this team, the way we battled today, especially after last week and the way we started today . . . the way I started today . . . threw an ugly interception," Favre began. "We knew their offense could score a lot of points. Did I think we would score that many, or that way, six TDs? I think it shows the potential that this team has.

"I don't think it's any reason to go out and start buying playoff or Super Bowl tickets."

"Brett, how did you feel about your performance overall? . . . We've been talking for weeks about you getting on the same page with your receivers."

"You know, throwing six touchdown passes was awesome," Favre said. "But that had nothing to do with how I felt like I played. I think it was just one of those games. I mean, I've played a long time, and I've had guys come up to me in the locker room and say, 'You mean it's the first time you ever threw six touchdown passes?' And . . . 'Yeah. It is.' But . . . it's just one of those things. But, more importantly, I felt like, for the most part, just the overall game itself, I managed it well . . . once again, take the touchdowns out of it. . . . I mean, it wasn't a lot of yards for the most part . . . completion percentage was good, could have been better. . . . I wish I had the one decision back . . . fortunately we didn't give up any points out of that. But it wasn't perfect. The one good thing I'll say about this team that I've noticed in the short time I've been here is, like last week after the game, the way guys took ownership for the way we played last week I think is so important. We go out there, it's a tough loss, it'd be easy to point fingers, it's early in the year. But, as I've told guys throughout my career, taking ownership and handling success to me is almost as important, if not more important. And so in a game like this, it would be easy to . . . 'We're there. We've arrived.'"

Favre won't let those thoughts infiltrate his locker room. Pennington was the same way. There isn't a head coach alive who wants his team to think it's the Lombardi Packers. Parcells would reserve his most pointed tongue lashings following victories rather than defeats. "I think there's a lot of things we can get better at, and I'm pointing at me first," Favre said. "It was by no means perfect . . . that's the way we have to look at it, because that's the truth. But I'm pleased, because it was a win. I've won games before, been a part of some great wins where I threw no touchdowns, I threw several picks. Those wins were just as sweet as a win like this. A win's a win."

In the interview room, a young man held up what resembled a plastic cheesecake hat for Favre. "What do you think about the notion that Jets fans view you as a cult hero, and now they've invented a cheesecake hat in your honor?" he asked. It's the kind of silly self-serving publicity stunt you see all the time at Super Bowl Media Days.

"I don't know what to say," Favre said, and laughter filled the room. "For the first time in my career I have nothing to say!"

The kid asked, "Would you want to wear it?"

"I'm so hungry right now I could eat a cheesecake," Favre said, smiling.

More laughter.

The kid decided to press his luck. "Can I give it to you?"

"No thank you," Favre said softly.

The questions kept coming for Favre, and as several reporters began shouting them out, Speight, standing to Favre's left by the door to the locker room, bellowed, "Whoa, whoa, whoa. This'll be the last question. We'll take it right here from Rich."

Rich Cimini, Jets beat reporter for the past two decades, asked Favre if he had asked for the ball Coles had given him after their third touchdown connection.

"No, he gave it to me," Favre said. "Not too many times in my career has someone given *me* the ball. I don't want to make a big deal out of it, he just said, 'Hey, I've already had two today, here's one for you.' And . . . I'll keep it. I'll put it up in my trophy case, I'm honored that . . . and I told Damien Woody, not to really change the subject, but I told Damien on the sidelines late in the game, I said, 'I'm very, very happy I'm here.'"

So were Coles and Cotchery. Cotchery had caught only two touchdown passes in 2007. He had three in four games with Favre. "We've been saying all along it was gonna take a little time," he said.

But after a day like this, every Jet, from Woody Johnson on down, had unmistakable visual evidence that with Favre, nothing is impossible. Or impossible is nothing. Whatever Schottenheimer called worked. "It helps when Brett gets in a zone like that," Cotchery said. "It was fun out there playing today."

While Favre was turning back the clock, Rodgers was knocked out of a 30–21 loss to the Bucs with what was diagnosed as a sprained right shoulder. That sound heard across the country was the gnashing of teeth in Green Bay: was it possible that Rodgers's consecutive games streak as starting quarterback could be ending at—gasp—4?

Rodgers rehabbed that Monday and Tuesday and attempted a few handoffs Wednesday. The Packers, like the Jets, were 2–2, with a home game against the Falcons next. Favre and the Jets had their bye week.

"Every year, regardless of whatever team it is, they always seem like they say the bye week came at a good time," Favre said. "I'm used to the bye week actually being a little bit later. As far as physically, I could play this week. Everyone says, "How do you feel?" I don't know if I know what feeling good feels like anymore, but I can still go out and play, drag myself out there and be productive. Mentally, sometimes as you get older, you need to, as you say, recycle and recharge the batteries. Young guys, they just follow along. If the old guys complain, they complain. They don't know any different. Sometimes it's good to just get away. I mean, it's going to be a long, twelve-week run as opposed to breaking it up halfway. You know, it is what it is. It came this week, so it's at a good time."

He was asked whether there was a point when he knew he made the right decision. "I don't know exactly," Favre said. "I'd like to say when I first got here, but that would probably be a lie. It took a little while. I knew I was going to be here when I accepted that trade. When did I feel comfortable and felt like it was the right move? I don't know the exact time. To me, the most important aspect of the whole transition was liking the group of guys I was going to be working with and the coaches. There are no guarantees from after that how you'll play, how the team will play, and how we will gel together. I know that if we get along well and enjoy working together, I knew there was a good group of guys from a talent standpoint. When people at home ask me, either when they come up or on the phone, 'What do you think?' my response has always been, 'It's really a good group of guys that I enjoy working with.'"

It was an older group of guys than he had played with a year earlier, when the Packers were the youngest team in football. "As far as the talent is concerned, I really think that the talent pool is about the same," Favre said. "There are a lot more veterans here, but we're all new to each other. That's a big difference. I think when I say that this team has a lot of potential, I really believe it. The question is, can the chemistry come together pretty quickly? I think you're seeing flashes of it. It took a couple years for that to happen in Green Bay. Last year we kind of exploded, but we had been playing together for a couple years. There were a few new faces. It's like with the Giants last year, something clicked. What that was, I don't know. I wasn't in their locker room. This team, I don't want to say we can be the Giants, we have a long ways to go, but we have the makeup that can be pretty good."

But he was the Straw That Stirred the Drink. Their Namath. Their AFC Offensive Player of the Week.

"Joe Namath, it goes without saying how great he was not only for the league but for this organization," Favre said. "It just goes to show you how hard it is to do certain things. It's been that long since it [six touchdown passes] was done. That's not a bad one to be ranked up there with. As sweet as it feels to do that, it would feel a lot better if we just continue to win. One of the things I said in the press conference the other day was, 'Don't expect this every week, don't. I mean, it would be great, but don't.'" He smiled. "I just hope we win football games. Whatever happens after that, happens. That was a first, and I've played in a lot of games. Nothing ceases to amaze me."

To Favre, simpler was still better. "We have enough really right now to go into the rest of the season and have success," he said. "I don't think we need to add stuff. If one play was successful and we only ran it one time, why go and add a new play?"

There was a question about his relationship with Daboll, and Favre decided to give a quarterly report on all his new relationships. "It's been great," he began. "It's a little bit strange being that the GM and I are the same age. The head coach is younger. The quarterback coach is younger. The offensive coordinator is younger. Every player is younger." He chuckled. "Woody [Johnson], he's a little bit older than me. I think that's the only one," Favre continued with a smile. "I think when you're committed to what you're doing, and I've always considered myself coachable, I would hope that every coach that's ever coached me would agree to that. It doesn't really matter. Our relationship has been great. First of all, he knows that I'll make mistakes. I know that as well. Second of all, he knows I'm willing to do whatever it takes to correct those mistakes. As much as I've played, as much as I've seen, as much success as I've had, it doesn't really matter. What matters is what I do this year. He knows that. He knows from just the small amount of time he's been with me, he has no reservations of saying, 'Brett, you need to do this, you need to read that this way.' But in a way that is good for both of us, and vice versa, I think if I see something differently than maybe he sees it, and that goes for Schotty and Eric.

"I'm here for one reason, to help this team win. It's not about me. I think they know that. . . . I knew when I came here that there would be some questions. 'Okay, we have a guy with a lot of experience, but is he going to want to do it his way or our way?' Understandably so. I think they all would tell you, 'He's here as a Jet. He's willing to do whatever it takes to win.' That's true. Am I going to make mistakes? Sure. I hope with each week there's less and less and more production. We'll see what happens."

For once, Favre was all ears—and all eyes—right before the bye week. "This is a little bit different only because, in the past, when we had meetings during the bye week, my eyes were open, but they were closed, if that makes any sense," he said and smiled. 'Oh yeah, I heard you, Coach.' Yeah right. Then I needed to look over, 'What did he say?'" The tiny press room erupted in laughter. "This is obviously different because I'm still learning."

The Jets appeared ready for takeoff. Their legendary quarterback was suddenly leading the NFL in quarterback passer rating and touchdown passes.

OUT OF THE CANYON

Cincinnati • At Oakland • Kansas City • At Buffalo • St. Louis

F avre returned home for three days for some R&R. "Didn't do much of anything," he said. "Yard work. Pretty boring. Going home for three days . . . it's good, but also you see all the things that need to be done and . . . get stressed out. Come back to a nonstressful job. Pretty simple." And everyone in the press room chuckled.

Mangini and the Jets had been saying all the right things about the Bengals, all but calling them the best 0–5 team in the history of the NFL. "I know probably what [head coach] Marvin [Lewis] is telling 'em: 'Hey guys, you're better than our record indicates,'" Favre said. "And they are; they really are. I think we all look at that team and say, 'It's just a matter of time that they explode.' Now, trying to convince every one of those guys of that is always a difficult task."

Even though Favre led all quarterbacks with 12 touchdown passes and a 110.2 quarterback passer rating, the Jets were 2–2. The Bills were 4–1. The Patriots were 3–1. Even Pennington and the 2–2 Dolphins were in the hunt. Favre knew the last thing he should expect from himself was another six-touchdown outburst.

"It seems like that game was a month ago," he said. "And one thing I've learned throughout my career . . . what you did last week—how good you were, how bad you were—really doesn't matter the following week. Once you kick it off, it's a new team, it's a new day. Week-to-week changes, season-to-season changes, expectations obviously are different from one week to the next. I think for us, for any team that I've been fortunate enough to play on, it's important to expect a lot of yourself, but not get caught up—and Eric and I have had this conversation several times—not to rest on what you've done in the past. And like for me, coming here, for example, there was so much that you could look back to that I had done over my career and think that that would be enough or is enough to carry this team. And really what matters is how I play this year . . . how I carry myself as a leader and teammate. I mean, that's the only thing that matters—not how many touchdowns I've thrown in the past."

Lost in all the euphoria over the sudden ignition of Favre and the passing game was the sagging running game. Jones had gained only 37 yards against the Chargers and 46 against the Cardinals.

Favre said of him, "One of the things that I'm very impressed with is his leadership and his character . . . really a likable guy . . . he's an outspoken guy but not in a negative way . . . he's always the one calling us up, breaking a team down . . . after a tough loss, he's the first one to speak up in the locker room. Those are things that you can't coach. . . . There'll be weeks where he gets a hundred yards, there'll be weeks where he gets forty. There'll be weeks where I throw four touchdowns, there'll be weeks where I may not throw any. And I don't think it's a reflection of . . . losing a little bit. . . . Thomas can't break the long run anymore, Thomas can't do this. . . . I don't think it has anything to do with that—I *know* it doesn't. I think Thomas can break one at any point. But we have to be able to—or any team, really, for that matter—if they're gonna put too many in the box, you have to be able to throw the ball. If they drop back and play coverage, you have to run the ball. It's really as simple as that. . . . I think that a lot of our passes have been opened up by the running game, and you don't have to rush for a hundred before you do a play-action, and we've thrown two deep balls for touchdowns—one against Miami and one last week—they were *all* up in there for the run. . . . I think Thomas is a heckuva running back."

The Jets schedule over the next five weeks was quite forgiving: Cincinnati at home; at Oakland, coached now by someone named Tom Cable because Al Davis had whacked Lane Kiffin; Kansas City at home; at Buffalo; and St. Louis at home, coached now by Jim Haslett because Linehan had been fired. There was no reason why the Jets could not be 6–3 before their November 13 showdown in Foxboro.

"It's a work in progress; obviously, it's gotten better," Favre said. "But to sit here and say that I'm as comfortable as I was in my last few years in Green Bay, I'd be lying to you. But I'm working hard at it, and I like the open dialogue and the way we're going about it. Anyone has an idea, we speak up, we talk about it. Once again, we're trying to keep it simple, but yet within the confines of this offense. And Schotty's been great working with me, and I hope he can say the same thing. I'm not trying to change this whole offense, I'm trying to be productive in this offense, but try to get the terminology out as quickly as possible . . . if there's checks to be made, do that . . . and roll with it. I think it's been pretty productive up to this point. I think it . . . I know it should continue to get better. As long as we stay healthy and stick with the plan, I think we'll be okay."

Favre and his receivers were meeting every day after practice to study tape, bounce ideas off the wall, and shoot the breeze in a relaxed setting inside the facility. "It gives us an opportunity to see what he sees and what he is thinking," Coles said. "Of course, again, nobody knows what Brett is thinking at the time. His philosophy will go one way during the meeting, but when Sunday hits and he looks at the pictures, he will come up with something totally different. The meeting is to keep you on edge and give you an idea of what direction or his train of thought is going to be on Sunday. For the most part, it's everybody trying to get a better understanding for him."

The captivated owner included. Johnson remembers asking Coles in the cafeteria what it was like catching Favre's fastball. "And so he took his shirt down and showed me the piece of his skin, kind of torn off a little bit," Johnson said. "I said, 'You better catch it in your hands!'"

Before Favre had left for his break, a dead animal—howling team-mates speculated that it was a wild turkey—was deposited along with its blood and guts in linebacker Eric Barton's locker. Favre was the prime suspect.

"That was pretty good," Barton said. "Definitely up there." He was the victim because he had accidentally run over a goose.

"It definitely had the wow factor," said Faneca. "I've never had a dead animal brought into the locker room, so yeah, it's up there."

"I hope that the animal rights activists find out about it, whoever did it, that cruel person," Barton joked.

That cruel person wasn't Favre.

"All of a sudden, he got a letter from PETA [People for the Ethical Treatment of Animals]," Tratner said.

It was actually a dead goose.

"I didn't even do that!" Favre told Tratner.

The Jets kept the culprit's identity under wraps. "He felt bad because Favre was catching grief for something that he did," Speight said.

The airhorn was Favre's pet trick. "You know the little blowhorns?" Keller asked. "He'll be dead serious, installing plays, just talking about, 'Dustin, you have to do this, Laveranues, Jerricho, whatever, you have to do this' . . . just in the middle of this very serious meeting all you hear is toooooooooot—just loud as can be. And you just look over and you see Favre with the biggest smile on his face, just crack-ing up, like, 'I scared the hell out of you guys, didn't I?' He just car-ried it in his pocket."

"He loves the airhorn . . . he's got it on him at all times," Faneca said. "The funniest thing, though, is for about probably the first three weeks he was doing it, nobody knew who it was. I knew who it was, and a couple of people did, but for some reason, people would hear it and they'd be like: 'Who *is* that?' And I had told him that, and he just loved it to death, and I think that just took off."

"He scared one of the [assistant] coaches [Jimmy Raye] one day," Cotchery said, and chuckled.

"When we were at lunch, we'd hear it from like a team meeting," Cortez Robinson said.

On several occasions, when the players would deplane the club charter, Favre would swipe one of the adhesive name tags affixed to the top of one of the seats belonging to the operations staff and slap it on the back of the unsuspecting teammate directly in front of him.

Then there was the rubber snake. Favre would sneak up behind an unsuspecting foil with it for the desired effect. When Lori Nickel, who had covered Favre for McClatchy Newspapers, visited Florham Park in December, she quickly learned that little had changed with him. "Oh," she said with Tratner within earshot, "he's still got the rubber snake."

Well, it was actually a different rubber snake, a black one. "We used to have a container of gum . . . Bazooka Joe gum . . . and we keep it in a bucket, and there was a rubber snake in there, so when people reached for a piece of gum, they would see the snake," Robinson said. "So he thought it was funny, and he just always played with it."

"Whenever somebody wasn't paying attention, he'd throw it at their feet, or throw it in their locker," Gilmore said.

"The thing that struck me," said Speight, "was a lot of fuss was made about him, but he didn't make a fuss about himself. If he could rip off his face and put another face on, and take off that right arm so he'd be unrecognizable, it would all be fine with him."

Favre would also ask unsuspecting victims this simple question: "Do you like duck meat?"

One Jets employee chuckled as he repeated the punch line: "If you said, 'Yeah, I like duck meat,' he'd say, 'Well, duck under here and get you some,' and he'd grab his nuts."

Practice—even game day—had become a new experience in Jets World. "An unsuspecting coach not paying attention, he'd pants 'em," Schottenheimer said. "He slapped my ass a couple of times pretty good. It was a pregame ritual to get me going. He'd get a good running start and get somebody on the ass. You always had to be alert when Brett was behind you."

Friday, October 10 was an eventful day in the Jets family. At 7:43 a.m., Mangini's wife, Julie, gave birth to their third son—Zack Brett Mangini. It turns out that Mangini committed to Brett as a middle name during his wooing of Favre. Luke Harrison, his firstborn, was named after

Rodney Harrison, and the William in Jake William, his second son, was chosen for none other than one William Belichick, before the relationship between the coaches turned arctic cold.

And maybe, just maybe, the fact that Zack Brett's first day on this earth happened to fall on Favre's thirty-ninth birthday would prove to be more omen than coincidence. "The odds of the child being born on the same day as my birthday, I don't know what the odds are," Favre said. "He told me that today was the day and I asked, 'Well, is he still going to be Brett?' He said, 'Yeah, Zack Brett.' The odds, in some respects, are a lot like me. What were the odds of me ever coming to the Jets?

"It is a pretty cool thing."

There was more good news two days before the game: the Bengals announced that Carson Palmer had been scratched with an elbow injury. His replacement would be Ryan Fitzpatrick, a 2005 seventh-round pick of the Rams out of Harvard who had thrown three interceptions and lost a fumble in a 20–12 loss to the feeble Browns on September 28.

Namath had weighed in on Favre at his March of Dimes charity golf tournament on Long Island. "I'm optimistic. Who isn't?" he said. "This is the most exciting beginning of a season we've had in some time. This is a tremendous lift in terms of expectations and excitement." Namath, over the years, always stressed the importance of a quarterback's offensive line. And it was his defense that suffocated Earl Morrall and Unitas in Super Bowl III, and fullback Matt Snell who helped him keep the Colts off the field. "I've been watching him a lifetime; the man is great," Namath said. "Brett's a Hall of Famer. We know what Brett's going to do for the most part. If the Jets are a good enough team, they'll be serious contenders. If the rest of the team can't own up, Brett's in for a long season."

He could have guaranteed it.

Because on this bright sunny afternoon, Favre would have to be rescued by his teammates.

Before you could say Ochocinco, the 0–5 Bengals had taken a 7–0 lead when Favre lost a fumble that Chinedum Ndukwe returned

17 yards for a touchdown. "Don't worry about it," David Bowens told Favre on the sideline. The Bengals, contrary to popular opinion, did indeed watch game film, and so the coaches installed a game plan that would prevent Favre from strafing them the way he did the Cardinals. So Favre, who over the previous few years had added patience to his considerable arsenal, took what they gave him, and the Jets took a shaky 17–14 lead into halftime.

But here's the thing about Favre: you can give him a mile, and he'll take an inch for only so long. Inevitably, his trigger finger will begin to itch and twitch, and he'll try to take that mile. So as he peered across the field to his left from the Cincinnati 23 on the opening possession of the second half, he knew that Franks wasn't open at the 3. And didn't care. Favre let loose, and Marvin White intercepted.

"Sometimes you make good decisions, sometimes you make bad decisions," Favre said. "But you have to be able to roll the dice, and you gotta go down swinging, within reason, and you gotta trust the guys around you."

He decided to trust Cotchery early in the fourth quarter down the right sideline and watched helplessly as Jonathan Joseph deflected the missile into the waiting arms of Corey Lynch at the Cincinnati 2. "I felt like in both situations, neither guy was wide open, but I like

my chances one-on-one with those guys," Favre said. "I think more times we'll make that play or it'll fall incomplete."

Even a day later, Favre would have no regrets. "If I had to do it over again, I probably would take the same shot with Jerricho one-on-one," he said. But not with Franks. "The one to Bubba, I just should have thrown it away," he said. "I felt Bubba had leverage on the guy, and really thought the ball was thrown far enough where it would fall out of bounds. That was one of those you shouldn't throw. The one to Jerricho, it just happens."

It's all part of the deal with Favre. You take the bad with the good, because there has been so much more good. "That's the cost of doing business when you're gonna throw into tight spaces," Mangini said.

The Jets were fortunate that Fitzpatrick was the opposing quarterback. Return man Leon Washington, meanwhile, was repeatedly positioning Favre with a short field, and the defense was reminding

Fitzpatrick that he wasn't playing against Columbia anymore. So, clinging to a 20–14 lead in the fourth quarter, Favre needed only to direct a 41-yard drive that culminated in Jones's third touchdown of the day. The final was 27–14. An ugly win like this is in the eye of the beholder. "I think it goes without saying how important not only having balance on offense but in all three phases of the team is to be productive," Favre said. "I don't believe in ugly wins. I believe a win is a win, and that one felt as good as any win I've been a part of in recent memory."

Favre's 71.3 completion percentage was his highest after five games for his career. He talked optimistically about simply getting the ball into his playmakers' hands, and he was quite happy with his coterie of playmakers. "I think that there is no reason why we can't complete twenty-five, thirty balls, depending on how many you throw, week in and week out," he said.

The 1–4 Raiders had been blown out in New Orleans. Quarterback JaMarcus Russell looked overmatched. Rookie running back

Darren McFadden had been hampered by a toe injury. It was time for Favre to strike while the iron was hot.

"I love to stockpile victories but I don't think that you can assume any game will be easy," he said. "In the situation we're facing now, we're aware the teams we are facing haven't been that successful. Never can anyone, especially us, take anyone for granted. I'd like to say we can go in and that no doubt we should win this game and win the next game. Our worst enemy—and this comes from day

one, my first game I ever played in—is ourselves. If we can play the way we're capable of playing and clean up some of the little things, we should be fine. We can't worry about who we're playing and their record."

Favre and the Jets were still a work in progress. But at least they could see the progress. And in this NFL, where parity runs rampant, a work in progress can sometimes be good enough.

"I think each week with this team, there's a lot less doubt," Favre said. "I'm not going to say that we're going to go on a winning spree. I'd like to think so, but I think there are some positive vibes taking place here and that's how you start winning. Things start kind of happening and you go, 'Okay, that didn't happen to us in the past.' You just kind of start believing in that and good things fall in place."

He reminded everyone that he didn't have to throw six touchdowns every week, and mentioned nothing about a big hit to his fully extended arm from Bengal defender Jonathan Fanene. "I'm not here for stats," the winningest quarterback in NFL history said. "I'm here for wins."

As for Pennington, he was coping with a heartbreaking, last-second 29–28 loss in Houston on a day when he hit Patrick Cobbs on a fleaflicker off the wildcat for a 53-yard touchdown. "It hurts," Pennington said.

Favre's most dramatic win, the one that to this day tugs at the heartstrings of American football fans, came five years earlier in Oakland, one day after his father, Irvin, the man who had been his coach growing up, succumbed to a heart attack. Favre decided to play, and summoned the strength to throw for 399 yards and four touchdown passes (all in the first half) in a tearjerking 41–7 Monday night victory over the Raiders. Now, many gray hairs later, he would be returning to Oakland.

"It was obviously a tough time," Favre recalled, "but one of those games that everything I seemed to do was right. Guys around me made me right . . . it was a game that we needed to win . . . didn't know if I would play . . . ended up playing. Had a half, probably, better than any full game I'd ever played in, so. . . . It was a special game but it carried a lot weight obviously."

Favre had learned of his father's passing at the end of a Sunday round of golf with several teammates. "I think from the time I found out, I really felt like I was gonna play," he said, "'cause I knew we needed to win the ballgame. So it was a question of, 'Could I play, and help this team win?' was really the most important thing for me. I knew my dad was wanting me to play and all those things. But the shock of it . . . really when I went out for pregame the next day, I'd forgotten everything I'd studied all week. I couldn't tell you what coverage they were gonna play, what particular checks we had . . . in pregame warm-ups, throwing just ten-yard passes with [backup] Doug [Pederson], I was all over the place. Even though I had dressed for the game, I was more concerned at that point, 'Well, if I can't throw it to Doug here in pregame warm-ups, what makes me think I can complete a thirty-yard crossing route?' So . . . your question would be, 'Well, okay, what changed?' I just felt like, as I have in different times in my career, you don't really feel right in pregame, or you're not as accurate in pregame—you should be fine in pregame, but there are times where you don't feel up to par, but it turns out better than you think, and that was one of those cases. I said, 'Well, once they start chasing me, and live bullets start flying, I'll be fine.' But it was more than fine."

Favre could be certain that the warm reception he received that night would not be waiting for him this time. "One of the things I remember about that game in particular," Favre said, "was Oakland fans are not the politest fans in the National Football League, but I remember getting a standing ovation when I was introduced—the offense was introduced that night, and I didn't know what to expect. Believe me, I didn't expect them to give that type of ovation, but . . . I can't tell you how many signs were in the stadium, and we got a police escort after the game, Deanna and I going back to the airport—we chartered a plane—that was probably the best police escort I'd ever seen. . . . We never stopped, not one time. And it just seemed like the whole experience, as bad it was from their stand-point, couldn't have been any better."

He recalled that his wife flying to his side helped him to no end. "She asked me on the phone when I first talked with her if I wanted her to come out, and I told her no," Favre said. "Well, she ended up coming anyway, and that helped me through. I still think that I would have been fine without her, but it sure made a big difference for her to come out. I shouldn't say she surprised me. I had a feeling she was gonna come out."

Rachel Nichols from ESPN, who was assigned Favre duty by the Favre-obsessed network, wanted to know more about their partnership/relationship.

"I would consider it fifty-fifty; I don't know how many marriages can look at it that way," Favre said. "She's helped me in all the decisions I've made . . . has stuck with me in times where she probably shouldn't have. There was about a two- or three-year stretch there where it was a lot of things that were happening to us as a family. But she, as usual—the woman seems to be the one who stands tall through it all, and that's the way she was in other cases."

Favre's wife had endured her own battle with breast cancer and written a book—*Don't Bet Against Me! Beating the Odds Against Breast Cancer and in Life*—about it. "It's funny how you can impact people when you don't think that your situation can," Favre said. "I know for a woman losing her hair—and I hate to use that as an example—but that's a very tough thing to go through. But she stood tall through it, and listened to me gripe and grumble about [the Packers] losing games and things like that, and she got up and made breakfast for the girls and for me, and drove 'em to school, and did all the things that other moms do. But it made her stronger, and made our family stronger. You just never know—sometimes you're hit with unfortunate circumstances, but in the end, I think it makes you stronger, and that was the case with us."

Deanna let her husband figure out whether he wanted to stay retired by himself this time. "She didn't say a whole lot this time," Favre said. "In the past, she was like, 'Hey, I think you need to go back, I think you need to give it up,' which are the same things I'd been saying. She said, 'I'm not saying anything. I think you still can play. I think at times you still want to. But ultimately it's your decision.' Which I told her, 'That doesn't help a bit!' But it was the right approach. Ultimately, it was my decision, but we're happy we're here, and see what happens."

He didn't expect a flood of emotions to overcome him come game day. "Maybe going out on that field the start of the game will bring back some memories, but it's been a long time, a lot of games, and just the way I've handled things throughout my career, I hope that it's not anything big one way or the other. It's just another game, one that we need to win. Obviously I'm with a different team, but in some ways the circumstances are the same—we need to win this game. And hopefully it'll be nothing more than that."

Favre saw blue skies ahead. "I feel like each week I'm getting more and more comfortable with the offense," he said. "I think this team . . . I see a lot of potential. Maybe outside looking in, in the past, you saw a lot of potential, but I don't know if guys . . . it's almost like they anticipated something bad happening. And it's kinda hard to change that way of thinking. I mean, I haven't heard that, I haven't discussed it with anyone, but I think good things happen when you start believing that good things will happen. It's been a long time, but that's kind of what we started out in Green Bay thinking. They had lost there for so many years, and Mike Holmgren was trying to change that way of thinking, and whether it be get rid of some of the guys that felt that way, or able to change the mind-set of those guys, is different places that you go. But you look at this team, there's a lot of good players on this team, both sides of the ball . . . but I think more so than anything, it's a mind-set. Every game you play is tough. But I think for us, the games we've lost, we could easily have won. And I think if we continue to believe that we can win any game, and that we can make every play, and not anticipate something bad happening, that rather anticipate good things happening. . . . I'm not gonna sit here and make predictions, but I think people can see that there's some improvement from this team."

Favre, asked where he had gotten the perception that the ghosts of Murphy's law had lived for forty years with the Jets franchise, said, "I don't sit here and listen to talk radio and read the papers—no offense, but you do hear things."

Favre next revealed an insecurity that befalls most aging athletes when he began patting himself on the back. "Like the way I play, which is not perfect every game, but I play with a lot of enthusiasm and I try to have fun, but I try to bring that in practice as well," he said. "And I've heard from numerous guys, 'You know, we just didn't have that as much in the past.' And winning obviously is a lot more fun than losing. But I've been in seasons before where we are winning, and it hasn't been as much fun, for whatever reason. And what I try to bring regardless of it was here, or in Green Bay, is have fun every day, it's a long season and, believe me, it's a game. It's a game, I keep saying that. And if you lose sight of that, it won't be as much fun, and I don't think you'll be as productive. So if you have fun doing what you love to do . . . I love doing this, and I hope the rest of our guys love doing it. . . . But there's nothing more enjoyable than doing it as a team, and celebrating as a team, as opposed to individuals. But I see a lot of good guys on this team, I see a lot of good players, and it's just a matter of putting it together. . . . Chemistry to me is the most important aspect of being a winning football team. Not the most talented team, but it's chemistry. And I think this team has a lot of potential as far as chemistry is concerned, and I see that getting better each and every day."

All well and good. Favre's on-field joy and Everyman persona have forever been infectious charms. But he would ultimately be judged the same way all the Jets quarterbacks from Namath to now had been judged—by wins and losses. The Jets did have twitches of fun with Todd, with O'Brien, with Testaverde, with Pennington. None of them won a championship. Favre, even as he turned thirty-nine, wasn't here merely to make the game fun again for a team that had been 4–12. He was here to get the Jets a championship, or at the very least within sniffing distance of one.

But what if Favre couldn't pull it off this year? Might he consider returning in 2009? Of course, that wasn't a question you ask Favre after 3–2. It's a pertinent question for him only weeks and months after another season ends.

"I haven't even thought about next year, obviously," he said. "I really am excited about being here. And, for me, I'm taking it game by game. I don't see how you can look at it any differently, I really don't. My job is to lead this team, and hopefully go into Oakland and win this football game, and then we'll go from there. I mean, it's always a game-to-game basis. When I was young, in my third, fourth, fifth, sixth, seventh, eighth year, you're always thinking past that. You're always thinking next contract, you're always thinking, 'Gotta get to the Pro Bowl,' you're always thinking Super Bowl, you're always thinking those things. And it seems like as a young player, you're always thinking more individual things. And for me, I've been fortunate enough to achieve all those things, way more than I ever set out to. And I don't know if there's too many guys who've been in my situation. Records and all those things never really meant a whole lot to me, and I guess from some people's standpoint, they go, 'Well, that's easy for you to say, you have them all.' Good and bad.

"So for me, it's hard to explain the situation I'm in. I often wonder, or have wondered myself, just like other people have, 'What the heck are you doing?' You know? 'You got it all. Why continue to put yourself through it?' Well, I love to play the game. It's a different situation here in New York . . . but I'm really excited about it. I don't know what's gonna happen in the end. The only thing I can control is this week, and the type of leadership that they brought me in here to show. I think I'm doing a good job of that, but I expect to play at a high level, and that's what I'm looking at each week—play at a high enough level to give your team a chance to win. But more importantly, bring a type of leadership that you have brought in the past. And if you can continue that, fine. We'll take it week to week and then at the end of the season I'll assess how I played this year and talk with the Jets and we'll see from there. I think it's way premature to even think about next season."

They call the Oakland Coliseum the Black Hole, and this time Favre was swallowed up in it.

He looked old. His arm looked old and tired. He missed open receivers. He forced a goal-line interception into double coverage for Cotchery and cost his team a field goal. "He actually slips, Dustin gets interfered with by two guys, it's illegal contact, he's running a cross route which would have pulled both guys out of the play," Favre would say. "Instead, they both hit him, one of the guys that hits him falls into the place where Jerricho's coming, which is where he slips. It's one of them how they didn't call a penalty I have no idea. But if he's able to get through on his crossing route, we'd probably have a touchdown."

A miscommunication problem between Favre and Cotchery resulted in what appeared to be a killer interception with just under three minutes left, after placekicker Sebastian Janikowski had broken a 10–10 tie when the Raiders special teams duped the Jets with a fake punt as upback Jon Alston rumbled 21 yards. "I got desperate at that point," Favre would say.

And he was taking a beating.

"We didn't blitz Favre much, but we damn sure hit him," Oakland defensive coordinator Rob Ryan said. "Those guys were knocking the crap out of him."

CBS showed a clip of the Fanene hit, after which Favre rotated his arm, and legendary play-by-play man Dick Enberg revealed that Favre had told him his arm was sore.

Fanene, a 6-foot-4, 295-pound defensive end from Pago Pago, American Samoa, recalls smashing Favre to the ground in the third quarter. "I got him good," Fanene said. "We were in our nickel package. We have a stunt inside. When I came around, he was backing up a little bit. His eyes got big—my helmet was right there on his chest. When he released the ball, that's when I tackled him. He made a little noise on the ground; he said the F word." Where exactly did Fanene land? "On his right side, on his throwing side, on that chest and right arm," Fanene said.

Fanene was asked whether he noticed that Favre's arm affected him from that point on. "Pretty much, yeah," Fanene said. In fact, when Fanene returned to the sideline, he remembers defensive line coach Jay Hayes telling him: "I think he got hurt on that play."

Could this have been the hit that changed the course of the season for Favre and the Jets? "I'll say a little bit," Fanene said.

But Favre always keeps on keeping on, had made a living snatching victory from the jaws of defeat, and as silver-and-black storm clouds rained desperation on him, he was fortunate enough to get one last chance, at his 5-yard line, with 1:24 remaining.

He found Stuckey for 31 yards on third-and-10, and Brad Smith on a slant for 18 on third-and-3, and suddenly Feely was lining up for the last-second 52-yard field goal that would force overtime.

Feely hit the left upright.

But wait—Cable had called time-out in a foolish attempt to ice the veteran kicker.

Feely nailed the next one, and Favre, seemingly in disbelief on the sideline, cradled the top of his helmet with both hands. "To be in that position and make it was awesome," he said.

Normally, in situations such as these, Jets fans would be making reservations for a stay at the Heartbreak Hotel. But Brett Favre was here to change all that, right?

While the Jets had showed some fourth-quarter imagination with a direct snap to Smith that gained 6 yards and a 36-yard reverse by Smith, it was nevertheless troubling that only 2 of Favre's 34 regulation passes had traveled more than 20 yards.

Favre had it first in overtime. It seemed too good to be true: Favre versus Russell with the money on the line.

Except Mangini inexplicably and inexcusably coached as if he were the one saddled with Russell. The Raiders lined up eight men in the box and practically dared Favre to beat them, and yet Mangini and Schottenheimer decided to put the ball and the game in the hands of Jones, who had been heroic with 159 rushing yards.

It seemed like another cruel joke. Jones running three straight times first-and-goal against the Patriots was bad enough. This was worse. The Raiders were a dysfunctional laughingstock—a tomato can, in boxing terms. Al Davis's "just win, baby" mantra had become a distant memory in Oakland. The Raiders (14 penalties) were trying to give the game to the Jets. And the Jets couldn't take it.

Favre would have three possessions in overtime. The Jets offense gained all of 45 yards. The playcallers called eight runs and six passes.

One man's pain is another man's gain. A rookie defensive end named Trevor Scott, out of the University of Buffalo, was having himself a dream day. Scott had sacked Favre in the third quarter and once more in the overtime. "If you told me about ten to fifteen years ago that

I would be sacking Brett Favre, I would have told you you're full of crap," Scott said. "All week, I was thinking, 'I've got to get to Favre. How cool would that be if my first sack in the NFL is against Favre?'

"I kept attacking, kept attacking, and finally got to Brett."

Finally, Russell found Javon Walker for 16 yards and tight end Zach Miller over the middle against a busted coverage for 27 more, and Janikowski lined up for what would be the longest field goal in Raiders history, 57 yards.

"I didn't even look," Favre said.

Raiders 16, Jets 13.

Favre, battered physically and emotionally, limped barefoot to the podium for the postmortem. "One of the toughest losses I've ever been a part of," he said. "I came here to win games like that. That's what's disappointing for me."

He wouldn't second-guess his coaches. "We made some plays, but we could never just finish it," he said.

He seemed so distraught that hardened, longtime writers found it too uncomfortable to interrogate him about a report by Jay Glazer that he had helped the Lions prepare for their week 2 game against the Packers.

His teammates were angry and embarrassed by the loss. Only pretenders lose to a team like the Raiders.

"I do feel it's much easier to feel sorry for yourself after a game like this and that's the thing we have to guard against," Favre said. "If we are fortunate enough to win this game next week, then we are right back on track, obviously. Whatever track that may be."

They were way off track, and Favre's schizophrenic offense had yet to find its identity. Bombs away against the Cardinals, duck and cover against the Raiders.

Favre had thrown for fewer than 200 yards in four of his six games as a Jet. He was averaging a career-low 9.9 yards per completion. Pennington, meanwhile, was averaging 11.8.

Remember the old joke that the only man who ever stopped Michael Jordan was Dean Smith, his former legendary basketball coach at North Carolina? Well, now there were Jets fans wondering whether the only coach who could ever stop Favre would be Mangini.

Pennington and the Dolphins fell to 2–4 following a 27–13 loss at home to the Ravens. He missed open receivers, called an ill-advised quarterback sneak on second-and-16, and had an interception returned 44 yards for a touchdown by Terrell Suggs. "I shouldn't have made the throw," Pennington said.

Favre awakened Wednesday morning to a *New York Daily News* headline that blared: IS IT TIME TO WORRY ABOUT FAVRE'S ARM? The New York media were searching for an answer. Was there any other logical way to explain Mangini coaching as if he still had Pennington behind center?

But reporters who filled the tiny press room at Florham Park for the 10:30 a.m. press conference had an even more pressing agenda: Lion Gate. Or, perhaps, Lyin' Gate. Favre had quickly shot off an e-mail to longtime ally Peter King of NBC and *Sports Illustrated* calling Glazer's bombshell "total B.S." But in the days that followed, Lions head coach Rod Marinelli lent credence to Glazer's report when he refused comment on it. Glazer emphatically stood by the story. ESPN, meanwhile, which owned a veritable army of correspondents and reporters friendly to Favre, ignored the story.

Until now.

Because now Favre, wearing a green Jets shirt and his Titans throwback hat, was coming clean, and squirming in the hot seat as he did. That the NFL issued a statement that it would not have been against the rules anyway was of no comfort for the legions of Packers fans who lived and died with him. If Favre had tried to sabotage the Packers' season, to them it would have been an act of treachery. That the Packers won the game 48–25 excused nothing. Favre's integrity, his iconic reputation, his everlasting legacy, they were all dangling precariously on a tightrope.

Had he really gone from Brett the Jet to Benedict Brett?

"That week," Favre began, "Matt Millen [who was finally fired as Lions GM after years of ineptitude weeks later] called me. Matt and I are friends, and was inviting me to come to his place to hunt—I think he lives about an hour from here. But I'm sure his intentions were to fish me for information, just asked me how we attacked 'em last year . . . we attacked 'em pretty good. Didn't give him any game plan . . . I haven't been in that offense in over a year. . . . I don't know what else to tell ya . . . it was pretty simple."

Not quite. Favre never should have originally denied Glazer's report. It inspired Glazer to hit the airwaves in defense of his story. Someone asked Favre if it angered him that he had to stand there answering to it all, an absurd, kiss-ass question to say the least.

"I wouldn't say anger," Favre said, "as much as 'Here we go again.' I wish those guys well in Green Bay. I have a lot of friends, not only as far as teammates are concerned, but coaches, and just people in general there. It's unfortunate the way some of the things went down this off-season, but no hard feelings—it's business. I'm happy to be here; I'm trying to get ready for the Jet—excuse me—get ready for the Chiefs. Learning this Jets game plan has been difficult, and to be spending whatever amount of time giving away another game plan is totally not true. It's ridiculous for both sides, really. It's unfair for this team, and it's unfair for those guys up there trying to play too."

Favre revealed that his conversation with Millen lasted "fifteen, twenty minutes." But some of it involved football. More than enough time to spill some significant beans. And there existed the possibility that Lions coaches were listening in. Favre said he had no idea whether they were or not. "We did talk about hunting, and he said he had a bulldozer or some tractors if I needed to go relieve some tension, and in the process wanted to know . . . more or less, I think the question he asked was, 'Anything in particular that you guys did to us last year?' or 'how you looked at us' or whatever. I couldn't tell you what Detroit runs this year, I haven't watched them. And I can vaguely remember what they did last year."

Favre remembered that he completed 22 straight passes in the first 2007 meeting with the Lions. He was asked if he told Millen some of the strategy the Packers used against the Lions. "We went empty formation [no backs] and we just kept throwin' completion after completion," he said. If that was all Favre told Millen, no harm, no foul. Because even Rich Kotite could have picked that up on film. If. "I don't want to make this any bigger than what it is; I don't know what else to tell ya," Favre said. "I haven't sat in their meetings to know what they're callin', or how they're gonna attack, or how they're gonna use Aaron Rodgers. I can assure you, it wasn't anything. And I would almost be embarrassed to say that if I gave more, it was the wrong information because I think they beat Detroit rather soundly. And I bet it was pretty much the same things we've run in the past."

Favre wanted to make it clear that he did not call the Lions, which is a moot point. It doesn't matter whether he called Millen or Millen called him if he gave up privileged information. "Nor," Favre said, "did I call Tony Romo." (This was a reference to the previous week, when Romo, who had sustained a broken right pinkie against the Cardinals, called Favre to ask for advice. The Cowboys were reeling under Wade Phillips, and Romo tried desperately to play against the Rams. But Jerry Jones didn't want to risk losing Jessica Simpson's better half for the rest of the season, and forty-year-old Brad Johnson started against the Rams and lost.)

Favre offered that he and his teammates had asked former Cardinal Calvin Pace if he could provide helpful tidbits before the Cardinals game. "Let's see if this story turns out to be bigger," he said.

Of course it was bigger. Favre was the face of the NFL, especially with Brady gone for the season and Peyton Manning struggling. Besides, when a player changes teams, his new coaches and teammates would be derelict if they made no attempt to pick his brain before a game against his former team. But to reveal state secrets of his former team to a division rival? It may not be an indefensible offense to the NFL, but it sure would be to the Packers.

"Yeah, I played for the Packers for sixteen years; we played against the Lions a bunch," Favre said. "It's no secret what we did against 'em. I don't have a playbook from Green Bay . . . I didn't send a playbook. I didn't call him and say, 'Look, if you do this, you're gonna win the game.' I didn't do that. It's common, it happens every day. It happens more than you know. Don't think for a second when Mike McCarthy left in '99 and went to the Saints and we played 'em the next year and they put it to us, that he didn't tell his guys what he thought. There's nothing wrong with that."

Tannenbaum said, "I thought it was very overrated; I think people talk all the time in the league about trying to get insight on an opponent."

But Favre's bitter parting with the Packers only added a sinister intrigue to the story, and he knew it. Packers cornerback Charles Woodson was quoted as saying Favre was guilty of "sabotage" if he had reached out to Millen, an accusation that had Favre accusing Packer powers-that-be of "brainwashing" their players. The report struck a nerve inside the Green Bay locker room.

Said defensive end Cullen Jenkins, "I don't know if he's done it or not. It's one of those things, personally, and I don't know the situation, but I just think it's kind of messed up how he left here. Hasn't talked to Aaron [Rodgers], wished Aaron good luck or anything, but he's called everybody else, called Tony Romo and stuff like that. I don't have nothing against Brett personally. But I think in his position, he could at least show a little more class, a little more respect to Aaron in that regard. If that was the case, if he did talk to the coaches, I could see if he told his coaches if they were going to play us. That's all right. But if you go out of your way to talk to another team, nah, I don't think that's right."

Woodson: "He contacted them? I don't respect that. If they called him and he gives them information, that's one thing. But to seek a team out, because you know I guess you're trying to sabotage this team, you know I don't respect that. I know he's been the greatest player around here for a long time but there's no honor in that."

McCarthy: "I would say it's disappointing. I'm not really in tune with the whole report and so forth. . . . I really have no comment on that stuff."

That Favre was having as hard a time helping the Jets win as he apparently did for Millen and the Lions didn't aid his cause. It made him look vindictive. Remember how he had emphatically told the world at his introductory Jets press conference in Cleveland that he was not a traitor? Well, try telling that to a growing segment of Packers Nation, which was warming to Rodgers.

"Believe me, I'm trying my best to help this team win, the New York Jets," Favre said. "And spendin' no time trying to make sure the Packers lose. I got enough on my plate, believe me. I wish those guys well. And I'll say it again—it's unfortunate the way some things went down. I was at fault; I felt like they were at fault, in some areas. But it's over and done with, it's business, it happens all the time. And I guess because it's Brett Favre it's a bigger deal . . . it's a bigger deal for other people than it is for me."

Unless and until Millen is called before a grand jury and testifies otherwise, Favre wasn't going to have to sweat the way Roger Clemens did during his congressional steroids hearing. Or the way A-Rod did following his steroid confession. "Nothing happened; nothing happened that was any different than happens any other day," Favre said. "But the fact that I was in Green Bay for so long, what happened this off-season, that makes it a big deal. I am who I am, I'm a part of the Jets, trying to get ready for the Chiefs, I don't have time to be dealing with other issues, especially other game plans, so . . . I wish 'em well up there, I really do."

Finally, Dave Hutchinson announced that he had a football question, and a look of relief swept across Favre's face. Hutchinson wanted to know if Favre felt the Jets had been too conservative.

"After we left the Arizona game everyone thought we were on track," Favre said. "Throwing for four hundred yards is great—Kurt Warner did that against us but he lost. We are trying to find a balance; no one's at fault here. We have capable guys, not only in the passing game, but we obviously have capable guys in the run game. How we mix the two is a work in progress. But I like our game plans, I like the way Schotty calls the games. We have to be more consistent 'cause I can assure you if you watch tape like we do, there were plays to be made individually, me included. Numerous plays that I could have made that I didn't make . . . it's tough on a playcaller, it's tough on a head coach, but we had to execute individually the game plan. There's always better plays out there regardless, and that's the way it always works. But we'll be fine."

Now, what about all those shots he took in Oakland? How was the shoulder? "A little sore today, but I mean, that's been two days . . . long flight," Favre said. "But I could play today; I could. I think I'll practice today too." He smiled and was off to practice.

• • •

Favre's next immediate concern was the revelation three days before the Chiefs game that Coles had suffered a concussion in Oakland. And Cotchery (shoulder) looked as though he was going to be a gametime decision. That meant the possibility that Favre's starting receivers would be Stuckey and Smith. The crisis was averted when Coles, whose concussion was mild, was cleared to play. Cotchery improved quickly enough to join him.

The Chiefs were one of the three worst teams in the league, along with the Lions and Bengals. Running back Larry Johnson had been suspended by head coach Herm Edwards for violating team rules. The quarterback was Tyler Thigpen, because brittle Brodie Croyle had been knocked out for the season with a knee injury, and veteran backup Damon Huard (thumb) was unavailable. Favre and the Jets and restless, exasperated Jets fans needed a blowout victory in the worst way, and this was the perfect foil. Thigpen (2 TDs, 4 INTs) had a league-worst 44.3 passer rating. The 1–5 Chiefs, who had lost 14 of their last 15 under Edwards, ranked 31st in total defense (402.2 yards per game) and 29th in total offense (257.3 yards).

Jets fans were unhappy with Mangini and Schottenheimer for letting Favre be Favre when they needed to let Thomas Jones be Thomas Jones, and vice versa. Two days before the Chiefs game, Schottenheimer met the firing squad and pooh-poohed the notion he had been too conservative in overtime in Oakland.

"There's nothing that I would really do differently," he said. "I felt really good with the way we were running the football. I don't think it was that unusual from what we do, other than the Arizona game. I was fine with it."

Schottenheimer had run Jones on the first two plays of each of the Jets' three overtime possessions. "I don't get caught up in the criticism. . . . We're a game-plan-specific team," the offensive coordinator said. "This week's plan is going to be different than last week. You try to mix in personnel. You try to mix in schemes. Just to keep the defense guessing."

The defense was guessing right much too often.

The Jets hadn't had a 100-yard rusher and 200-yard passer in a game. Only 49er quarterback J. T. O'Sullivan, who was on the brink of losing his job, had thrown more interceptions (10) than Favre (8). It was not lost on the glass-half-empty crowd—and certainly not on the Packers decision-makers—that Favre had tossed 47 interceptions in 2006 and 2007.

As Namath and the '69 Jets, honored at halftime on the fortieth anniversary of the greatest moment in Jets history, looked on, Favre completed five consecutive passes on his opening possession before an 18-yard touchdown pass to Washington gave the Jets a 7–0 lead.

It would prove to be another tease.

Because Favre was shamefully being outplayed by Thigpen, who would finish 25-of-36 for 280 yards and two touchdowns out of a spread offense.

And Favre was taking another beating. There was concern about that thirty-nine-year-old right arm when he hit Faneca's shoulder on a follow-through, and again when he stayed down for a brief period following an interception by rookie cornerback Brandon Flowers on a pass intended for Cotchery when he was blasted from behind by defensive end Tamba Hali and Faneca fell on him. Clemens began warming up. Thigpen to Tony Gonzalez soon tied the game.

Favre came back for the next series, and Washington (274 all-purpose yards) should have given the Jets a 14–7 halftime lead with 1:48 remaining on a dynamic 60-yard touchdown romp thanks to a nice block by right guard Brandon Moore. But Thigpen's 11-yard touchdown pass to Mark Bradley, ruled incomplete before a video review, tied it with four seconds left before intermission.

What was particularly mystifying was the Jets' game plan—the Chiefs owned the worst run defense in football. And yet Favre was throwing. To one receiver (Coles) who was cleared to play after suffering a low-grade concussion. To another (Cotchery) who had a bum shoulder. As a quarterback who was giving new meaning to the phrase "to err is human." "We thought we had real good opportunities in the passing game," Mangini said.

Namath, in a television interview during the third quarter, expressed concern about "the overall concept of our team, not the quarterback, right now. I know they are trying, but today they are making Kansas City look good. A quarterback is gonna get hit, no doubt about that, but the accumulation of the bumps and bruises must have [Favre] at the most fragile as at any point in his career."

He was right. Except nobody around Mangini's Jets was willing to admit as much.

The Jets actually trailed 17–14 and were driving when disaster nearly struck. Chiefs linebacker Derrick Johnson dropped what was likely a gift touchdown when he stepped in front of Stuckey at the Chiefs' 8-yard line. Jones's 1-yard touchdown run gave the Jets the lead.

Favre had a chance to bury the Chiefs the next time he had the ball. He faced third-and-2 at the Kansas City 8. As Favre backpedaled, he floated a pass over the middle intended for Stuckey. Except Stuckey was nowhere to be found. Much to the horror of Jets Nation, Flowers intercepted and returned it 91 yards, and just like that, the Jets trailed 24–21 with 7:48 remaining.

Stuckey, according to Mangini following the film review, had given up on his short crossing route when Flowers cut in front of him. "[Stuckey] should have kept going on that," said Mangini. "Worst-case scenario, if the guy does catch it, you have to be able to make the tackle."

Stuckey second-guessed himself for not holding Flowers before he had a chance to intercept the ball. "I tried to get in front of [Flowers], but he gave me a little bump that kind of got me off my route and I bumped into the safety," he said.

The same fans who began making Super Bowl hotel reservations in Tampa when the Favre news first broke only knew that Favre had just thrown his third interception of the afternoon, and they savaged him with boos.

"I've heard them in Green Bay before," Favre would say. "I don't blame them, but it was a little premature, as we see now."

Favre soaks up the sights and sounds in warm-ups before his first—and only—Jets-Giants preseason game.

Favre awaits the start of the Jets-Giants preseason game with rookie offensive tackle Nate Garner.

Favre confers with Eric Mangini during the home opener against the Patriots.

Favre eagerly awaits the next series of play calls from quarterbacks coach Brian Daboll during a six–touchdown day against the Cardinals.

Chansi Stuckey appears open in the right flat, but Favre finds Dustin Keller (not shown) open over the middle for a touchdown against the Bengals that was nullified by a penalty.

Favre uncorks one over the middle during a 28–24 victory over the Chiefs.

Favre rolls right before hitting Laveranues Coles (not shown) across the field

Favre's stunning 27-yard naked bootleg sets up the first Jets score against the Bills.

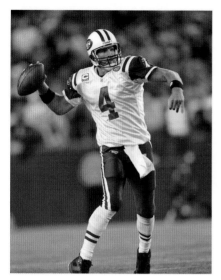

against the Patriots in Foxboro.

Favre trots out for the final second half of his Jets career, against the Dolphins.

Chad Pennington and his Dolphins teammates wait in the tunnel before the season-finale showdown against Favre and the Jets.

Favre finds a throwing lane against the Dolphins thanks to Nick Mangold (left) and Alan Faneca (right).

Pennington, under pressure from C. J. Mosley (No. 69), hits Ronnie Brown short of a first down.

Favre celebrates a touchdown pass to Laveranues Coles to give the Jets a 6–0 lead against the Dolphins.

On the sideline, Franks, who saw so much Favre magic firsthand as a Packers teammate, offered words of encouragement.

"Keep slingin' it, kid," he said.

No one, however, has ever needed to worry about Favre turning gun-shy.

The Jets were lucky that Edwards was on the other sideline, playing *not* to win the game. Thigpen, in a zone, took over at his 20 with 5:20 left and handed off three straight times to running back Kolby Smith, three-and-out. "We were backed up," Edwards said. "We just felt we could make a first down running the football." Washington's 37-yard punt return—during which he carried punter Steve Weatherford on his back—positioned Favre at the Chiefs' 46.

In essence, this was the season right here.

"I believe that's why they brought him in here," Coles said. "No matter what the circumstances are, he always gives you a good chance to win. I know he's a little old, but he can still play." He laughed.

Favre found Stuckey for 18 yards, Keller for 5, and Washington for 5 more. Now, 15 yards from the Great Escape, Favre heard Schottenheimer, up in the press box, blare into his headset, "No

matter what happens, just throw it up to LC." Favre had Coles in single coverage against Dimitri Patterson down the left sideline, and made a back-shoulder throw that Coles snared with his right hand as he twisted to shield Patterson near the front pylon. Only one minute remained. Asked if he deliberately underthrew Coles, Favre said, "Yeah, actually I wanted to put it a little more behind him than I did. It was a fade route, the guy played it high over the top with his back to me, so I was going to try the back shoulder and I did, but not as much as I would've liked."

It was his forty-first career fourth-quarter comeback.

"For the most part, I still feel like I can throw it with the best of them," Favre said. "I don't feel like I throw as well as I did ten years ago, but I would still put it up there with the top guys in the league. I assume that I can take hits like that all year long. I may be kidding myself, but I'm just expecting to keep throwing."

Favre exhaled when Drew Coleman broke up Thigpen's fourth-and-1 pass from the Jets' 31-yard line for Will Franklin with

21 seconds left. "I knew one thing: I'd go down swinging, however that may be," Favre said.

Favre (28-of-40 for 290 yards, 2 TDs, 3 INTs) looked on the bright side. "It's easy to smile and feel good about yourselves as a team when you win a game like that," he said. "We have some things to clean up, but 4–3 is not too bad right now."

But how bad was his throwing shoulder? "I feel okay," Favre said. "For thirty-nine, I don't feel too bad."

But Jets players were privately wondering about the playcalling. Referring to his interceptions, Favre joked, "They seem to follow me wherever I go." But no one was laughing.

Meanwhile, Pennington (22-of-30, 314 yards), down 16–7 to the Bills and facing a moment of truth, rallied the Dolphins with the help of a breakout game from Ted Ginn Jr. (7-for-175 receiving) to a 25–16 victory. "We could have folded," Pennington said. "We didn't do that."

Mangini parried reporters with his own brand of damage control on Monday. If the Jets offense had an identity, apparently only Mangini and Schottenheimer could define it. "I think you're always looking to try to classify things, but our identity is the fact that it's game-plan specific," Mangini said. "It can be heavy emphasis on the run; heavy emphasis on the pass; it could be no-huddle; it could be empty [backfield]. It's not just one package. It's the package that we think is going to help us move the ball and score the most points."

But why not run the ball down the Chiefs' throats? Their defense had been gashed for 207 rushing yards per game, for crying out loud. Take away Washington's 60-yard touchdown and the Jets accumulated only 75 yards on the ground. "They also had a very young secondary, starting two rookie corners, two second-year safeties, and had not gotten a lot of pressure on the quarterback, so all those things are pretty positive," Mangini said. "I feel really good about Jerricho. I feel really good about Laveranues." Better he should have felt good about Jerricho and Laveranues in overtime against the Raiders. Better he should have felt good about Jones against the Chiefs.

"I would say Oakland wasn't particularly strong against the run and we ran it for [242 yards] and scored thirteen points," Mangini said. "So you can look at it either way."

Favre's interception total had swelled to 11, tying him with O'Sullivan. Once against the Raiders and once against the Chiefs, he was intercepted when Cotchery broke off his route. Mangini argued there was enough carryover from one game plan–specific game plan to the next. "It's not a total overhaul of the offensive system," he said. "It could be the same play, just a different formation."

But didn't Pennington have to learn a new system in Miami? One glance at the league statistics was akin to a punch to the gut of the anguished Jets fan—Pennington had thrown only three interceptions and owned a passer rating of 100.5. Favre's was 89.5.

The 4–3 Packers seemed to be reveling in Favre's travails. Following their bye week, two days before a big game on the road against the Titans, the Packers decided this was the perfect time for them to announce a new five-year, $63.5 million contract for Rodgers. It meant everything to Rodgers, who had a year and a half left on his rookie contract. It meant he was the Quarterback of the Present *and* Future.

"I appreciate the commitment that they've made, and I plan to reciprocate that commitment in my play and hopefully prove to them that they made the correct decision giving me this extension," Rodgers said.

He had thrown 12 touchdowns with 4 interceptions and owned a 98.8 passer rating. But equally impressive was that he had played the last three games with a sprained throwing shoulder—a lesson in toughness he undoubtedly had learned from Favre.

In a statement, Packers GM Ted Thompson said, "As we talked about in the past, we try to be proactive in our discussions with our current players, and we felt like this was an appropriate time to try to come to an agreement with Aaron. We feel like this is good for the organization and the players, and we will continue this approach as we move forward."

Deanna Favre decided this was the right time to again stand by her husband's side. On the Favre family Web site, she blogged:

Over the past weeks, we have been deeply affected by the various media reports and accusations that have unfairly questioned Brett's loyalty, fairness and character. . . .

Most hurtful are those media reports who would like you to believe that Brett is eaten up with bitterness over his split with the Packers. Still feeling some grief, sure . . . but not bitterness. Yes, in the beginning, Brett was angry and hurt with the way things ended, but how could he not be? Brett gave most of his career (and his adult life) to the Packers. They were more than just an organization but also became our home away from home and our surrogate family. We will always love the Packer fans for making Brett more than just the focus of their applause on game day, but as part of their families, too. Again, how could any of us not be hurt and brokenhearted about such a loss of connection? Thus, certainly, Brett does not, in any way, hold a vendetta against his former team. But that has not stopped some from scrutinizing his every move and blaming him for so many things that simply are not true. Some incidents, like the locker room pranks appear funny (but they are still untrue). . . . Others, like the questionable phone calls to other teams, are hurtful, distasteful, and . . . still untrue as they have been reported. . . .

But, lately Brett has reminded me of what is truly important and what is not. . . . Not long ago when he re-prioritized his life, he asked himself the question "Who will be here after football is gone?" The answer was his family. So at that moment, our family became priority one for him. Brett reminded me that at the end . . . it is his family, their opinions and their love that matters the most to him. People will have to believe what they will. They have known his character for 18 years, and they will have to trust that, although teams change, a man like Brett Favre does not.

Deanna—Coach Deanna—sat down with Nichols for ESPN's *E:60* and offered this gem: "Sometimes I watch film with him, [and] he's like, 'You know, I really—I just didn't make good decisions in this game and I missed a lot of plays,' and I'm like, 'You know what, sit in the pocket [and] watch the play happen.' He is so used to getting rid of the ball quick. It really helped. The next week, he threw six touchdowns."

Just what Coach Mangini and Coach Schottenheimer needed to hear, right?

Indeed, bringing Favre to the Big Apple was a not-so-subtle attempt to whip up a frenzy for the personal seat licenses at the new Meadowlands Stadium. An eight-day online auction for the Coaches Club section had brought in gross revenue of $16 million as 620 of the 2,028 PSLs had been sold on StubHub.

The Jets had set a $5,000-a-license minimum and required that buyers purchase at least two to sit in the Coaches Club—marketed as two of the best two thousand seats in sports—behind the team's bench. Club members will be able to stand on the field, five yards off the Jets bench, or step inside to a private twenty-thousand-square-foot bar and lounge designed by Nobu architect David Rockwell. The final prices for the auctioned Coaches Club licenses ranged from $10,000 to $82,500 each. The licenses in the section are fees for the right to buy season tickets that will cost fans $700 a game in 2010.

Mangini and Favre met to discuss the offense as they customarily do on Tuesdays. A possible season-changing game in Buffalo was five days away. Mangini never put the onus on any one man; it is always the collective group with him. But that by no means absolved Favre of blame.

"He has to know when to just throw it away, just get rid of it, and sometimes there's nothing there, and that's okay, throw it away," Mangini said.

The offensive line, of course, needed to protect better, and the receivers, aside from the problematic task of getting on that elusive same page with Favre, were challenged by Mangini to be more aware of danger. "If that ball has a chance to be intercepted, you better do whatever you have to do to make sure that it doesn't; and if it does, you better become a defensive player and make a tackle," he said.

Mangini was asked how he weighs the risk/reward with Favre. "You just stress, 'Don't hit on twenty,'" he said. "Sometimes it's okay to stay, and see what the dealer has. You're not trying to reel him in, and not trying to coach him out of being a good player, you're just trying to reinforce that everything needs to be . . . calculated risk."

Were some of those interceptions a case of Favre hitting on twenty? "I haven't played the position, and he's gotten twenty-one when he's hit on twenty in the past," Mangini said.

Lion Gate, meanwhile, wasn't going away so fast. The first question for Favre at his Wednesday press conference centered on his reaction to his wife's blog, and whether the Glazer report had been a distraction to him.

"It's not the first time we've either gone through things as a family or dealt with . . . not all stories are positive, and families are families—you stick up for one another, regardless of what situation you're in," Favre said. "Obviously this is a pretty unique situation being a pro football player and doing it for a long time, and because of that, you're in the public eye and things happen, things are said. . . . I would stick up for my wife as well. But . . . it hasn't lingered . . . hasn't distracted me. I hate to say I'm used to it—it's just part of it. Positive stories, or good things being said about you, how you handle those are to me equally as important. You start believing all the hype, good or bad, I think you're on your way out. I probably am less affected by those type of stories than my family. Understandably so."

Favre said that he had spoken to Millen after the story broke. "Nothing was wrong; nothing was done illegally," he said. "He doesn't have to apologize to me."

It was pointed out to Favre that Glazer had stood by his story 1,000 percent. And the story had Favre spending an hour on the phone with Millen. "Great," Favre said. "Let him stand by it, I could care less. I got the Buffalo Bills to worry about this week. I didn't call the Lions, I'll say that again. He can stand by whatever. I'm trying to get ready for the Buffalo Bills."

And Mangini's blackjack analogy? "I used to always take hits on sixteen, or fifteen," Favre joked. "Believe it or not, I'm not a gambler. I know it sounds crazy."

It sure did.

"Believe me, I'm well aware of what is expected of me . . . how important it is to take care of the ball," Favre said. "I'm trying to take care of the ball, to be high-percentage passing, but also productive. Being thirty-for-thirty for a hundred yards is not very good. Points are the most important thing. . . . If we can just eliminate some of these mistakes, just a little bit, we can be highly productive."

The 5–2 Bills, coming off a loss in Miami, were tied atop the AFC East with the Patriots. "They're no fluke," Favre said.

He was asked if this was the toughest challenge he has faced, taking a 4–12 Jets team to the playoffs at the very least. "I would think it is probably the toughest challenge up to this point," Favre said.

Mangini knew a crossroads had arrived. It was Thursday when he lowered the boom behind closed doors and, in an urgent attempt to wake the Jets from their lethargy, threatened jobs. No one—except Favre, of course—was safe.

"Fill your role or somebody else will step in and fill it if you can't handle it," was how Coles remembered it.

"It was just post-practice, and it wasn't anything that dramatic," Mangini explained. "It was just stating the obvious that a lot of these young guys have really pushed and improved, not just young guys, but different guys that have been in roles, that they have pushed and improved. As that's happening, the people that are in those current roles need to maintain their level of performance, or improve their level of performance, because it is a meritocracy and we're going to play the best players. I just wanted to remind everybody that that's the case and there had been a lot of progress by players, and they were pushing for playing time."

Tratner had noticed the increase in the number of fans at the road hotels once Favre arrived. The day before the Buffalo game, Jim Nantz and CBS producer Lee Barrow waited for Favre in a street-level restaurant. Phil Simms, who was driving from Buffalo to Syracuse to watch his son Matt play quarterback for Louisville, had done his due diligence by telephone. "We had to get [Favre] to the production meeting through a back entrance," Tratner said.

November in Buffalo is always a crapshoot, but sunshine and forty-eight-degree temperatures awaited Favre inside raucous Ralph Wilson Stadium. After all the turbulence, Favre and the Jets clearly needed to make a stand and announce themselves as contenders once and for all. Nothing brings a team together more than an us-against-the-world triumph in hostile surroundings. The Bills, with second-year quarterback Trent Edwards, rugged running back Marshawn Lynch, and deep threat Lee Evans, were a nice little team, but on this day they would be missing defensive end Aaron Schobel, their best pass rusher, clutch wide receiver Josh Reed, and starting guard Brad Butler. Still, a struggling Favre gave them hope. "The tape speaks for itself," defensive end Chris Kelsay told the *Buffalo News*. "Everybody who's ever played with Brett realizes the risk and reward. He will throw a lot of picks, because he takes a chance."

The outside cries to let Favre be Favre had died down significantly. If the Jets only barely survived the quarterback's self-inflicted wounds against the Chiefs, there was no way they would be able to live with them and beat a real team. The game plan against the Bills was to let Favre be Pennington.

"It was hard to pass up a little dink right in front of me," Favre said. "If you have a touchdown, great. But try to move the chains. Control the clock. Manage the game, or whatever."

He managed just fine.

A first-quarter screen to Washington gained 40 yards and set up a Feely field goal. Before the day was through, Favre would throw six times to Jones for 38 yards. Of course there were deep shots in the game plan, but they were afterthoughts. "It's something that not only this year but throughout my career I've been willing to do," Favre said. "We tried to play the percentages."

Down 7–3, Darrelle Revis stripped Edwards of the ball on a blindside blitz and recovered at the Buffalo 6. But Favre dropped the shotgun snap from Mangold and Jones had to recover. The Jets settled for a field goal when Favre didn't see Coles wide open in the back of the end zone and threw the ball away.

Mangini, after the Bills were flagged for ineligible man downfield, errantly accepted the penalty, giving Edwards third-and-16 from the Jets' 30 instead of the likely prospect of a 43-yard Rian Lindell field goal attempt. Edwards connected with Roscoe Parrish for 22 yards when Coleman fell down.

But Gang Green, which stuffed the Bills' running game (30 yards) all day—Lynch missed over a quarter with nausea—had Mangini's back. Kris Jenkins, dominant all day (2 sacks), demolished Edwards, Parrish stumbled coming out of his break, and Abram Elam intercepted and was off to the races, chased futilely by Lynch, 92 yards to pay dirt. Jets 13, Bills 7. "It was just something I had seen on film," Elam said. "My coach gave me good keys on what to expect and I just believed what I saw."

Washington, in one of the smartest special teams plays you will ever see, had the presence of mind to field a Lindell kickoff with one foot out of bounds, enabling the Jets to start at their 40 instead of their 8 because it was ruled out of bounds. A Favre slant to Cotchery went for 35 yards, to the 7, where Jones ran it in to make it 23–10 late in the third quarter.

But here Favre, falling backward and hit by blitzing linebacker Paul Posluszny as he threw a wobbly out to the left side for Cotchery, single-handedly turned the momentum back to the Bills. His 12th interception of the season was returned 42 yards for a touchdown by Jabari Greer. Now it was 23–17 with 10:53 remaining. The place exploded. A jolt of electricity surged through the Bills. "I'm thinking, 'Boy, this ain't good,'" Favre said. He was overwhelmed with a sense of doom. "Believe me," he said, "when I walked off the field after that pick, I thought, 'We don't stand a chance.'" Jenkins tried to encourage him on the sidelines. "Just relax," he told him. "You've been playing forty-eight years. What are you getting upset about?"

Favre was brought to the Jets to steady the Good Ship Woody during times of distress, and here was one of them all right. First he needed to steady himself. "Nervous as hell," Favre would remember feeling. The nerves, thankfully, left. Favre engineered a 14-play smashmouth drive that consumed 8:41 and culminated with a 31-yard field goal by Feely. He threw no pass longer than six yards but was 5-of-5 with two third-down conversions. A 23-yard run by Jones behind Faneca was the biggie. "That drive," Favre said, "was one of the most important drives for us offensively all year. Not only because it helped win the game, but it was a statement drive."

Favre (19-of-28, 201 yards) didn't throw a touchdown pass. And didn't care. "You don't have to throw six touchdowns to win a football game," he said, repeating a line he had used from time to time after the Arizona game. "That win felt as good as any win I've ever been a part of." He had clearly gotten sentimental in his old age. He'd won a Super Bowl. He'd won two NFC Championship games. A midseason road victory over the Bills felt as good? "I'd love to throw seventy-yard bombs on every play, but that's not the way you're gonna win every game," Favre said. "And that's not how we were gonna win today."

He was giddy enough to poke fun at himself when he said, "I didn't throw a touchdown pass . . . at least not to us." And everyone laughed.

Later that night, the Patriots would lose in Indianapolis, leaving the Jets in a three-way tie atop the AFC East with the Pats and the Bills. And lo and behold, Pennington and the Dolphins had beaten the Broncos in Denver and were 4–4. At his Monday press conference, Mangini was asked whether he had examined the trade for Favre given Pennington's surprising success.

"There is so much other stuff to do," Mangini said. "All I examine is how we're doing, the things that we're doing and the opponent that we're playing. That's not something that I do on any kind of weekly basis or monthly basis or quarterly basis."

For the record, Pennington's numbers at the midway mark: 7 TDs, 4 INTs, 95.2 passer rating.

Favre: 15 TDs, 12 INTs, 87.8 passer rating.

Rodgers: 13 TDs, 5 INTs, 95.3 passer rating.

Incredibly, after all the gnashing of teeth about Pennington's weak arm, he was averaging 8.2 yards per attempt. Favre was averaging 6.9.

Favre's edge? He was 5–3. Pennington and Rodgers were 4–4.

Pennington (23-of-40, 281 yards) was 4–4 because he completed six passes during a 15-play, 80-yard, eight-minute touchdown drive that iced a 26–17 victory in Denver with 3:10 left. "Coach Sparano told us to go out and win the game rather than sitting back and watching," he said. "Now we have to keep it going."

Newly hired head coach Al Groh and GM Bill Parcells couldn't wait for the 2000 NFL Draft.

Testaverde was thirty-eight and coming back from a ruptured Achilles'. But finding a Quarterback of the Future was an afterthought in the Jets war room. Not even Michigan's Tom Brady, who somehow lasted until the sixth round before the Patriots pulled the trigger, was a consideration. Pennington was the marquee name, but Parcells and Groh were determined to rebuild the Jets defense, and with the twelfth and thirteenth picks selected defensive end Shaun Ellis and pass rusher John Abraham. "We didn't even go into the draft to take a quarterback," player personnel director Dick Haley said at the time. "As much as we liked Chad, we figured somebody else would take him." But when their next turn came at eighteen, Pennington was still on the board. He was a skinny kid with big feet, and he didn't have the biggest arm, but he did have an accurate one, and he did have a 3.75 GPA in broadcast journalism at Marshall, and he did have a 38-to-12 touchdown-to-interception ratio, and he did lead his team to a 13–0 record, and he did rally his team from a 23–0 deficit to beat Western Michigan 34–30 in the last minute of the Mid-American Conference title game.

Parcells and Groh couldn't pass.

Pennington, who expected to be a 49er, a Steeler, or a Bronco, was delighted—even if there wasn't a Cracker Barrel in sight. He looked forward to learning his craft under a pro like Testaverde, and an offensive coordinator like Dan Henning. "I think if you look at some great quarterbacks—like Joe Montana, my idol—he didn't have an overpowering arm," Pennington told the *New York Times*. "Quarterback has to do with accuracy and leadership. This is the best situation of all the teams. I don't have to worry about going in and starting."

So he was a sponge as Testaverde grunted in the weight room, and diligently studied film. Pennington threw five passes as a rookie. The Jets finished 9–7 and missed the playoffs when Testaverde threw three interceptions in the regular-season finale in Baltimore. By the time the next season started, Pennington had a new head coach and new offensive coordinator.

Groh stunned new owner Johnson when he left for what he called his dream job at his alma mater, the University of Virginia. The ever-mercurial Parcells, spurning Johnson's overtures to return to the sidelines, opted for television, an interim resting place for him. Before leaving, he recommended a former scout from his Giants days, Terry Bradway, for the vacant general manager job. Johnson, no Wellington Mara when it came to football pedigree, hired Bradway, who'd worked for seven years under Giants GM George Young and was instrumental in the drafting of perennial All-Pro tight end Tony Gonzalez in Kansas City. Bradway turned to Tampa Bay assistant coach Herm Edwards, who was best known for his role in The Fumble, that ignominious bit of Giants history in which the Eagles cornerback scooped up a last-second Joe Pisarcik fumbled handoff and raced into the end zone with it to win a 1978 game that caused an uproar and upheaval around the Giants. Edwards had also been Chiefs defensive backs coach and a scout in the organization.

Edwards predictably hitched his wagon to Testaverde as Pennington, who married longtime sweetheart Robin and took his playbook on his honeymoon, worked feverishly at his craft. One day in training camp, as I waited to interview him after the morning practice, Pennington wouldn't leave the field. Cornerback Aaron Glenn lined up on his right and free agent wide receiver Phil McGeoghan lined up on his left and Pennington worked on his long ball.

"I'm gonna succeed because of the hard work that I've put in and because of the examples that I have seen," Pennington told me in his Tennessee twang, "through my father, through players like Vinny, through the support I have; that's why I'm gonna succeed. And the second reason why I'm gonna succeed is because of the passion that I have to succeed. I'm not gonna give up.

"Who knows? It may not be here. You never know what's gonna happen in this league. You may be here one day and get traded the next.

"But wherever I am, I'm gonna succeed, and I'm gonna try and make my team better."

New York has scared plenty of players. Todd would have been better off starting anywhere else. Dave Brown would have been better off following someone other than Simms. Even Alex Rodriguez and Roger Clemens were shaken in the beginning as Yankees. New York didn't scare Pennington. "I think being a quarterback here can be very gratifying, very satisfying," he said, "but there's no doubt about it, there's a lot of pressure. But I put so much pressure on myself to do well that there's no one that can put any more pressure on me than me. You have to deal with the criticism and go on about it. But there's one thing that Vinny has taught me; that is, if you love what you do, it doesn't matter what anybody else says."

This was one driven young man. "I have a passion about this game not to be just another quarterback, not to be just another NFL player," Pennington said. "That's what I think about constantly, when I'm at sleep at night, when I'm on vacation, when I'm in there working out. Not just being one of the best, but being *the* best. That's hard to do, and that's lofty, but you gotta set 'em lofty to get there."

When the 2002 training camp started, Pennington believed he was ready, even though he had thrown all of twenty-five NFL passes. "They have to see it to believe it, and when they see it," he vowed, "then they will believe it." Testaverde had led Edwards to the playoffs, only to lose the wild-card game in Oakland. His hold on the job was not airtight.

And Testaverde struggled mightily out of the gate. The Jets were 1–3, and Edwards knew that his team was in desperate need of a spark that could only come with a quarterback change. Early in the first quarter in Jacksonville, Testaverde was sacked by defensive tackle Marcus Stroud and had to be helped off the field.

The Chad Pennington Era began right then and there.

The Jets lost, but Pennington (21-of-34, 281 yards) showed promise. "I guarantee you one thing," he said. "We're gonna get this thing turned around."

It was hardly a Namath guarantee, but it would have to do.

And, like Namath, Pennington would back it up.

Edwards that week handed the keys to the kingdom to the Kid. "Talk is cheap," Pennington announced to reporters, "so after today there's not gonna be any more talking, there has to be action on the field." Asked what kind of quarterback New York should expect to see, starting with the Chiefs that Sunday, Pennington said, "I'm gonna be a winner, bottom line. This is about winning games, and that's what I'm focused on, that's what we're focused on, and I'm only a little piece of the puzzle to this. But we're gonna be winners as a team, no doubt."

But first he needed to be a profile in courage when he learned that his wife's father had been diagnosed with leukemia that would claim his life the following summer. For three hours, he fought to block out the tragic news. He was 23-of-30 for 245 yards, two touchdowns, and one interception in a 28–25 loss to the Chiefs. "I don't really care what history says, what the facts are," Pennington said. "I think we can turn it around and still make a run at it." Then he beat the Vikings 20–7, and the run was on. "I gave him the nickname 'Franchise,'" Coles said. And from this point, Pennington grabbed the franchise by the throat and took it on an exhilarating magic carpet ride to the playoffs. He was a fiery leader, not averse to head-butting teammates during pregame introductions. He became the toast of the town, a star in a city that lusts for star power. Pennington led the NFL with a 104.2 passer rating and 68.9 completion percentage. He had thrown 22 touchdowns and only 6 interceptions.

The Jets would be hosting Peyton Manning and the Colts in the wild-card playoff game. Days earlier, Pennington wore a green T-shirt with a white "NY" above the heart inside Weeb Ewbank Hall. "This is what it's all about, this is me, the New York Jets," he said, looking down and pointing to the "NY," "and that's what I'm proud of.

And I'll be proud of being a Jet as long as I'm here. It's not about me, it's about the Jets."

On a euphoric field of dreams, Pennington (three touchdown passes) and the Jets routed Manning and the Colts 41–0. "I am so proud of my teammates to see in every one of them that they are not complacent," Pennington said. "To me, it's special when you're able to step in the huddle and see the intensity and focus in the eyes of your teammates."

Pennington and the Jets crashed inside the Black Hole in Oakland the following week. Pennington, a cauldron of hyperactivity, was intercepted twice and lost one fumble in a 30–10 drubbing. Four months later, seated inside Houston's, a restaurant not far from the Jets facility, he was still stung by the defeat. "It will linger until we get past the second round of the playoffs," he said. He managed a chuckle. "In that game, I should have lined up at linebacker."

I asked him if he had any doubt that he would one day win a Super Bowl.

"I don't look at it that way," Pennington said. "I have no doubt in my mind that *we* will win the Super Bowl. It's not gonna be just me."

He had two years left on his contract. "Right now, short-term goal, I would like to be here another seven years," Pennington said. That would take him through the 2009 season. "That would give me a ten-year career in one place, and that would be amazing."

Simms was Parcells's idea of a quarterback in large part because he was football first. Parcells had little regard for what he termed celebrity quarterbacks. He would have loved the young Pennington. "If you want to be on every billboard in the city, you can," Pennington said. "But that's not my goal. I'm a football player first. I'm not a celebrity."

His luck began to change in the 2003 Jets-Giants preseason game. Linebacker Brandon Short blitzed, and Pennington suffered a dislocated and broken left wrist. He returned to play ten games of a lost season.

Still, Edwards and the organization loved him, and the Jets rewarded him with a $64 million contract. But the injury bug bit him again in November 2004 when he suffered what was announced as a strain of the right rotator cuff. He missed three games, and when he returned was intercepted three times in a loss to the Steelers. His big-game prowess was called into question, and after riddling the Seahawks 37–14 at home the following week, he had to be talked into meeting the media by a public relations aide. He was sacrificing his body for his team, and all the nattering nabobs of negativism (thank you, William Safire and Spiro Agnew) in the media wanted to ask was "Why can't Chad and the Jets win a big game?" In the interview room, Pennington took no questions for the first time.

"Here's the way it's going to be: The difference today was that we executed, and for the first time in a long time offensively we set the tempo running the ball [229 yards] and passing the ball. We were able to get into a rhythm and we just kept it flowing, and the biggest thing we tried to concentrate on throughout the game as an offense was to not let up, not even breathe, don't let those guys breathe. Just keep going, keep pressing forward, keep mixing it up, both run and pass. And answer the play of our defense with our own good play by putting up some good points, and we were able to accomplish that both running and passing.

"Great win for us, and now we're excited about the future of our season. Kind of put the [9–7] ghosts of 2000 behind us, and got our tenth win, and went ahead and put that to bed, and we're excited about the last two games of the season now to build some momentum to the playoffs, and . . . actions speak louder than words. There's not a lot that needs to be said; there wasn't a lot that was said between players this week. It was just the look in their eyes, the look in my eyes, that, hey, we know what we have to do, we don't need to really talk about it. We know what we have to do on the field, it doesn't matter what you do off the field, what you say off the field. It matters how you perform on the field. And as veterans, we were able to step up and make some things happen, and it was a great win for us.

"That's my statement, and I'm sticking to it. Thank you."

The back page of the Monday *New York Post* blared: JUST WHINE, BABY.

In the press room inside Weeb Ewbank Hall later that afternoon, Pennington made the mistake of lecturing the media. "I'm privileged and honored to play for the New York Jets," he said. "But guess what? You guys are privileged and honored to be a beat writer for the New York Jets. It is not your right. It is a privilege."

At that point, Ken Berger, then the Jets beat writer for *Newsday*, shot back, "It's our job." Pennington retaliated, "And it is a privilege. You took that job. You have an opportunity to be around some of the greatest athletes in the world." Eesh. Writers who had always found him engaging and insightful gave him a mulligan. A simple case of a good guy having a bad moment.

The Jets lost their last two games but backed into the playoffs when the Bills lost to the Steelers. No one gave them a chance to beat the Chargers in San Diego in the wild-card playoff game. Not with a one-armed quarterback saddled with what the world would later learn was a torn rotator cuff.

So imagine everyone's surprise when Pennington hit Santana Moss with a perfect 47-yard bomb over cornerback Quentin Jammer to give the Jets a 14–7 lead in the third quarter. As he ran toward the end zone to congratulate teammates, Pennington (23-of-33, 279 yards, 2 TDs) looked toward the Jets bench and flexed his bicep. The left one, of course. The Jets appeared to have a 17–10 victory when Barton elbowed Drew Brees on a fourth-and-season incompletion from the Jets' 3 in the final seconds for an unnecessary roughness penalty. Brees found tight end Antonio Gates for the touchdown that forced overtime. On the sideline, Barton pleaded with his quarterback. "Hey," he said, "I need you to get me out of this." Pennington looked him in the eyes and told him, "I got your back, man."

When San Diego rookie placekicker Nate Kaeding missed a 40-yard field goal in overtime, Pennington had Barton's back.

From his 30, Pennington hit a diving Moss for 18 yards and Justin McCareins for 11, and not long after LaMont Jordan rumbled for 19 yards to the Chargers 15, Doug Brien booted the 28-yarder for a stirring 20–17 victory.

"That's what playoff football's about, the quarterback being able to drive the offense down the field," Pennington said.

He nearly willed his way past the Steelers the following week in Pittsburgh to the AFC Championship game, but Brien missed two field goals in the final 2:02 of regulation, including a 43-yarder with four seconds left, and the Jets lost a 20–17 heartbreaker. "We came close," Pennington said. "But close only counts in horseshoes and hand grenades."

Offensive coordinator Paul Hackett, a play-not-to-lose pariah in the eyes of most Jets fans, resigned, and was replaced by Mike Heimerdinger. Edwards decided that if anyone could come back from a torn rotator cuff, it was Pennington. Indeed, as hope springs eternal in the summer, Pennington declared, "It's pretty amazing but it's the first time in three years I haven't felt anything as far as throwing the football." But it turned out that Edwards had placed too much trust in his quarterback's iron will. Pennington wasn't ready when the regular season started. He fumbled six times in Kansas City, and several weeks later against the Jaguars, the shoulder gave out. But when backup Jay Fiedler was knocked out of the game with a shoulder injury, Pennington implored Edwards, "I can do it. I want to do it."

Once again, Edwards let his unyielding faith and belief in Pennington override his common sense. A feeble-armed Pennington was intercepted in overtime as the Jets lost 26–20. In the interview room afterward, a defiant Pennington refused to even think about abandoning his team.

"They'll have to cut it off for me not to play," he said. He knew the deal, though. And it killed him inside. "It tests your willingness, your mind and your confidence."

Years later, when I asked him for the low point, he would reveal exactly how much it tested him. "A couple of days after the game when I was sitting in the doctor's office, and talking about the MRI, talking about all the different possibilities, and not knowing what's gonna happen. Normally as an athlete, you have a goal, you have a challenge in front of you, and you always go after that challenge. When you're sitting there after an injury, you have no goals, you have no challenges—all you have is questions, it's very hard to deal with."

I asked how close he came to just saying, "It's not worth it."

"I never got to that point," he said. "But I know that it was a situation where it took me probably two to three weeks just to regain that energy and focus to start the journey back. There was a good two- to three-week period there I was just totally drained, not only from being injured the second time, but drained from all the hard work and effort that I put into my first surgery."

I asked Pennington whether he regretted playing with that first torn rotator cuff.

"Absolutely not," he said. "Athletics is about people stepping out on the athletic field and doing something extraordinary, and trying to overcome the odds. That's why people are drawn to athletics, and you never know when your last game, when your last play is gonna be, and to me, it's disrespectful to the game to try to plan your future in athletics. You can't do that, 'cause you never know what's gonna happen."

He would need another rotator cuff surgery, of course, and few expected him to play for the Jets again when Edwards, unable to secure a contract extension from Johnson following a 4–12 season, bolted to a soft landing in Kansas City as the Chiefs' new head coach. The new regime—Mangini and Tannenbaum, who had replaced Bradway, who had been reassigned in the scouting department— asked Pennington to take a pay cut from $9 million to $1 million. With no one knocking down his door, Pennington ultimately accepted an incentive-laden $3 million offer.

He rehabbed with the eye of the tiger at IMG Academies in Bradenton, Florida. He showed up at training camp bloodied all right, but forever unbowed, ready to get off the deck and remind the doubters what he was made of, an inspiration to one and all. "I think it's real easy when you have setbacks and adversity to really look at it negatively and throw a pity party for yourself," Pennington told me. "And I just want to use this opportunity to show people that even when you get hit in the mouth twice, and even when you get stung twice and looks like there's no light at the end of the tunnel, that there is as long as you maintain the right attitude and focus on where you want to go and what you want to do. And that can definitely be an inspiration to anybody that's gone through anything. Dealing with a shoulder injury . . . that doesn't even compare to what some people go through on a daily basis."

All of a sudden, he was thirty years old, armed with an appreciation for how precious these opportunities are for someone who has
come eyeball-to-eyeball with his own athletic mortality. "I look back,
this is my seventh year, and it's flown by," he said. "But I'm not where
I want to be and I have a huge goal to help this organization win, help
our team win, and that's what I want to take advantage of." He was
proud that he had somehow been able to defy the odds. "Medically,"
he said, "I'm not even supposed to be here."

In each of the first two games, he threw for over 300 yards. For the
first time in his NFL career, he played the full schedule. He clicked
with Schottenheimer, the new offensive coordinator. He got Mangini
to the playoffs before losing the wild-card game to the Patriots in
Foxboro. He was the Comeback Kid. Through it all, the self-doubt,
the physical and emotional torment, he never let go of his Super
Bowl obsession, and here he was, on the eve of his eighth (and final,
as it turned out) season opener as a Jet, still dreaming that improb-
able dream. "Since I was drafted, in April of 2000, it's been on my
mind . . . every day," Pennington told me. "And it stays on my mind
even when times are hard, and you feel like as an athlete you don't
know if you can make it through two-a-days. . . . That's the one thing
that keeps me coming back, keeps me getting up the next day and
doing the same thing over again." But on this day, the very day that
Belichick was nabbed for Spygate at Giants Stadium, Pennington
sustained a high ankle sprain, and was never the same the rest of
the way. Teams loaded eight in the box and dared Pennington to
beat them, and he could not. The Jets were 1–7 when Mangini made
the switch to Clemens, who hardly distinguished himself and forced
Mangini to declare an open competition in 2008.

The winner, of course, would be Favre.

Saying good-bye wasn't easy for Mangini—Pennington epitomized
all of the core values that Mangini believed in. Pennington put on a
brave public face, but he was wounded. He understood all that jazz
about this being a business, but how could he not suddenly feel that
all the blood, sweat, and tears he had shed for the franchise meant
nothing now? Loyalty, however, is a one-way street in the NFL. It
hit Pennington almost immediately that the Jets had decided that

he was not the right man to deliver that elusive second Super Bowl championship for them. And it hurt. And it never stopped hurting. And probably never will.

Weeks later, in the days leading into the 2008 season opener against the Jets, Pennington touched briefly on his inner emotions in a conference call with reporters. "I would be remiss if I said I'm emotionless," he said. "I'm a human being. All of us have emotions." But he was a Miami Dolphin now, and proud to be one. "But my whole goal is to stay focused entirely on what I need to do to learn my responsibilities and help us win. It would be a disservice to my teammates and to myself if I put too much into the emotional part of this and not being able to go out there and perform well and not giving us a chance to win."

The Dolphins were lucky to have him.

For Brett Favre and the Jets, the Rams were next. The Rams had responded immediately to Haslett, stunning the Cowboys and then the Redskins at FedEx Field, but had come back down to earth and were bringing a 2–6 record to Giants Stadium. Bulger had settled

back in under center, energized by a rising star in rookie wide receiver Donnie Avery, a gamebreaker with scary speed. But franchise running back Steven Jackson (quad injury) had missed the previous game against the Cardinals, a 34–13 loss in St. Louis, and was so questionable midweek that Haslett was getting someone named Kenneth Darby ready for the Jets. And Antonio Pittman. Haslett, with the 28th-ranked pass defense, sounded as if he would rather be facing the young Unitas than Favre. "I think he may be the best player that ever played the game, at least the most competitive player that ever played the game," Haslett said. "I love the guy. If I was building a football team and somebody said you could have one player . . . that's the guy I would take, because I love his competitiveness, his arm strength, his mobility. The guy is unbelievable. . . . He's everything you want in a quarterback."

This was the day after Barack Obama had been elected the first African American president, and inside the Jets locker room, Kris Jenkins, who to his credit had resurrected his career and his life following battles with the bottle and depression, took time off from disrupting opposing offenses to talk about the history that had been made a night earlier. "I really enjoyed being able to be alive and see history being made during my generation," he said. "The thing that a lot of people have always stuck on with this election is race and to me it didn't matter. I really just wanted to see the best candidate be elected, and the thing is, I think that the best candidate in this election happened to be black or mixed or whatever you want to say, but I think that he is a great man. I think he really kept his cool in a really tough situation and I think as a country that is what we need. We need somebody that is going to be able to keep their cool and be able to think effectively during this time of crisis because we are in a bit of a situation right now with the country. It's just not one thing and when I look at the situation I have to be honest and realize what is best for my kids. I think a lot of people sometimes look past a lot of situations in a bigger picture because they are looking out for their personal benefit, and I can't be selfish enough to think about keeping all of my money, or being in a better tax bracket, because I have to make sure that I do my part for the world to be a better place for my kids, and if there is going to be a grown man who is going to step up and try to bring in that type of change so my friends can walk around and be comfortable, safe, and secure in their lives then I am going to welcome that and that's it. I am not looking at this from, like I said, a race standpoint or anything like that. I am looking at this as a parent. I am a patriot, I do love my country, and I have a brother that is out fighting war and I wish he wasn't there. I wish he was home safe, but I am still going to support them because he chose to stand up in a way that most people are afraid to do and so with that being said, I want what is best for this country and I think as a country we need to tighten it up. It's not just on one person to make a difference. It's not just on one person to be perfect. It's on everybody to make a difference and everybody to understand that one person, even though he is president, he is not going to be perfect, but you still have to support the person that you elect and you have to be there to demand the type of things as a society that you want. I am just trying to be the best person that I can be, honestly."

This was the day when the questions about Favre transforming into a game manager came fast and furious. He had just two 20-plus-yard completions in Buffalo, thanks to yards after catch from his receivers. Favre took one shot downfield, an incompletion to Coles. "I joked with Phil Simms before the game, the day before, about managing the game. . . . I kinda joked, I said, 'I never really believed in that.' I think you play the game, and whatever's asked of you, you do. I managed the game the other day, as bad as I hate to say that. I got no problems doing whatever it takes to win, believe me. I'm not gonna leave out of this room, and walk out, and say, 'I lied to 'em again.' All I want to do is win. That felt really good the other day.

"And I tell people this all the time, for me, at this stage in my career, there's not one thing left out there for me to achieve. Not one thing, that I've set, as far as goals, other than, 'I'm gonna come here and play for the Jets,' and that's to win here. That's it."

Favre volunteered that he spoke to Simms while the former Giant was driving to see his youngest son play at Syracuse. "He was just asking me about how I felt like I was playing and things like that,"

Favre said. "I said, 'It's been exactly what I thought it would be.' I don't know how we got on the subject of managing the game or whatever, but I think we were talking about my arm bothering me or whatever. He was not asking me that—he was asking me if I've gotten a lot of questions about that. I told him, 'Yes.' I said, 'Everyone thinks that my arm's bothering me so I'm managing the game or whatever.' Which he knows better than that, but . . . like he said, the last thing he said, 'Hey, whatever it takes to win,' and that's true. Whatever it takes. And, who knows? From week to week that changes."

Mangini asked Favre to play more like Pennington in Buffalo—even Simms in 1990 under Parcells—in part because of the Bills' defensive philosophy that aimed to take away the deep ball, and in part because of an emerging rushing attack and defense. Football isn't rocket science, but it's more than just football Xs and Os these days with all the chicanery and disguises.

"You know what? I think nowadays it has to be, to be totally honest with ya," Favre said. "More teams are going to that, not only offensively, but defensively." But what, Hutchinson wanted to know, would Favre say to people who say that maybe he should indeed be more of a game manager? "To be honest with ya, I don't really pay a whole lot of attention to what people are sayin'," Favre said. "I've had so much advice throughout my career—good and bad, some directly, some indirectly. All I know is this is eighteen years, I'm still playin', this team is tied for first place, and that's not too shabby. So . . . could be better . . . I could be better . . . but in my seventeen years of playin', seventeen and a half, I could have always been a little better. I'm always tryin' to achieve being perfect; that's never gonna happen. I don't know if anyone's ever been completely perfect, but I'm still tryin' to achieve it." If nothing else, the perfect answer.

Given their inexcusable loss in Oakland, and their life-and-death survival against the Chiefs, the Jets had no right to look past the Rams to a Thursday night Armageddon against the Patriots in Foxboro the following week. Then again, given human nature, and given the fact that Jackson had been declared out, Mangini addressed the danger with his team. This was no time to let down, not with the Dolphins hosting the battered Seahawks, quarterbacked by Seneca Wallace, not with the Patriots and Bills colliding in Foxboro. "We do a good job here, Eric does a good job, this whole organization, of concentratin' on now," Favre said.

They sure did. And it helped that the Rams, not long after kickoff, did a good job of concentrating solely on when the bus waiting outside Giants Stadium would take them back to the airport for the flight home.

Favre couldn't have picked a more gracious opponent. Once upon a time, he was Matt Ryan, the Falcons' rookie wunderkind who was being hailed as the best young quarterback since Peyton Manning, able to scoff at the reminders his barking body would insist on giving him during the course of the week following a particularly violent beating. But when you are thirty-nine, the barking is much louder, and lasts much longer. And this time, it followed Favre all the way to Sunday morning warm-ups. "I felt my age today," Favre said. "That happens from time to time."

So Favre passed the baton on his opening drive to Jones, who looked frisky and fresh and ran for 20 yards up the middle on the first play from scrimmage and the 13-yard touchdown that gave the Jets a 7–0 lead. Soon after Favre's 54-yard bomb deep down the middle to a wide-open Keller, it was 10–0. Favre's play-action froze the linebacker, and the safeties rolled outside to double Coles and Cotchery on each side of the field. "As soon as he snapped the ball, I looked downfield and the safeties just completely split," Keller said. "So, in my mind, I knew it was coming to me."

This burgeoning chemistry between Favre and Keller was of no small significance. Favre has forever had an affinity for his tight ends, from Mark Chmura to Keith Jackson to Franks to Donald Lee. "He's what I call a 'tweener,'" Favre said days later. "He's like Gates, where he can line up at wide receiver, but he also can line up at tight end and block. The problem that that presents to other teams is, 'What type of matchup do we want to put up against him—do we want to bring in a nickel, do we want to bring in a dime, do we want to bring in lesser of an athlete and play him man-to-man, and then potentially have him beat us deep like he did the other day?' Also, the blocking threat. We can line him up at X. We can line him up at Z. We can line him up at Y, which is traditionally where he's going to line up. You can put him in the backfield, but you don't want to overload him. He'll tell you he's got it all down and he'll be ready. The thing is, five years from now, he'll look back and say, 'I thought I had it.' We want to ease him into it and allow him to do what he does best right now, not have him overthink. We know he can run a Go route, we know he can run a slant, we know he can block. Let's just let him do that and not overthink. The sky's the limit for the guy."

The sky was falling on the bumbling Rams. Elam, on a beautifully timed delayed blitz on which he duped left tackle Orlando Pace into thinking he was dropping into coverage, strip-sacked Bulger, resulting in a room service fumble that Pace turned into a 50-yard touchdown—his first score since high school. It was 17–0.

The rout was on.

On Jones's 2-yard touchdown run early in the second quarter, Faneca pulled right and knocked linebacker Will Witherspoon back

to St. Louis. Favre hit Keller with a 1-yard touchdown pass and Feely nailed a franchise-record-tying 55-yard field goal, and by halftime the Jets led 40–0, the most one-sided halftime lead since the Packers were annihilating the Bucs in 1983. The Jets scored on every one of their seven possessions. Never before had a Favre-quarterbacked team scored 40 points in a half.

"The mantra at halftime was to remember the Arizona game, and we did," Favre said.

Favre threw only two passes in the second half, acquiescing to the wishes of his offensive linemen, who felt compelled to plead, "Brett, don't throw it."

Jones (149 yards) was on his way to a three-touchdown afternoon, tying Martin for the club mark. He seemed to get stronger and more determined with each carry, and it inspired his offensive line, which inspired him. "I'm lucky to be able to run behind those guys," Jones said. "They're one of the best offensive lines in the league." Tannenbaum had stolen him (and a lower second-round pick) for a high second-round draft choice before the 2007 season, when Jones scored only one rushing touchdown behind an inferior offensive line. Now he stood atop the AFC with 750 rushing yards, with eight rushing touchdowns to boot. The smashmouth Jets finished the day with 206 yards on the ground.

"We're starting to show our identity," Woody said.

It was 47–3 with 11:09 left when Mangini finally pulled Favre to give Clemens mop-up duty. Mangini blamed his insecurities on the Cardinals storming back from that 34–0 halftime deficit. Puh-leeze! Warner wasn't the quarterback, and Fitzgerald and Boldin weren't the wideouts. The Rams were mailing this one in. If Favre had suffered some freak injury, Mangini would have been excoriated. Favre should have been out of the game in the third quarter.

If every game was this easy for him, Favre would probably sign up for another ten years (okay, maybe another ten months). Given the Silence of the Lambs pass rush, Favre could have fielded another call on his cell phone from Millen while scanning the field for open receivers. He wasn't sacked. Not once. The Jets defense forced five turnovers that led to 27 points. Kerry Rhodes registered his first interception of the season, broke up a goal-line pass that was intercepted by Hank Poteat, and recovered a fumble. It was the blueprint Mangini had been seeking: complementary football, he called it. The offense complements the defense, which complements the special teams, which complements the offense . . .

"That's what we're capable of doing," Favre said. "It comes down to us believing we can play this way. If we keep playing games like this, we'll be hard to beat."

The surging Dolphins were demonstrating that they, too, were hard to beat; Pennington set the tone on his opening drive with a 39-yard touchdown pass to Ginn off a fleaflicker in a 19–17 victory over the Seahawks.

Cheers rang out in the Jets locker room when Mangini informed his players that the 47–3 romp marked the biggest winning margin in franchise history. What excited Favre as much as anything—and was about to torment Belichick—was the emergence of Keller, a nightmare matchup for linebackers and safeties. The charismatic rookie (6-for-107 receiving), becoming more involved in the "21" personnel package—two backs and one tight end—finished with his first 100-yard day. In the locker room afterward, Favre made the kid's day. "I wish I had you when I was younger," he told Keller.

Better late than never. Favre threw only 19 passes and was not intercepted for the first time in eight weeks. "Throwing touchdown passes is fun and throwing for a lot of yards is fun, but nothing is more fun than being in a football game like that," he said. "It was awesome."

THE MOUNTAINTOP

At New England • At Tennessee • Denver •
At San Francisco • Buffalo

The likelihood is Mangini began looking ahead to the Patriots sometime during the second half, but heaven forbid he should admit as much. When he was asked about the showdown, Mangini said, "I've had only five minutes to think about it."

You can bet that every waking minute from then on was spent thinking about the Patriots.

The Border War was only four days away.

Mangini's record against Belichick was 1–5.

First place in the division was on the line.

It was only the biggest regular-season game between the two teams since the Jets beat the Patriots 30–17 in Foxboro with a playoff spot on the line on December 22, 2002.

The Patriots were still the team to beat, even if Harrison, outside linebacker Adalius Thomas, and running back Laurence Maroney were missing, and defensive end Ty Warren was a surprise scratch before the game. They still had Vrabel, still had Bruschi, still had Seymour on defense, and still had Moss and Welker on offense.

And of course, they still had Belichick. And they had beaten the Jets eleven of the last twelve times they had met. But that hardly meant that Favre, or Faneca, or Jenkins, or Pace, or Woody were suffering from any inferiority complex. They had lost only one game to the Patriots in green and white, and that one came at a time when team chemistry was clearly lacking. Then there was the curious arrival of ex-Patriot Ty Law, a stunning signing that had the conspiracy theorists nodding their heads in agreement. Law, who was a Jet in 2004 under Edwards, would help school the younger Jets players in the Patriot Way. So what that he hadn't played a down all year? Even if, at age thirty-four, he had little or nothing left, maybe at least it could serve as a psychological shot across the New England bow.

"I know what Bill and the Patriots are saying: 'Hey, they have to beat us. We own the division,'" Favre said. "If we're playing games like we played today we'll be hard to beat. Very hard to beat."

This was Obama's time, this was his moment, and now these Jets believed this was their time, this was their moment. There was a feeling spreading like wildfire among the Jets that the Patriots were ready to be had. "Guys are starting to believe we have a good football team and it's showing on the field," Woody said. "The biggest thing I see is, we've developed a swagger. When you do that, it's a powerful thing."

That swagger, to a large degree because of Favre, was about to mushroom.

He had unretired to play in games like these. The Jets had brought him to New York for this game, more than any other, to beat this team. At his Wednesday press session, Favre was asked if he was feeling extra pressure. That impish grin creased his face.

"I haven't really thought about it," he said. "That may be true. Then again, it may not be. That may have been why we brought Kris Jenkins in. Let's put it off on Kris." The reporters laughed.

But you bet Favre knew the deal. "I know exactly what this game means, the weight it carries," he said.

Favre found a familiar way to cope with the stress. He and Szott, a fourteen-year NFL veteran offensive lineman and fellow Ed Block Courage award recipient, would steal away to Upstate New York for an occasional overnight hunting trip. "We spent a lot of time together,"

Szott said. "I was probably one of the few guys in the building older than him. He's got a passion for deer hunting as I do. He wouldn't do any other kind of hunting. We connected on that level."

Once Favre's head stopped swimming, by the middle of October, he and Szott would frequent the Jets owner's farm, sometimes on Friday afternoons for a couple of hours before nightfall. "It was great just to ride up and back and discuss everything from A to Z away from the complex," Szott said.

Favre was generous with imparting his wealth of knowledge to Clemens, as the quarterbacks enjoyed a healthy relationship. "The neat thing we did, some evenings after a game, or after watching film [on Mondays], we'd drive out and look at the deer and BS," Clemens said.

Favre's only other refuge was inside a small nook behind the equipment room where he could tend to e-mails on the computer between meetings—an arrangement other quarterbacks have and one he had in Green Bay over his last several years there.

Belichick, meanwhile, was placing his Patriots on Defcon 2, the kind of high alert our military remembers from the Cuban missile crisis. Every NFL head coach props up that week's opponent as if his team is playing the Lombardi Packers, even if they are playing the Kotite Jets. But Belichick had made an art form of it. He often sounded as if someone would have to drag him and his team out from under the covers to the game.

"They have gotten a couple of big first quarters in the Arizona game and the St. Louis game," Belichick said. "They're pretty much running out the clock by halftime."

His players—those few who make themselves available while the necessary-evil media are allowed to stalk the spacious locker room for forty-five minutes—parrot Belichick so religiously it is almost comical.

"They're just playing very well right now," Cassel said. "They're playing with a lot of aggression and energy. They've been very opportunistic. They continue to get turnover opportunities because they make those turnover opportunities. Nine interceptions and nine fumble recoveries on the season, and four of them have been returned for touchdowns."

Then there was this gem from Welker: "We have to make sure we bring our A-game to have a chance."

Of course, if anyone knows how to play the media game, it is Favre.

"I think we're still trying to find our identity, for the most part, but with each week, I feel like we're getting better and better," he said. "Until we beat these guys, or until anyone beats these guys and knocks them off from the top, then they're always going to be the team to beat."

Favre was 2–3 against Belichick-coached teams. He was 18-of-26, for 181 yards, one touchdown, and one interception in the 19–10 week 2 defeat.

"I think he beats you with simplicity," said Favre. "Not that he doesn't give you different looks, but it's pretty simple. . . . They do a good job of disguising."

In the Gillette Stadium press box, Steve Buckley, a *Boston Herald* columnist, greeted me with a smile and said, "You're the talk of the town!"

My entire column, written for that day's *New York Post*, had been read over the airwaves by Arnold Dale and Michael Holley (*The Dale & Holley Show*) on Boston radio station WEEI. "Steve Sermon," Holley said with a chuckle toward the end of their reading.

Here it is:

FOXBORO—One man.

One man changed the course of history for two franchises.

The Patriots have won three Super Bowls since Bill Belichick told Woody Johnson to take that job and shove it.

And the Jets haven't been able to do a damn thing about it. It's time.

It's time for this head coach, it's time for this quarterback, it's time for these players to give their owner, to give their tormented fans, a great big belated bang for their buck.

Beat this man, already. Beat this team.

Beat this cheat who brazenly spied on you in broad daylight in defiance of NFL rules.

Beat this man and beat this team tonight so you at least give yourself a chance—a chance—to beat this man and beat this team to the Super Bowl.

Beat this man and beat this team tonight so you can use this game as a launching pad for the rest of your season.

No excuses.

Beat this man and beat this team without Tom Brady. And Rodney Harrison. And Adalius Thomas. And Laurence Maroney.

Beat this man and beat this team, *Brett Favre*: This was your mandate when the franchise whacked Chad Pennington and brought you to New York, to win games like these, to infuse your new team with undying belief, especially in the fourth quarter, to make the big throw in the big moment. Sure, sure, as a 39-year-old gunslinger you carry fewer bullets in your holster, but you still pack enough heat to keep defenses from ganging up on Thomas Jones, and all that savvy, moxie and guile, and shame on you if you don't know your new offense well enough to outduel Matt Cassel.

Beat this man and beat this team, *Eric Mangini*: This was your mandate when Woody The Owner [no relation to Joe The Plumber, as far as we know] decided that imitation is the greatest form of flattery and gave you and Mike The GM the green-and-white light to build Patriots South. You beat this man once, in your rookie 2006 season, and haven't beaten him since. Beat this man and restore the faith of a wary and weary fan base that longs to hail you as Mangenius again. Beat this man and you become the pupil who steps out of his mentor's shadow once and for all.

Beat this man and beat this team, *Mike Tannenbaum*: This was your mandate when you were promoted to replace Terry Bradway, who tried to beat this man with Herm Edwards and Pennington and could not. You endured a sophomore slump, but then Woody The Owner gave you the green-and-white light to morph into Scott Pioli, and $140 million later, here we are. Nose tackle Kris Jenkins, possible defensive MVP. Calvin Pace, pass rushing weapon. Alan Faneca, tough and fiery. Damien Woody, pretty smooth transition to right tackle. Oh, and Brett

Favre. Thought you didn't know much football. Thought you were a salary cap guy.

Beat this man and beat this team, *Woody Johnson*: This man stiffed you, walked out on you, told New York that he didn't want to be HC of your NYJ after one day on the job. Yes, he wanted to escape the giant shadow of Bill Parcells, GM at the time, but face facts, he wanted Bob Kraft signing his checks instead of you. So you formed your own Generation Jets management team and here we are. You didn't enjoy being 4–12, so what did you do? You silenced the naysayers who were certain you didn't want to win badly enough by opening your wallet and turning Mike The GM loose in free agency. You went 4 it by signing off on Brett the Jet, even if you knew it would help you sell those outrageous PSLs.

Gentlemen, your team is peaking, oozing swagger, finally finding its identity. You stand once more at the corner of Contender and Pretender.

Turn that corner.

Beat that man and beat that team.

He has never been more Beat-a-Bill.

There was rain in the forecast, but as game time neared, only a slight mist greeted the teams. The Jets were saying all the right things, as always, but privately they were a confident bunch champing at the bit to make a bold statement. So much was at stake, for the aforementioned Gang of 4: For Johnson, who was burned when Belichick spurned him, and burned further when Belichick won his three Super Bowls. Who turned to Tannenbaum and asked him to be the Jets' equivalent of Pioli, and Mangini and asked him to be the Jets' equivalent of Belichick. Who handed $140 million to Tannenbaum and asked him to get some big-time players.

For Tannenbaum, who was instrumental in prying Mangini from Belichick's staff seconds after replacing Bradway, who claimed he would be happier in the personnel department.

For Mangini, whose standing in the eyes of Jets Nation was shaky at best, following 4–12, following all the suspect playcalling that gave it an inherent fear that he simply did not know how to make Jet Favre work, as challenging as that would be for any head coach having a thirty-eight-year-old Hall of Fame icon quarterback foisted upon his team in the second week of training camp. Who was 2–5 against Belichick only if you count nailing him on Spygate as one of the victories.

And, of course, for Favre. Whether he liked it or not—and remember, he never embraced the role of savior—this was a defining moment for him and his new team. It was a defining moment for his New York legacy as well. It was time for him to grab this franchise, this team, this season, by the throat. Because if he could not get past Belichick and the Patriots here, with first place on the line in November, then a slew of morbid questions threatened to hound him and everyone around him and shroud the Jets in yet another round of doom and gloom:

What was the point in bringing him here?
What was the point in spending all that money in free agency?
Was Mangini the right man for the job?

The Jets were a Win Now team, and never was it more important to Win Now than now.

On third-and-8, Favre hit Keller to set up a 7-yard touchdown on a screen pass to Washington.

Favre immediately began marching the Jets on his next possession. After Smith, out of the shotgun, took the direct snap and ran 17 yards to the New England 4, Favre targeted Keller, who dropped what would have been a 4-yard touchdown pass and 14–0 lead. The Jets settled for a field goal.

It had become evident why Law had been signed: to help against Moss, and be rough and tumble with him at every turn. It forced Cassel to fixate on Welker, tight end Benjamin Watson, Jabar Gaffney, and Kevin Faulk. Moss wouldn't catch a pass in the first half.

The Pats had scratched to within 10–6 when Washington hushed the place with a 92-yard kickoff return.

Now Favre saw that Cotchery was being singled by cornerback Ellis Hobbs—the same Ellis Hobbs who had been victimized in the

final minute of Super Bowl XLII by Plaxico Burress—and decided it was time to take a downfield shot. And Cotchery wound up making a play that reminded some of David Tyree's Catch 42 in the Super Bowl just prior to Eli Manning's game-winner to Burress. As the ball descended, a diving Cotchery reached around Hobbs with his left arm and somehow corralled the ball for a 46-yard completion.

It was 24–6 when Cotchery caught Favre's next offering at the 2 and extended his left arm over the plane of the goal line.

Gillette Stadium sat shell-shocked.

When C. J. Mosley sacked a driving Cassel on fourth-and-3, it looked over.

It wasn't over.

Belichick had found something. He unleashed Cassel, operating out of the shotgun, and Mangini did not adjust. From his 33, with 1:40 left in the half, Cassel hit Gaffney for 12 yards, then Gaffney again for 8 more. Cassel, on a keeper, converted a fourth-and-1, and with 13 seconds and no time-outs left before halftime, found Gaffney against rookie corner Dwight Lowery to cut the deficit to 24–13.

The Jets defense steadied itself when the second half began, but the offensive playcalling had that all too familiar play-not-to-lose look. At a time when Favre & Co. should have displayed some killer instinct, they went into a shell, and only established the recently signed punter, Reggie Hodges. Twenty yards in total in the third quarter. "I promise you, we didn't change our approach one bit," Mangini said.

As the momentum began to shift, and the Jets staggered around Gillette Stadium, Favre could hear fans behind the visiting bench taunt his team with chants of "Same Old Jets."

If these were indeed the Same Old Jets, they would not be able to hang on. They would—dare we say it?—choke.

Cassel was working Welker underneath, and a 29-yard hookup positioned his 10-yard touchdown pass to Watson, too athletic for Pace. Belichick went for two, and got it when Cassel hit Gaffney, and it was 24–21, and Gillette Stadium could smell Jets blood.

Soon Cotchery fumbled, and Stephen Gostkowski's 47-yard field goal tied it.

Cassel, feeling it in the no-huddle offense, suddenly resembled Brady, except when he overthrew an open Moss downfield. Had the Jets defense turned too conservative? The Jets blitzed Cassel only five times in 32 passing plays after intermission. "We've pressured before, in that opening game I think it was last year, where Randy killed us," Mangini said. "It's all calculated risk. One thing with playing New England is they're very good at identifying those things and they're very good at making you pay a cost. It's usually not a small cost. It's usually a significant cost."

Favre and the Jets needed to make their stand right here and now. And they did. Jones gained 11. Favre hit Baker, and then Keller, and then Stuckey, for first down at the New England 11.

Favre, at the 7, couldn't find an open receiver and threw the ball away. But Vrabel was called for holding Keller. Following another defensive holding penalty on James Sanders, Jones barged in from the 1, and the Jets led 31–24 with 3:10 left.

Jenkins sacked Cassel, and the Pats punted.

It looked over.

It wasn't over.

Favre had it at his 23, with 2:24 left. Following a 5-yard Jones run, the Patriots called their final time-out, with 2:20 remaining.

Jones again, for 3 yards.

Third-and-2 at the two-minute warning.

And Mangini tried to get those longest yards with Jones rather than Favre, and came up a yard short.

Cassel would get one last chance.

He started at his 38, with 1:04 and no time-outs left. The Jets were in one of those prevent defenses that so often in their history only prevented winning.

"In that situation with 1:09 [actually 1:04] left and no time-outs, they are fighting against two different things," Mangini said. "They are fighting against yardage and they are fighting against time, and what you don't want to do is give up yardage and let them get out of bounds. When you play the type of defense that we were playing, we were going to be able to protect the sidelines, jam the receivers, and really the only open area is short and in the middle of the field where you want them to catch all the balls because that keeps the clock going. About sixteen seconds per play is what it typically takes. If you can make them go the long, hard way and eat up that time on the clock, you put pressure on them two different ways, and that is something that we played back when I was with the Jets the first time [under Parcells], in New England, and now here. It's not something new that was just developed for [Thursday night]."

So Cassel dinked and dunked and spiked his way down the field and now it was fourth-and-1 at the Jets 16 with eight seconds left.

Bowens nearly made the game-deciding sack, but Cassel escaped. He looked right for Moss, blanketed by Law near the right pylon. There was only one place Cassel could have thrown the ball to complete it, a place where only a sprawling Moss could catch it, and he did. Touchdown, upheld by replay, with one second left. Gostkowski's point-after attempt meant overtime.

"I couldn't watch," Favre said. "I saw the replay. But believe me, when you have Randy Moss, I don't care what he's done or hasn't done until that clock is done. Until it's over, when you got eighty-one, anything can happen. Matt Cassel played one hell of a football game and I don't know if you can make a better throw at the end of the game than he made, honestly. It was a great catch on Randy's part but that ball was thrown—I mean Ty Law has great coverage—you can't get any better than that throw."

Rhodes, calling tails, won his tenth consecutive coin toss.

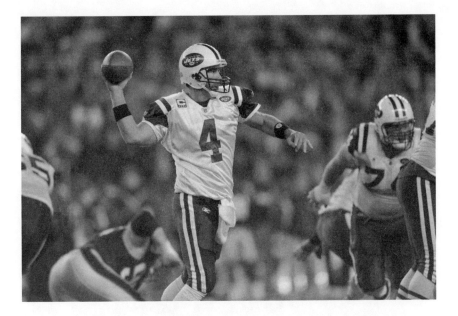

As fiery and emotional as Favre is, he was the stoic battlefield commander here, more interested in walking the walk than talking the talk.

"I didn't say anything, to be honest with you," he said. "It got to the point where there was nothing that needed to be said. We have a lot of veteran guys, guys that want to win and knew what was at stake. It was just a matter of making plays."

Favre started at his 20.

"'It's either now or never,'" Favre recalled thinking. "'This is your one shot.' . . . They were rollin' on offense, our defense was tired . . . it was all or nothing."

After all the times he had stared at moments such as these and refused to blink, you would have sworn Favre would be a remorseless assassin right then and there. Not even close.

"There was no one more nervous in that building than me," he said. "I'm no different than anyone else. Everyone's coming up, 'Hey, this is where you do your thing.' I'm thinking, 'My God! Why can't we make this easier?'"

"It's always amazing when you hear different great players who have done something tons of times talking about the nervousness they have," Mangini would say at his Friday press conference. "It's

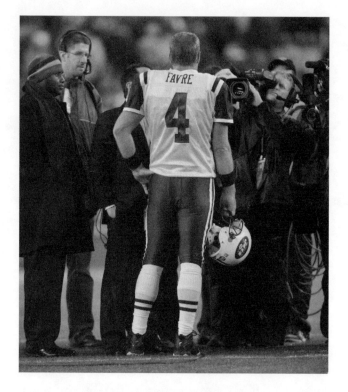

a great reminder that everybody feels the same way in different situations and it's your ability to face that nervousness, butterflies or whatever it is, and still execute. I think it's good for the young guys to hear that. It's good for the players that don't have the experience to hear that. Here is a guy that is going to the Hall of Fame. He has done everything there is to do in football and he still gets nervous. With all that being said, he has great poise and he is able to focus through that stuff and execute. You feel good when he has the ball."

Favre wore a mask to hide his anxieties. "You get into the huddle and you look into Number 4's eyes and you know you're going to have a chance to win," Washington said.

But Favre was sacked on first down. "Oh boy; this is not good," Tannenbaum thought.

Favre threw incomplete for Washington on second down, and suddenly it was third-and-15 at his 15, quite possibly third-and-season.

To lose this game, to this team, after leading 24–6, would have been catastrophic for the Jets' psyche.

Favre-to-Keller saved them. Favre found his rookie tight end over the middle, and Keller had the presence of mind and determination to bull his way past Meriweather for the first down, to the 31.

"I'd like to give you some secret, we just called All Go, four guys running vertical," Favre said. "I happened to look over and saw Coach Belichick telling them to get back. They got back but they pushed towards the slot and our two guys to the left, they pushed that way, it wasn't a blitz or anything like that, I won't say blown coverage, maybe they just thought I'd look down the middle of the field. Believe me, I was going to just buy some time and run around and make something happen and I was probably shocked as anyone."

Said Tannenbaum, "I thought the most incredible part of the play was when Dustin caught the ball; he knew he wasn't where he needed to be, and he had to like lunge to get the first down."

On second-and-6, Favre found Keller again for 12 yards. And again for 4 yards on third-and-1. "He hurt us tonight," Belichick would say. "We have to do a better job on him."

On second-and-10, Favre rolled right and threw across his body over the middle for Coles, for 16 yards, to the New England 24.

Now Washington for 4.

Jones for 2.

Mangini can kick the field goal here.

He doesn't.

Jones for 2.

Feely is ready.

The Pats call time. But Feely has been around the block. No one can ice him at this stage of his career.

And his 34-yarder is straight and true.

Favre was asked if he said anything to the fans who had chanted "Same Old Jets."

"No; Jay did when the ball went through," Favre said.

When it ended, Mangini walked over to Favre with a warm smile and locked him in a bear hug that lasted almost ten seconds, and patted him on the helmet. Tannenbaum greeted his players one by one with handshakes as they marched, big smiles on their faces, into the visiting locker room.

Tannenbaum hugged Favre. "I'm really glad you're here," he told him.

On his way into the locker room, Favre roared, "Bleep yeah!"

In the interview room, he was asked where this triumph ranked for him. "It ranks right up there near the top," he said. "Being in the moment, it's easy to say it may be at the top. It goes without saying how difficult it is to come here and win, not to mention the fact that the way we started versus the way regulation ended, they had all the momentum and every reason to win it. We could've easily folded. There were a lot of things in this game that happened based on the history, I'm sure most people were betting against us. We found a way to win the game and I think it says a lot about our team at this point. We've still got a lot of football left, but we have to be proud of the way we played."

Favre had to know this was one of those galvanizing, us-against-the-world triumphs that can launch a team's dreams. But he also knew that just because you slay a dragon doesn't necessarily mean a monster season is guaranteed. His was the voice of reason, and his younger teammates needed to hear it. "It wasn't the Super Bowl," Favre said. "We've still got a lot of football left, but that was fun, it was fun. . . . It's a big win, but the Patriots still have a lot of football left, they'll be right in the thick of it as always. We just gave ourselves a much better shot."

The owner marveled at what he had just witnessed. "When Brett's in the game, the other team can't relax," Johnson said six weeks before the start of the 2009 training camp in Cortland.

No one knew it at the time, but the owner's rapidly mushrooming expectations for his team would prove to be Mangini's undoing. "I was prepared to go to the Super Bowl that year," Johnson recalled.

Mangini was still beaming the next day. "It was a very good mood on the plane ride home," he said, laughing. "It's a very short plane ride home. It has felt long sometimes in the past, but this one felt very short."

He was energized by the way his team had begun playing complementary football, by the way it was finishing games. And, of course, by Favre.

"I think Brett just instills confidence in the group," Mangini said. "There is a sense of ease when he has the ball because you feel like he's going to get it to the right place. If the play doesn't look like it's supposed to look, he's going to make something happen that makes it right. I've watched him over time do that a lot. It's a lot more fun watching him do it for us than when he used to do it to us, whatever 'us' I was a part of at the time."

Away from the national spotlight, the Dolphins were flying under the radar. Pennington's fourth-and-5 completion to Ginn kept the winning field goal drive alive so that Dan Carpenter could boot the 38-yard field goal that gave the Fish a 17–15 victory over the Seahawks with 38 seconds left. "It was my first fourth-and-five with a minute or so left in the game," said Ginn. "It was probably Chad's twentieth. He's cool, calm, and collected. He went out there and got the job done."

Parcells stopped by the locker room to offer his quarterback encouragement. "It's so hard to win in the league," he said. "Enjoy every win."

Now another chance to make a loud statement across the league awaited the Jets. A road game against the 10–0 Titans was next. CBS's Simms sounded ready to board the Favre bandwagon. "The Jets remind me of a team that has the fever," he said. "The fever is winning and how much fun they can have doing it. They have some personality going for them. There are a lot of reasons for it. You have to give the coaching staff credit; Brett Favre and all the new additions. It's taken a while but they've all melded together. The Jets have absolutely become a fun team to watch in the NFL."

Indeed they had. Favre was asked what the victory over the Patriots had done for the team's mental state.

"I think time will tell, first of all," he said. "But there's no doubt that when we walked into the locker room after the game, we were on cloud nine. And I don't know if that's 'cause we beat the Patriots or we had five days off." Laughter. "A combination of both. This team is a veteran team, and regardless of if some of the guys were here last year or not really doesn't matter. I think the most important thing is we have guys who understand what we're capable of doing. . . . I think as each game is over, you're starting to see more and more confidence from a team standpoint—hey, you know, we can be pretty good. And I think that game, more than any game this year, probably did more for us in those respects than any game throughout the year.

"I think first and foremost the most important thing is to have confidence that you can win every game, and no matter what happens, or who you're playin', or where you're playin' 'em, it can be done."

The Titans' quarterback was another graybeard, thirty-five-year-old Kerry Collins. Titans coach Jeff Fisher had turned to the ex-Giant when Vince Young showed he was too immature to fulfill the obligations of the franchise quarterback. The thirtysomething quarterbacks all shared an appreciation for every game and every season, for seizing every moment. Collins was the Panthers' young franchise quarterback when Favre beat him and Speight in that 1996 NFC Championship game.

"I think you realize—I know you realize—that you're playing game to game," Favre said, "and your focus is so much different than it was as a younger player. You just appreciate the moment a lot more, 'cause you realize it won't be there forever, and this game could be my last. When you're twenty-two years old, you're looking for that new contract, you're looking for commercials, you're looking for . . . whatever. You just always say you're on scholarship still. As you get older, all you want to do is win, get by, and go on to the next game and win. I hear people talk about goin' back to school after they've been out of college for a long time, how much better they are at studying, or doing their work, and to me it's no different in pro football."

Mangini and Favre had been reminding one and all that the more you win, the bigger the next game becomes. "I think it's a measuring stick for us to find out who we are, and what we're capable of doing," Favre said.

With first-place Favre riding high, this was as good a time as any for one columnist to ask, "How hard is it for you to imagine not playing football this time next year?"

Nice try.

"Oh, I haven't even thought about it," Favre said. "I thought last year was probably—maybe not from a statistic standpoint—probably the best year I'd ever had playing, based on how young we were, and how we played the previous couple of years. And that was a dilemma I faced at the end of the season; I knew I was playing at a high level. And at thirty-eight, I know what everyone else is thinking—at some point, he's gotta fall off. And I agree. At some point. I don't know when that point will be. But I played last week like I expect to play; I thought I played at a high level, but that's what they brought me in here to do. I expect to play like that every week, and hope to. And I have people, friends, family, whoever, ask me all the time about next year. And the answer I give them, which is the honest answer, is I really don't know. I really don't know, and to be totally honest with ya, I really don't care. What I care about is trying to beat Tennessee. I don't see how anyone—aside from you guys—can focus on next year, when what we're tryin' to do right now is win, and do something this year. And I'm thirty-nine years old; I know that the better days are behind me for the most part. There won't be sixteen more years, or seventeen more years, and I'm tryin' to enjoy and help this team win now."

The beauty of Favre, then and now, is that the game is never too big for him—because he never lost sight of the fact that it is a game. "To me, you can have fun, and win at the same time," he said. "And I can only speak from experience, this is eighteen years, and believe me, there's nothin' fun about meetings, there's not a whole lotta fun in practice, there's not a whole lotta fun in losing. But you can make it as easy or as hard as you want to make it, and I try to make it as easy. And fortunately for me, because you can get the wrong impression from me, I think, if you don't know me, or at least early in my career, that I don't take it as serious as maybe the next guy. And that is totally wrong. My way of handling adversity is to joke, is to be loose about it. Not at any point in my career has it ever been taken lightly, that he took that play off, or we lost and to come back on Wednesday and he pulls a joke—ah, maybe he doesn't care. That's not true. No one is as competitive as me. And I firmly believe that today, no one has as much fun as me. I've had more people tell me that throughout my career— 'Man, we love to watch you play, and your enthusiasm,' and stuff like that . . . it's not fabricated. I love to play the game, there's nothin' like throwin' touchdown passes, nothin' like goin' into Foxboro and beatin' them when no one gave us a chance. There's nothin' like goin' to play the undefeated team in football right now, and all eyes will be on us. Hey, I hope we win the football game, I'm gonna do everything I can. But I'm gonna have fun in the process. And I hope that's what guys take from me, that you can still do your job, and have fun."

Mission accomplished.

"There's not a day that goes by that he doesn't come in and keeps things light, regardless of what's going on, he keeps it fun," Coles said in the vibrant visiting locker room after the Jets had dismembered the Titans 34–13. "He's a great person, he's a great guy. . . . I don't have to go into he's a great football player. That's something everybody already knows."

You could have called it Favre Fever.

"I think the offense, and even sometimes the defense, man, we feed off him, 'cause he's always up," Pace said. "And when you play with him, you're never out of a game. You're never out of a game, man. Blessed to have him here."

The Titans hadn't exactly captured the imagination of the betting public, and talk of a perfect season was muted, but they were a tough, smart, sound, blue-collar team with an elite head coach in Fisher. They led the NFL in fewest points allowed (13.1 points per game) and were tied for second with 15 interceptions. Defensive end Kyle Vanden Bosch, who had missed some time with a knee injury, was itching to get back to work against Favre.

"I'm looking forward to it," Vanden Bosch said. "He is going to be a first-ballot Hall of Famer, so anytime you get a chance to take the field against a player like him, you accept that challenge and you step up to it."

Favre, of course, never met a challenge he didn't like. Employing a deadly quick passing game out of the chute, he was 6-of-6 on the opening drive and just like that it was 7–0. It marked the sixth straight game the Jets had scored on their opening drive. "I tried to get it to our playmakers underneath, and let 'em make plays," Favre said. "That first drive was really a tone-setter, if you will. It sure sent a message that we were capable of scoring against this defense."

The message within the message was sent on the first play from scrimmage, a 16-yard completion to Cotchery off a pump fake. "First play of the game kinda set the tone," Favre said. "It was a one-man route designed to go to LC on a slant; Jerricho doesn't even have a route on the play, and the protection was so that I was gonna take two steps and throw it. I wind up taking three, and five more. It was a busted play slash great play."

With Vanden Bosch a constant menace, and defensive tackle Albert Haynesworth trying to be his disruptive self, Favre placed a premium on getting the ball out of his hand pronto, just as he had against the Pats. "I knew it going in that if you had to take seven steps, you better take seven and throw it; they were gonna get to ya," he said.

Favre further defused the threat with screen passes and his new trusted safety valve, Keller, who caught three third-down conversions and drew three penalties against the depleted, overmatched Titans secondary. "He's as fast as any receiver we have," Favre said.

Favre threw his first interception in three games, an underthrow for Coles (7-for-88, 1 TD) down the left sideline. But it was his 2-yard touchdown pass to Coles to make it 20–3 that titillated his teammates and his fans. Favre looked left for Keller (6-for-42) as he rolled right and threw across his body to Coles, engulfed by defenders in back of the end zone. "When I threw it, I thought, 'This is gonna be tight,'" Favre said, "but I felt like it had a chance. . . . It's one of those, to me, what I think I can offer, and have offered throughout my career. I always called it the [ex-Packers coach] Mike Holmgren syndrome: 'Oh no no no no— *good!*'" Favre smiled now. "It was good today," he said.

With Favre (25-of-32, 224 yards, 2 TDs, 1 INT) playing at such a high level, defenses were forced to pick their poison. The real eye-opener was the way the Jets smashed the Titans in the mouth, as Jones and Washington combined for 192 rushing yards. The Jets, with a time of possession advantage that evoked memories of the Super Bowl XXV Giants against the Bills, held the ball for 40:30. With Jenkins fresh, the Titans were held to 45 rushing yards. No one had pushed around the Titans like this. No one.

The Titans cut their deficit to 20–6 with 12:50 left, but Washington, using blocks from Brandon Moore and Damien Woody, romped

61 yards to pay dirt to seal the deal. Jones expressed his belief that he was playing behind the best offensive line in football.

Favre would say, "The best offensive lines are the offensive lines that play as one, not five guys, but play as one. I've played with some very good centers over my career. Nick has the chance to be the best I've ever played with. Athletically speaking, he's by far the most athletic. Frank Winters I played with, who was my roommate for twelve, thirteen years, is going to kill me for saying that, because he claims he's still the best athlete. Nick is very bright and has the right mentality. It starts with the center and it works its way outward. He has all the tools.

"Faneca is one of those guys that every team wishes they had on their team. He never complains, is always running, blocking, and doing something. I'm talking about in practice. He's always positive no matter what. He's a perfect fit for the side that Brick's [D'Brickashaw Ferguson] on, because I see a change in Brick. I wasn't here last year, but just from the start of the year to now, it goes without saying that Brick is ultratalented. Using that is the key. He's finding out day in and day out that he can be pretty darn good. Having a little spunk about you is not a bad thing. He got in a little scrap one day with Shaun Ellis. Everybody laughed. Most people were like, 'Man, we haven't seen that side of Brick.' Maybe Alan is rubbing off on him a little bit.

"Brandon and Woody, the right side, they're all playing great. Woody's got the best feet I've ever seen. The guy's got tremendous feet and a great personality. They're fun to work with. Brandon is probably our best pure run blocker. He's hard to move. He can move people. They've all had their share of scraps this year on the field, things that people don't see, where they're not going to take anything from anyone else. That's where it starts. They've been a blast to work with. I hope that the feeling is mutual. That's where it all starts, up front."

Favre drew merciless ribbing on a play where he lined up wide and was belted by Cortland Finnegan. "I actually thought about it from the huddle to when I lined up; they were ready to kill me on our sidelines 'cause they said, 'Cortland Finnegan's gonna drill ya,' which he did," Favre said. "It didn't hurt—I've been hit a lot harder, but no offense to him."

As soon as the Titans had been vanquished, Favre—a 77.3 percent completion mark over his last three games with five touchdowns—jogged up the ramp leading to the visiting locker room and screamed, "Woooooooo!" The big victories now, at this stage of his career, after what had transpired in Green Bay, felt better than he dreamed they could. "My career in Green Bay was awesome . . . it was better than awesome," he said. "Will I have a sixteen-year career in New York? I doubt it. But I'm gonna try to lump sixteen into one, and see what happens."

Packers fans, meanwhile, were tuning in to see what was happening with Favre. The Jets-Titans game was the most watched sports program in Milwaukee that weekend, according to a report in jsonline .com. With the Packers on their bye week, the noon Jets-Titans game on WDJT-TV (channel 58) had a rating of 14.6, or 132,181 households in the Milwaukee market.

The first question for Favre in the interview room: "Where should the '72 Dolphins send the champagne?" now that their perfect season remained in the history books.

"I don't drink," Favre said with one those mischievous smiles. "Twelve years ago I'da . . . " And the room broke up.

Twelve years ago he'da emptied every last bottle with his buddies. Now he was driving the AFC to drink.

"I'm not gonna sit here and say that we've established ourselves as the best team in football," he said. "All it says is that I think we beat the best team in football today—definitely if you go by record and the way that they've played . . . they have been the best team in football." It wasn't the time to inform Favre that the NFC Giants were the best team in football.

In the middle of an answer about how the developing chemistry on this team reminded him of his Super Bowl Packers, Favre recognized a face in the crowd, a member of the media, seated on a chair directly in front of him. "Mitch, it's good to see ya . . . Mitch, hometown . . . nice to see a familiar face for a change," he said with a smile.

Now he was ready to continue.

"I don't know if we were the best, or the most talented team in '96, '97, '98, whatever . . . we may have been . . . I think we had the best chemistry, by far," Favre said. "Talent sure helps, but talent alone will not get it done. This team . . . I start sensing a belief that, 'All right, we can get it done.' When we stepped on the field in '95, '96, '97, we were fourteen points ahead before the first kickoff. And I mean that from a mental standpoint. No one wanted to play us. And that, more than anything, is what got us to the Super Bowl. Once you kinda get that edge, you're well on your way."

Feely chuckled when it was suggested that the Jets had caught Favre Fever. "I think New York has, in general," he said, "and we'll all ride that train."

The No. 4 train.

Continued Feely, "I think that when you get in a situation like New England last week, go into overtime you're disappointed, and yet you know Number 4's going out there with the ball, there's a collective belief that he's gonna find a way to get it done. And I think that the guys that they've brought in here in free agency, not only are they star players for us on that field, but in that locker room and out on the practice field. They've brought an enthusiasm and raised the bar for everyone on this team."

The 8–3 Jets had reeled off five straight, averaging 33.8 points per game. They had averaged 168.5 rushing yards over their last six games. Feely, still alive and kicking as Nugent was forced to wait and watch, had booted 10 straight field goals. A number two playoff seed was within reach. "We feel like we can play any team, anywhere," Chris Baker said.

On the charter home from Nashville, before takeoff, Bubba Franks walked by Favre's seat and asked him how he felt.

"Like I'm thirty-nine," Favre said.

With the Giants steamrolling everyone in their path, the tabloids began trumpeting the prospect of a New York–New York Subway Super Bowl. The headline SUPE DREAMS surfaced first on the back page of the *New York Post* and weeks later on the back page of the *New York Daily News*.

Tannenbaum, who joined the Jets in 1997, knew better than to be swept away by the hysteria. "Going back to '97, you really try not to get too high or too low," he said.

Or going back to January 12, 1969, for that matter.

NFL commissioner Roger Goodell told WFAN radio that if the Jets and Giants were to host conference championship games at

Giants Stadium, the games would not be played on the same day. One game would likely be played at night on Sunday, January 18, and the other would be played on Monday night.

Pennington (three touchdown passes) engaged in a shootout with Cassel, but threw a crushing fourth-quarter interception to Meriweather at his 37 at a time when the Dolphins, 48–28 losers, were only 10 points down. "I have to go back and look at it," Pennington said. "I felt like I lost the ball a little bit. I left it high. I am sure there is always a better place to go with the ball. Hindsight is twenty-twenty. For the most part I felt like I stayed disciplined with the reads and we were creasing them here and there and really finding some holes, and it is one of them I would like to have back." Further complicating Pennington's uphill battle was the loss of his best receiver, Greg Camarillo, to a season-ending knee injury.

A day after the Jets had unofficially earned best team in the AFC honors, Mangold got his oil changed at an auto shop in New Jersey.

"I'm standing there just waiting around and two of the guys there working, they were sitting there by the water cooler just talking about the weekend's games and they were both talking Jets and Giants," Mangold said. "One of them kept trying to talk about the Giants and the other guy kept trying to talk about the Jets. And it was neat to see they were both able to go back and forth because both teams are doing well at this point in the season."

Tony Richardson had a question for an older man in an aging Jets hat at a Queens garage. "I asked him, 'You're a Jets fan?' and he was like, 'I am now. I hadn't put my hat on in a long time, but it's pretty exciting now,'" Richardson recalled. "So that was pretty cool."

Richardson, a throwback fullback, had also been invaluable to the dominant rushing attack. Jones was leading the AFC in rushing and the Jets were second in points—323—only 96 shy of the franchise mark set in 1968.

"The fact we've been able to run the football at our discretion has made all the difference," Favre said. "For a quarterback, if you can run the football the way we're running it, it sort of dictates to the defense. Do they bring an extra guy in the box? If they do that, then a slant should be there, a Go route, a back-shoulder throw, or whatever. We have guys from our receiving corps that can catch the ball at the line of scrimmage, get ten or fifteen yards. If you're a defensive coordinator, you're scratching your head, going, 'What do I do?'"

If you're the offensive coordinator, you don't take what the defense gives you, you take what you want. Said Schottenheimer, "A lot of people now are having to load up the box to try to stop the run, they're putting eight and nine guys up there so you can push it a little bit faster on the outside. Again, we have the plays to go up the field."

Montana and Walsh, Walton and Joe Theismann, they became one mind. Favre and Schottenheimer weren't going to achieve anything close. But this was the time of the season when they needed to click. "I've always been very comfortable with Brett," Schottenheimer said. "There has always been that fact that as you go further and further down the road, down the season, there are things you begin to anticipate. Where you had to talk about things in the past, now you're able to solve it between each other. You don't even have to discuss it. I don't know if you call it in the zone. We're playing pretty well. We have a very good feel for one another."

Favre wasn't complaining that he had only one completion of 20 or more yards in 32 attempts against the Titans. He was totally on board with Schottenheimer paring down the shifts and motions in favor of a more simplified approach.

"The philosophy hasn't changed, it's just that we've been executing the short passing game very, very well and that's a credit to the players," Schottenheimer said.

None more than Favre. "I don't know if I like the term 'managing a game,'" he said. "I think that's a polite way of saying 'don't lose it for us.' All I want to do is win. I'd like to think that I've won my share of games and I wouldn't trade it for anything."

Favre had completed 79 of 103 passes (76.6 percent) for 816 yards over the last four games, with only six completions of 20 or more yards. "I'm getting more comfortable with what Schotty likes to call and what he feels comfortable with," he said.

• • •

Broncos coach Mike Shanahan was impressed with the Jets' balance. "You have a good running attack and you have a good passing attack," he said. "Brett is able to take what the defense gives him. He doesn't always have to go downfield, but he's got the ability to do it. To me, that's what great quarterbacks do."

So here came one Thanksgiving Day when Jets fans could truly be thankful for their quarterback and their team. Only a year earlier, they had been humiliated 34–3 by the Cowboys on national television. Same Old Turkeys? Not a chance.

Or so they thought.

"I don't have to be told anything," Favre said. "You're on top of the world one day and at the bottom the next. We struggled early in the year, I don't think it really affected anyone, because look where we are now. I really don't think the success that we're having right now will affect us."

He didn't know his team as well as he thought he did.

The Jets were looking forward to a rousing welcome from their home fans—particularly Fireman Ed. "I miss the little guy with the fire hat doing his little signs on the video screen," said Jenkins. "I like that.

He gets me excited, actually. I know some guys on the team asked why I get excited. . . . I never got to experience something like that. We have some intense fans here and I'm glad to be a part of that experience."

It proved to be an experience he and the Jets would rather forget.

The Jets had serious interest in Cutler before the 2006 NFL Draft but rated Ferguson higher. Cutler had intrigued most teams that looked at him and saw a young Favre. He was a swashbuckler, all right, with a howitzer for an arm. Now the young gunslinger would be facing off against the old gunslinger. They even shared the same agent.

"The guy can be pretty darn good," Favre said. "He has been good up to this point. He'll continue to get better. He has the right mentality. He has all the physical tools you need. He has a real strong arm and moves around well. Barring some injury, he'll have a great career . . . I can see the comparisons. He's probably a little more advanced as far as being in a passing offense when he came into the league as I was. From a physical standpoint I see us doing a lot of the same things at that age."

Cutler was asked by the Denver media if his arm was stronger than Favre's.

"Yeah, I think so," Cutler said, and laughed. He had said his arm was stronger than Elway's early in the season. "What is Brett? Is he forty yet? Thirty-nine, soon to be forty? I think he may have given me a run back in his twenties, but I think I got him now." Yes, he did.

The so-called experts were expecting a shootout, and how could they not? The Jets were second in the NFL in scoring (29.4 points per game). The Broncos, decimated by injuries, were 26th against the run and 28th overall defensively. But then they were also third in the NFL in total offense, and Cutler (19 TDs, 12 INTs) was third with 3,036 passing yards.

But Favre, who struggled in the arctic elements in the NFC Championship game at Lambeau, found Mother Nature conspiring with Father Time as a cold, driving rain greeted him when he arrived at Giants Stadium.

Favre opened with a three-and-out on his opening possession— the first time in seven games the Jets had failed to score on their opening possession.

No problem. Plenty of time for Jones to run it down the Broncos' sorry throats.

One problem: on a day when the Bad Brett instead of the Good Brett would show up, the Bad Mangini and the Bad Schottenheimer would show up with him.

And, on the Jets' second possession, the Bad Bretts made one of those unfathomable, maddening play calls that drives infuriated Jets fans to vent to their favorite talk radio station.

Wide receiver Brad Smith, the former Missouri quarterback, took a shotgun snap and attempted a pitch to Cotchery, who bobbled the wet ball, and finally fell on it deep in Jets territory. But only for an instant. Broncos linebacker Wesley Woodyard jumped on Cotchery and forced the ball to pop out, and safety Vernon Fox picked it up and scored on a 23-yard touchdown run. Bad call by the zebras, but not reviewable.

"Brad made a good toss, I just couldn't get a grip on it," Cotchery said. "I had it covered up until the dude hit me. That's when it came out. The ball was slick, but in these times, you just have to focus more."

Mangini offered no sympathy. Referring to the Broncos, he said, "It didn't feel like it affected their ballhandling. Whenever you call a play like that, it's critical to get the ball first." After watching the tape, he accepted blame for not making sure the pitch was delivered underhanded.

Of course, it's even more critical not to call a play like that in those conditions, and if Mangini wasn't inclined to publicly second-guess his offensive coordinator, he didn't pretend he was Vince Lombardi either. He was speaking through clenched teeth when he volunteered that the Jets' Thanksgiving week preparation had fallen short of his standards. "I don't think we coached very well," he said.

To which Jets Nation roared: Amen!

Only when Jones was handed the ball did the coach resemble Mangenius. Jones, who lives in the weight room and owns biceps almost as big as Jenkins's thighs, burst through a hole on the right side for a 59-yard touchdown, the longest run of his career.

Cutler quickly got that one back with a 59-yard touchdown of his own, a sideline throw that rookie standout Eddie Royal caught against Abram Elam by the Jets sideline and ran to daylight. Mangini unsuccessfully challenged that Royal's right foot had stepped out of bounds.

It was 17–7 when Jones tried to rescue the Jets with a play that epitomized second effort and presence of mind. He had landed on top of defensive end Kenny Peterson at the end of an 8-yard gain but quickly recognized that he was never down by contact. He jumped to his feet, and Woody began screaming, "Go, go, go," as Jones raced to the end zone with a 29-yard touchdown run.

"[Peterson] tried to spin me around," Jones said. "When I was going down, I didn't feel my elbow touch the ground. I definitely didn't feel my back hit the ground. Once I came up and I was still on my feet, I just said let me just go ahead and at least score and leave it up to debate rather than just lay there."

Down 17–14, Favre took a shot down the left sideline for Coles (2 catches, 2 yards). "It was Double Go," Favre said. "We had Dustin on the outside to the right . . . hopin' maybe to get a mismatch with Dustin outside . . . they actually played zone, one of the few times that they played zone in that down and distance. And so, playin' zone, I knew the corner would be far off of Dustin. . . . I was looking off the safety the whole time . . . up to that play, he'd been leaning a lot towards LC's side, and just looked him off and just took a shot . . . tried to give LC a jumpable, catchable ball." It was overthrown, and Dre Bly intercepted. "I didn't even look at the receiver," Bly said. "I just read the quarterback, and he threw it right to me. Laveranues was just jogging." Cutler went right back to exposing the Jets pass defense. It was 27–14 at the half.

Jones had already rushed for 108 yards, on only 11 carries, in the first half. So with an entire half to go, there was absolutely no need to abandon him. But that's exactly what Mangini and Schottenheimer would do; Jones rushed only five more times, and finished with 138 yards.

Peyton Hillis, a converted 250-pound rookie fullback in tune with the Broncos' zone-blocking offensive scheme, was on his way to 129 rushing yards, the first 100-yard rusher against the 2008 Jets, who suddenly forgot how to tackle. Broncos center Casey Wiegmann had shockingly neutralized Jenkins, who had a 70-pound weight advantage and was being hyped as a Defensive Player of the Year candidate. Jenkins bolted from the locker room to duck the media and when he resurfaced in the middle of the week he pointed a finger at himself. "I can assure you one thing: our feet are back on planet earth. . . . I hate feeling like this," he said. "As far as I'm concerned, I can take full blame for the fact that I didn't get it done." No one on Gang Green had. Gholston didn't ingratiate himself with Mangini by failing to help slumping Thomas, Ellis, and Pace get pressure on Cutler. The sixth pick of the draft let Cutler escape down by the Denver goal line late in the third quarter and contributed one tackle in his part-time role. Paging Mark Gastineau, paging Mark Gastineau! "The biggest thing about sacks," Gholston said, "is once you get that first one, it can keep on rolling after that." Unfortunately, Gholston hadn't yet gotten that first one, and was careening toward Mangini's doghouse.

Cutler, operating out of three– and four–wide receiver sets, toyed with the Jets pass defense, which had clearly become the team's Achilles' heel. With Revis occupied with Brandon Marshall, tight ends Tony Scheffler and Daniel Graham would combine for 13 catches worth 149 yards. The Broncos had amassed 316 yards of offense over the first 20 minutes and 484 by the finish.

The rain hadn't relented as Mangini and Schottenheimer faced third-and-1 at the Denver 46 early in the third quarter.

No Jones.

Favre threw incomplete short for Smith. "They covered it," Favre said.

Now it was fourth-and-1.

No Jones.

Favre looked for Baker, didn't like what he saw, tried to run, and was buried by Mario Haggan.

"I just run whatever play's called," said Jones. "I don't get into the playcalling."

Neither did Favre, forever the good soldier. "The fourth-and-one was really one of those they're gonna have everyone up in there; it's one of those you play the odds," he said. "We have hit some big ones early in the year on those type of situations. And given the situation we were in, I thought it was good calls. . . . They didn't work, and I'm no different than anyone else, it's always easy to second-guess when they don't work. When they work, they're great; when they don't, they were the wrong call. I didn't think they were the wrong call; I give Denver credit. If I had to do it over again, I'd back [Schottenheimer] one hundred percent."

So did Mangini, who referred to the Jets' successful fourth-down conversion rate entering the game (8-of-9). "I felt good about those plays," he said. Jets fans couldn't help but recall that he felt good about the three running plays by the goal line against the Patriots too.

As Favre pressed to overcome a 27–14 deficit, three Broncos players (linebacker Spencer Larsen, hip/back), defensive end Ebenezer Ekuban (shoulder), and Bly (shin) fell injured on consecutive plays; conspiracy theorists were convinced this was a sinister attempt to slow down Favre's hurry-up shotgun offense.

"Just a bruise on my shin," Bly told the dying *Rocky Mountain News*. "You know Brett. Him being a savvy vet, when he sees somebody down, he likes to do a no-huddle, catch a defense off balance. I knew that, so I just laid on the ground and let the pain go away.

"But that's one thing you have to do. You have injuries, anything that's bothering you, stay on the ground, don't try to be Superman and rush back up because it can hurt your defense."

Mangini, in no mood to offer excuses at a time when he was upset with his team, took the high road. "With any injury situation," he said, "you take it at face value."

Cutler is compared so often to Favre in large degree because of that fearlessness that sometimes turns into recklessness. And now he threw across his body for Scheffler as he rolled right and the overthrow was intercepted in the end zone by Lowery, the struggling rookie corner who had lost his starting job to Law.

Favre got 34 yards on a screen to Washington, who put a beauty of a juke on Fox. Then 14 more on another screen to Washington. But he couldn't get his team in the end zone after first-and-goal at the 7. On third-and-goal, he pumped, brought the ball down, and was strip-sacked by Elvis Dumervil. Moore recovered the fumble. In came Feely to make it 27–17.

Favre, fourth-and-3 from the Denver 39, thought for a moment he was in business when he uncorked a beauty of a bomb down the right sideline for Cotchery with approximately 12 minutes left. Cotchery leaped for it at the 10-yard line, had it for a split second, then didn't

have it as Karl Paymah stripped it from him on their way down. Favre held his helmet in both hands.

When Cutler hit Brandon Stokley with a 36-yard touchdown pass over Elam with 9:26 left to play, what was left of the drowned rats disguised as Jets fans trudged to the parking lots.

"I'd rather play in snow," Favre said afterward. Perhaps he should have informed Mangini. "I've played in colder. It was just windy enough, and it was a steady rain the whole night. There were numerous passes that I felt like I easily would have made, or made a much more accurate pass . . . but the conditions got the better of me, I think, tonight."

Cutler, on the other hand, got the better of the conditions (357 yards, 2 TDs) and Favre tipped his umbrella to him.

"Be easy to write off our lack of production for the conditions, but that won't look too good, considering they did produce.

"He was the better man tonight."

Rhodes, however, wasn't interested in throwing bouquets to the trash-talking Cutler. The Jets, thanks in part to registering only one sack in 82 passing attempts, were now thirtieth in pass defense. "I don't like him," the safety said. "I don't want to talk about him. Any other questions?"

Well, yes: had the Jets been reading their press clippings? Favre (23-of-43, 247 yards, 0 TDs, 1 INT) didn't think success had spoiled the Jets. "I thought we've handled everything up to this point very well," he said. "We didn't play very well tonight; I don't think it was because everyone walked in this locker room prior to the game was thinking, 'We're the team to beat.'"

The 7–5 Patriots had been whipped at home by the Steelers to fall into a second-place tie with the Dolphins, who survived the Rams 16–12 thanks to three second-half Bulger interceptions. The 11–1 Titans had humiliated the toothless, winless Lions on Thanksgiving Day; the 9–3 Steelers were now in the driver's seat for the number two seed and the first-round playoff bye. "I think we were first going into this game, I think we're still first," Favre said.

The Jets had actually picked a relatively good time for a stinker. As they headed back to their bunker to regroup, a scandal of national proportions swirled around the Giants and consumed the local media. Super Bowl hero Plaxico Burress had brought an unregistered loaded gun into a Manhattan nightspot shortly after midnight that Saturday morning and accidentally shot himself. Antonio Pierce, the heart and soul of their defense, accompanied him, and was at the heart of an investigation by the NYPD for possible obstruction of justice. Burress, thankfully, was not seriously hurt; the bullet missed all of the potential catastrophic targets inside his right thigh and everywhere else. Pierce played in the Giants' thumping of the Redskins at FedEx Field. But the story escalated when Mayor Bloomberg called for Burress to be prosecuted to the fullest extent of the law, which in this case meant three and a half years in the slammer. The Giants, heartened that Burress was not hurt but sick and tired of his irresponsibility and refusal to wake up, suspended him and placed him on the nonfootball injury list, marking the end of his season and, eventually, the end of his Giants career.

As the Jets prepared to fly out to San Francisco, Pierce, who was not charged, and the Giants were trying to rise above the distractions as they had done for the past two seasons and clinch the division title at home against the Eagles.

Unbeknownst to the general public, the Jets were already privately dealing with a distraction of their own.

Favre showed up for his weekly press conference wearing a wool cap. It was December. One of the columnists asked him how helpful the Jets' absence of off-field distractions had been for them. "A good example is look at the Giants—they're playin' pretty good," Favre said. "They've dealt with that all year—different issues. They're dealing with being Super Bowl winners—that's a huge issue. But they've managed to deal with it exceptionally well. . . . I give Coach Coughlin a lot of credit; he's handled it very well. The guys that handle that team have handled it very well. They've managed to just go out and focus on the job at hand. But it's nice to not have to deal with issues . . . it's part of it. . . . You never know when it's gonna come, and how it will come, whether it be on-the-field or off-the-field issues. In order to play a long time you gotta have a lot of luck . . . on the field, obviously . . . but you also have to be smart off the field and manage your success as well as failure if you want to play a long time."

Two days later—two days before the 49ers game—the news that Ellis, a defensive co-captain and a Jet since 2000, had been arrested on charges of possession of marijuana and possession of drug paraphernalia hit the papers.

From the moment they arrived, Tannenbaum and Mangini had talked about the core values they hold dear to their heart, and winding up on the police blotter was not one of them. They'd rather field a team of Boy Scouts than have a single Pacman Jones in their midst.

"He is disappointed with himself and has apologized for his actions," Tannenbaum said in a statement. "Personal conduct is important and an area that we stress to the entire organization. Shaun has been a leader on this team and I am confident that he will handle this in the appropriate fashion. The legal process will run its course and the league will handle this matter."

Said Mangini, "When the incident took place, Mike and I gathered as much information as we could. We sat down with Shaun and discussed the situation with him. We expressed our disappointment with what happened. And Shaun did exactly what I expected Shaun to do, which was to take full accountability for his actions and expressed his disappointment to us, to the fans, to his family, to his teammates, to himself. At that point, we disciplined him internally."

Ellis did not face immediate discipline from the NFL and therefore would not miss the 49ers game. The Jets fined him a reported $10,000. "People will judge," Ellis said. "They have a right to do so. It was my mistake, and I am fortunate everything will move forward and the fans still embrace me."

Favre was having age-old issues of his own. He grew defensive when he was asked whether in recent years he had worn down at the end of the season, reminding everyone that he had played well in a blizzard against the Seahawks prior to the 2007 NFC Championship game. In his view, he played well against the Giants—up until his overtime interception, that is.

"At some point, I gotta fall apart . . . I'm not gonna lie to ya," Favre said. "It's like any car—you drive it long enough, it's gonna fall apart . . . you're gonna have a flat tire, somethin's gonna happen. At some point, I'm gonna fall apart. But . . . right now I'm still together, so . . . I don't know what else to tell ya. As long as they [Jets ownership and management] want me, as long as I can still play at a high level and feel like I can, we're goin' about it as usual."

The Jets had lost in San Diego and Oakland but Mangini wasn't about to change the routine by leaving on Saturday for San Francisco instead of Friday. "At the end of the day, you wake up and play football," he said. "East Coast, West Coast, Mars, Mexico, London . . . rainy, hot. You've just got to go out and play with whatever it is."

The 49ers had responded to interim head coach Mike Singletary, who had replaced Mike Nolan. For all the talk about offensive coordinator Mike Martz and his big-play attack, and quarterback Shaun Hill, who was tabbed by Singletary to replace the turnover-plagued J. T. O'Sullivan, and ageless Isaac Bruce, and dangerous Frank Gore, the Jets had no right losing to a 4–8 team.

Mangini must have spat out his breakfast oatmeal on Sunday morning, however. The *San Francisco Chronicle* printed an unflattering story, from Coles's point of view, about his relationship with Favre. It turned out that Coles and Favre were joking with each other in the locker room shortly before Coles's conference call with the Bay Area media days earlier. Favre suggested that Coles tell them that they just don't get along. But what could Mangini and Tannenbaum do anyway? Scold Favre for drumming up another one of his practical jokes? They had far larger concerns.

"I read that whole transcript, and I think those were very selective comments," Mangini said. "I've talked to Laveranues; I've talked to Brett. . . . I think their goal is exactly the same—that LC wants to do everything he can help us to do to win and so does Brett. It's not a function of personal goals or anything like that. LC is not like that."

Here are snippets from the original transcript.

Q. What are the differences in how you're being used?

A. Well of course, I mean it's different. Now, we're in a quarterback-driven offense where he pretty much has control of everything, where before the offense was pretty much driven through me. Now that we have a lot of guys that can make plays, and now all of our skill positions are making plays, now I just kind of become just a role player instead of a guy that teams had to prepare for. So my role is drastically changed based on the order of importance of the football coming to me.

Q. And has that been difficult for you to handle?

A. No, I'm not a fussy guy. I mean whenever you have guys that can make plays and give us an opportunity to win, just like I feel like I do, then there really isn't much that you can say. You just sit back and take a role. The coaching staff has been pleased with the way I've handled things, and that's all you can look forward to with that—being looked upon as a great teammate and a great team player.

Q. What is that role? You said you were a role player but what role do you serve now?

A. Basically, you just follow the plays around [Favre]. This is his offense. Our running game has taken off and then when we do throw the ball, there's really no level of importance, where at one point in time it used to be where I was the guy that was put in the position to get the ball most of the time. Now I just play my role and if the team decides to take me away, we've got other guys that make plays. Basically, I just do what I'm supposed to do and that's my role.

Q. How challenging is it for a receiver to adjust to a quarterback with his arm strength? Is the ball on you more quickly than you're used to? Is it harder to catch?

A. No, it's the same thing. I mean it's football. Anytime you're playing ball, a lot of the guys have good arm strength. Kellen Clemens has a strong arm and other guys have strong arms. Day in and day out I catch balls from the Jugs machine. The ball probably comes out harder from there than it does from anywhere else, so there's nothing different about it.

Q. You don't sound entirely thrilled to have a future Hall of Famer as your quarterback.

A. Why would you say I'm not happy with it? It doesn't bother me at all. I get up and come to work every day. I'm cool.

Favre had this to say about Coles's interview: "I wasn't on that call with him. I haven't found one receiver that thinks, 'Okay, the five passes you threw to me this year were plenty.' He's a competitor. His locker is right next to mine. He knows where I stand. I know where he stands. I have no problems with Laveranues at all. None. I'm doing my best to get him the ball. He's made great plays throughout his career. He will continue to make them, probably long after I'm gone. He knows that there's no personal vendetta towards him, or towards me. Laveranues is one of those who will tell you what he feels or what he doesn't feel, without thinking. Is that a knock against him? No. That's just the way he is. That's what makes him special. . . . It was not a slap towards me at all. It doesn't bother me one bit."

At least there was no rain when Sunday arrived, and no Nate Clements, the 49ers' elite cornerback.

Parcells sometimes would say that God is playing in some of these games (not nearly enough on the Jets' side, of course). Maybe He had seen enough. Maybe He would mercifully start removing the forty-year curse.

Yeah, right.

Singletary, hardly terrified by Jet Favre, opened the game with an onsides kick that was recovered by Brad Smith at the Niner 46.

But on third-and-2, Keller started to run before the catch and made a grievous drop that would provoke Mangini's ire. The head coach would sit the rookie down days later for a little chitchat. "The rookie period is over," was how Mangini explained it to the media. "We've graduated. When you play a significant amount, you have to perform at a consistent level."

Now it was fourth-and-2 at the 38. Time for Favre to make a play, right? Time for Mangini to make a statement and set a tone and trust his quarterback and his offense and seize the moment, right?

Wrong.

Mangini inexplicably summoned Hodges. Another playing-not-to-win moment that drives Jets Nation bonkers.

In came Hodges to pin the Niners inside their 10, right?

Wrong.

Touchback.

Hill (285 yards, 2 TDs, 1 INT), naturally, showed up as Montana. The Jets failed to keep him in the pocket, and he riddled Gang Green by keeping plays alive with his legs. Tackle Joe Staley recovered a Jason Hill fumble in the end zone and it was 7–0. The 49ers would fumble five times—and the Jets could only recover one.

Favre scored on a 2-yard run, and Jones tied it with a 17-yard romp in the third quarter. It was his 12th rushing touchdown, tying the club record set by Martin in 2004.

Gore (ankle injury), meanwhile, had been replaced in the second half by DeShaun Foster. This was the perfect time for the Jets to exhibit some killer instinct and reclaim their swagger.

The 49ers took a 17–14 lead with 14:44 left on a 32-yard field goal by Joe Nedney. But Washington returned the ensuing kickoff 99 yards for a touchdown.

Flag.

Holding on James Ihedigbo.

Hill, who completed passes to ten different receivers, hit Bryant Johnson for a 3-yard touchdown that made it 24–14 with 6:05 remaining. The heat was about to be ratcheted up on Mangini and defensive coordinator Bob Sutton to become more aggressive and dictate to offenses for a change. The Jets were blitzing approximately one-third of the time on passing plays, to little avail. Lowery, for example, had a clean shot on Hill and missed. Alarmingly, Jenkins was wearing down, because this time it was center Eric Heitmann who was the thorn in his side. Referring to Jenkins (one tackle, one forced fumble, one encroachment penalty on a fourth-and-1 gamble by Singletary), Staley said, "I didn't really hear his name at all." Rookie right guard Chilo Rachal: "The coaches told us how difficult it was to take him head-on, so we concentrated on hitting him on the hip to change his direction."

Favre, who was 20-of-31 for only 137 yards, was intercepted by cornerback Walt Harris with 1:52 left to play. Against the Broncos

and 49ers, the Jets were a combined 4-of-21 on third-down conversions. "We knew we were going to have to keep Brett Favre off
the field as much as possible," Heitmann said. Oh, really? And why
was that, exactly? Mangini bemoaned the fact that the Niners owned
a 39:49–20:11 time of possession advantage, but in truth, he and
Schottenheimer had abandoned Jones (10-for-56), dredging up the
old what-came-first-the-chicken-or-the-egg argument.

Coles and Cotchery combined for just two catches for 15 yards.
Keller was 2-for-14. What happened to yards after catch? Remember
when Favre was comparing Coles and Cotchery to Jennings and
Driver? The 49ers took away the bubble screens and quick slants,
and Mangini and Schottenheimer never made the necessary adjustments. Favre, who sensed something was wrong with his arm, threw
five deep balls to Coles and Cotchery—four incompletions and an interception. "I think teams have penciled in on what we've been doing,"
Coles said. "They've done a great job and you have to give them credit.
I think our coaching staff, now, is trying to make some adjustments."

In other words, Mangini and his staff were being outcoached.

Simms offered an obvious adjustment. "The Jets did throw deep
but they were all balls down the sidelines," he told the *Newark Star-
Ledger*. "What I consider deep balls is having the wide receiver run
a deep in-cut, deep outs, making a double move. You have to set up
your receivers by giving them more opportunities."

Simms said that opponents had indeed figured out the Jets' short
passing game—screens and quick passes to Keller—and it was
Schottenheimer's mandate to solve it. "I think teams have decided
to just play the Jets a little more aggressive and see what happens,"
he told the *Star-Ledger*. "And when teams do that, you have to show
them that you're capable of doing something else.

"That's why I find these last three weeks of the season so intriguing. I want to see how the Jets handle it, how they react to these past
two losses. What do they do schematically to get themselves back on
track? I'm not saying they have to reinvent themselves, but they have to
change. Do they throw the football down the field more? Will the wide
receivers be the first read and give them more chances to make plays?"

Probably not. Because Favre's worst fears were being realized: he
was breaking down. The Lamborghini was suddenly an Edsel. In an

effort to relieve some inflammation in his shoulder, he received a cortisone injection after the game. "Something he felt good about doing, in concert with our doctors," Tannenbaum said. No one inside Mangini's police state—especially in a Spygate world where a star player coming down with a common cold is hushed for competitive reasons—was about to call ESPN with the news. Not even Favre.

"They knew that it was affecting me to a certain point," Favre revealed on the day he retired. "That was probably the only time where I really had doubts, after that game. I made some throws during that game that I made throughout the season that I thought, 'Okay, that's what I do.' I just felt like after that game there were some throws that, whether or not we would have caught them, I don't know. I could have made better throws and I threw it, and it didn't end up where I wanted it to. That to me was an eye-opener."

The body could no longer achieve what the mind could conceive.

Favre was clearly more alarmed about his arm than Mangini and Tannenbaum. "He feels like he was a diminished-skill player; I never felt that way," Tannenbaum said.

There was no excuse for the other side of the ball, however. For Republican presidential loser John McCain, it was "Drill, baby, drill." For Jets fans, it was "Blitz, baby, blitz."

"We definitely have been reacting a little bit more," Rhodes said. "Teams are coming out and abandoning their game plans. They're not doing what they usually do. They're doing, I guess, what they see from a prior team or something and they try to exploit it in a different way. We're going into the game more in a reaction mode anyway. Teams are figuring out what they want to do against us from the previous game. They're going outside of their box. They're not doing what they like to do. They're doing what they've seen has been successful against us."

So, uh, why not adapt and change the scheme?

"You've got to talk to Coach about that one," Rhodes said. "I have no answer for that one."

Shaun Hill had a blast outplaying Favre. "That was really neat to play against him and for our team to come away with the win," he said. "That is something I'll be able to tell the kids and grandkids way on down the road."

• • •

Even more bad news accompanied the Jets on their depressing cross-country flight back home. The Patriots had stormed back to beat the Seahawks, and the Dolphins had subdued the Bills 16–3 in Toronto. It meant the Jets found themselves in a three-way tie for the division lead.

"I don't sense desperation," Favre said. "We're still in decent shape. If we continue the way we're playing, we won't be. . . . We need to continue to stick together and get back to the way we were playing several weeks ago."

Jets Nation, which always senses desperation, was in need of a group hug at best, more therapy at worst. To wit: the following e-mail I received that night from a Stephen from Maplewood, New Jersey: "Steve I don't know if you go to the Jet press conferences, but if you do, please ask this question of Mangini: 'At least Herman Edwards got the Jets to the playoffs. Meanwhile, you're kicking on fourth and inches in your first two possessions against one of the worst teams in the NFL. Now NE might be tied with you, and you gained no ground against Pitt. What's your excuse, you fat bastard?' Thanks. Last week I could understand. But not this."

My response: "Is that you I see on the Whitestone [Bridge]?"

Stephen from Maplewood's response: "No, the GW. It's higher."

Then there was Benigno.

The losses to the Broncos and 49ers had struck that throbbing green-and-white nerve inside him long before he hit the airwaves at 10:06 a.m. on Monday, December 8.

"We gotta open with the disgrace that right now is the New York Jets," Benigno said to WFAN cohost Evan Roberts. "And there's no other way to say it—an out-and-out *disgrace*!"

Benigno was certain that the Patriots would win their last three games, imperiling the Jets' playoff chances. "In my mind," he said, "if the Jets do not run the table and win this division outright, Bro, they're not making the playoffs."

Other gems:

"Their pass rush right now, they might as well be counting five Mississippis before they go after the quarterback . . . you had receivers running open all over the world, guys I've never heard of—they were coming *out of the stands to catch passes*, some guy named Ziegler . . . I mean, *what's goin' on here*? They made Isaac Bruce look like he was twenty-five, not thirty-five, or whatever he is, and the coach . . .

"I have about had it with Eric Mangini. And I'm gonna say this right now: if they do *not* run the table and win this division, if they blow the playoffs this year, don't make it, Mangini's gotta go. Done. Out. Good-bye. Throw as much money as you can at Bill Cowher. . . . I've had it with this guy—have another *chipotle burger, Eric.*"

Roberts interrupted: "Don't get on his girth. What does that have to do with anything?"

"Maybe if he was in a little better shape, maybe he could think a little clearly!" Benigno screamed.

Benigno, watching the game on television at his home, had screamed expletives when Mangini punted on that fourth-and-2 at the Niner 38.

"W-What are you, an idiot?" he was screaming now on the radio. "I *couldn't believe* . . . and you *knew* Hodges was kicking the ball in the end zone. Did you know that?"

Soon Benigno was railing at the downfield passing game, or lack thereof. "Every time Favre throws a bomb down the field, you'd think he was in the Punt, Pass, and Kick competition to see how far he can throw it because there's no receiver within twenty yards of it!" he screamed. "Do you ever see a Jet receiver *in the picture* when Favre throws a deep ball?"

His last line before the break: "Hey, here's the bottom line—they win these next three games and win the division, you know what, Eric? The doughnuts are on me."

Benigno had calmed down, but only slightly, a day later over his cell phone. "I still think there is a conflict with [Favre] and the head coach," he said. "I don't think these guys are on the same page." He was disgusted that the Jets could recover only one of five 49ers fumbles. Referring to Ellis's failure, he said, "If it was a joint, he woulda found a way to hold on to it!"

Gholston's lack of progress wasn't irritating only Mangini. "Can the guy freakin' make some kind of damn impact? I mean, Jesus Christ!" Benigno roared.

If Mangini couldn't rally the troops, in Benigno's mind this would be a "monumental collapse" that would rank with any in Jets history. "Bill Parcells, Bill Belichick, Eric Mangini—what's wrong with this picture?" he asked. "It's like Sonny, Michael, and Fredo.

"We got Fredo."

Linebacker David Bowens was asked if the Subway Super Bowl talk had been a distraction.

"It may have been; personally it wasn't for me," Bowens said. "You can say it was a distraction because of what happened the last two weeks, but if it was, it can't be. We can't allow things like that, it's the 'old lobster trap.' You just can't fall into that. Sometimes you have to turn the television off for a while, watch movies all week like I do and don't pay attention to it."

Mangini's good-natured banter with the media had disappeared. His face had turned to stone immediately after the game, and now at his Monday afternoon press conference. "If there hadn't been a sense of urgency," he said, "there certainly will be now."

Behind closed doors that day, he showed his team the face and voice of urgency. "It's kind of like the angry father," Bowens said. "He yells at his kids, but he doesn't hate his kids and wants his kids to do well. He can only say so much and then something has to be done. I guess it's gotten to the point where he sees so much potential that we're not playing up to, it just frustrates him."

A day later, ESPN's John Clayton speculated that Cowher, still filling his football void at CBS, just might be a candidate for the Jets job should Mangini fail to rally the troops and miss the playoffs. It seemed like a reach at the time—Tannenbaum was a huge Mangini booster—but imagine how the owner might feel if Pennington were to outduel Favre on the last Sunday of the regular season to cost the Jets a playoff berth.

Favre, at his Wednesday session, held up his half-full glass. "I expect us to make the playoffs," he said. "I didn't expect us to lose the last two games, but I don't know if too many people expected us to win five straight—maybe our team did. If we're able to win five straight and accept that, then we have to be willing to deal with these two games that we've lost and figure out a way to turn it around. The bottom line is we're 8–5 and we're tied for the division. . . . There are three games left. We can't worry about the remaining two. We have to worry about this one. It will be tough, obviously, especially based on the way that we've played the last two weeks. I expect us to make the playoffs. I would hope that every guy in the locker room feels the same way. Why think any differently?"

Because you are the quarterback of the New York Jets, that's why.

"Oh, there they go again, the old Jets," Favre said. "Why wouldn't you say that? I consider it a challenge. Pardon my French, but, hell, I don't know what's going to happen. I really don't. I'm aware of what's happened here in the past for the most part. But to be quite honest, I don't care. I care about what's happening in the next three weeks."

Favre talked about growing up a Saints fan in Mississippi, back when they were so bad they were dubbed the Aints. "I never quite got to wearing a bag over my head, but I was close," he recalled. "And I was miserable. I'm sure Jets fans probably feel the same way I did growing up as a Saints fan. I think it's a huge challenge for us—a fun challenge. We would have liked to have won these last two games, but we're in a good position. Let's ride the wave, see what happens. And at the end of the year, regroup and hopefully it was good enough. But we still control our own destiny."

And Favre held their destiny in his thirty-nine-year-old hands. Favre Time, or Father Time?

"What is Favre Time? Magic, or whatever?" Favre said and smiled, and the room broke up in laughter.

Favre again absolved the playcalling. "What we've done in the last two weeks really hasn't been, as far as playcalling, any different than the five games that we got on the hot streak," he said. "We just didn't execute. People want to say, 'Well, they figured out the short passing game,' or 'You guys can't throw deep.' No one has figured out anything. It's a matter of execution."

But could he possibly be the cold-blooded executioner who won a Super Bowl twelve years prior?

"I've always looked at myself as, if I'm on the field I give you an added edge," Favre said. "That's not being cocky. I think every player should feel that way, whether I've won a Super Bowl or not. A lot of these guys don't even remember. I brought my Super Bowl ring for the first time on the plane the other day, just to show the guys, more or less to prove to them that I did play in a Super Bowl." Laughter. "'Hey, I didn't know you won a Super Bowl.' I don't know if it gives us an edge. It proves that I've been there. It's kind of like what you were talking about, 'Oh, Same Old Jets.' Just like that doesn't matter, the fact that I was on a winning Super Bowl team really doesn't matter. It helps, I would assume. Ty Law, he's played in a few. Coach Mangini, he has a couple Super Bowl rings. It helps, but what matters is the guys in the room now. What kind of statement are they going to make?"

Perhaps Favre should have showed them his Super Bowl ring in the huddle.

Ominously, the owner began wondering whether he would get a Super Bowl ring of his own. It wasn't Favre who troubled him as much as it was the defense.

"They were taking some of the players and putting onus on them rather than looking at it in more of a cohesive way," Johnson would say in June 2009. "We put a lot of emphasis on the quarterback. So the quarterback is playing well, we did well, because you kept the defense off. You win championships with defense. We had to change our patterns to be more effective."

The young Brett Favre might have been able to lift the team on his shoulders. Not this Brett Favre. "We couldn't stop the run or the pass, and that's always a problem," Johnson said.

Did Johnson think Favre's arm was showing signs of deterioration? "No. I didn't see anything different," he said.

There was no inclination on anyone's part to sit Favre for a week. But something needed to change and fast. "It would have been good to do something different than we did because we had a better team than was showing up on the field. . . . We weren't managing the team very effectively," Johnson said.

Mangini, in an effort to refresh his players, shortened practices by thirty minutes before the critical Bills game.

Favre rested his arm that Wednesday. But the cortisone shot had helped immeasurably. "It did feel better," he said on the day he retired. "That Thursday practice probably was my best throwing practice throughout the year, but then it went downhill again after that." That Thursday night, the defense held a cathartic players-only meeting, organized by Ellis, Revis, Rhodes, and Pace, at a local Ruth's Chris Steak House. "A lot of guys stood up and said what they had to say personally," Revis said.

If God wasn't playing for the Jets in San Francisco, perhaps He had a hand in the heaven-sent schedule. The Bills had lost six of their last seven games, and had scored a field goal in each of their last two defeats. J. P. Losman was making his second straight start in place of Trent Edwards (strained groin muscle). Marshawn Lynch, who rarely speaks with the Buffalo media, decided to man up and point the finger at himself for the Bills' offensive woes.

Or perhaps God put Dick Jauron on the sideline with the game on the line.

Favre came out determined to get the ball in the hands of Coles (three catches for 7 yards in the previous two games) and Cotchery. He found Coles on a deep 22-yard crossing route on the first play. The shocker was Favre taking off on a third-and-1 bootleg around left end (sand dial, please) for a 27-yard gain—his longest run since 1998. Fran Tarkenton? Not exactly. He was tackled out of bounds and came up laughing—and no doubt breathing heavily.

"It probably shocked everyone," Favre said. "I really thought I was going to score. I was about twenty yards down there when I realized that I was slower than I thought."

The Bills answered Jones's 2-yard touchdown run—his club-record 13th rushing touchdown (and 15th overall)—with a successful fake punt and 35-yard romp by Lynch, but when Favre hit Cotchery on an out route for an 11-yard touchdown, it was 14–3.

Against a team looking for an excuse to quit, this was the time for the Jets to resurrect the killer instinct that had buried the Rams.

Instead, after Paul Posluszny came up with an interception that bounced off Coles and cornerback Leodis McKelvin, and Roscoe Parrish returned a punt 56 yards, the Jets found themselves staring at a 17–14 deficit and listening to the angry boobirds.

Then the one player capable of a game-changing play made one. Washington, in what was inexplicably his lone carry of the day, electrified the stadium with a 47-yard run that gave the Jets a 21–17 half-time lead. It was his tenth play of 40 yards or more, best in the NFL. "Leon is one of the most explosive players in the league," Jones said. Someone needed to remind the head coach and the offensive coordinator.

The Bad Favre showed up for the second half. He uncorked a third-and-17 bomb down the right sideline for Cotchery that was underthrown by five yards and intercepted by Terrence McGee, and soon it was 21–20. It was Favre's league-leading 20th interception.

"I underthrew it," Favre said. "I was thinking they would play Cover 2. I really was thinking checkdown, [but] they played single safety. So that gives you an opportunity to take a shot." Then he uttered words that must have sent shudders through the entire organization, and knowing nods back in Green Bay: "Maybe I don't have the arm I once had. I don't know."

Maybe he had been hiding an injury after all. Maybe he was being strangled by self-doubt. Maybe Father Time was imposing his will on the thirty-nine-year-old quarterback. Maybe he was kidding. Maybe all of the above. Or maybe, as it was revealed days later, Faneca had been driven back into him as he released the ball.

"I think we as players should always take a lot of the blame and never point fingers or anything like that," Favre said. "That's the way I am. I assumed on that play, without watching the film, that I underthrew him badly. In hindsight, it was underthrown and I actually either stepped on Alan or he stepped on me. . . . I was not able to finish the throw. I felt like I got bumped on the play, but I had to watch the film. I didn't want to sit there and say I bumped into someone. If you go in and you talk to Daboll or Schotty, they probably would say, 'You probably should have just dumped it off.' They're probably right, but Jerricho did actually run by McGee. . . . I'm not going to sit here and lie to you, I don't throw the ball as far as I used to, but if I have to throw the ball eighty-three yards in a game, it's the last play of the game and we're throwing a Hail Mary to win, we have problems anyway. But that's a throw I can make."

He continued, "I knew when I left that podium there, 'Oh, here we go, old Favre.' I was just being honest with you. There are a lot of throws that I can make that other guys can't make. That's one of them that I can make, there's no doubt about it."

One throw he used to make in his sleep, over the middle to a wide-open tight end—sailed ridiculously behind Keller.

While anxiety-riddled Jets fans were noticing on the scoreboard that Pennington was beating the 49ers, McKelvin's 100-yard kickoff return gave the Bills a 27–24 lead—until it was called back by a holding penalty.

Whew!

But then Mangini and Schottenheimer infuriated Jets Nation by calling three consecutive passing plays—all incomplete—while pinned inside their 5-yard line. Brilliant, boys, brilliant.

Lynch (21-for-127) had dominated the Jets all afternoon, and now here came Fred Jackson, Lynch's backup. Jackson kept his legs churning and carried several Jets into the end zone for the 11-yard touchdown that gave the Bills that 27–24 lead with five and a half minutes left.

Favre went three-and-out.

Losman took over at his 22 with 4:20 left.

The Jets looked like dead men walking. There would be no coming back from a disaster like this. Mangini was about to be as popular with Jets Nation as Belichick.

"They were running out the clock to win the game and our season was riding out," Woody said.

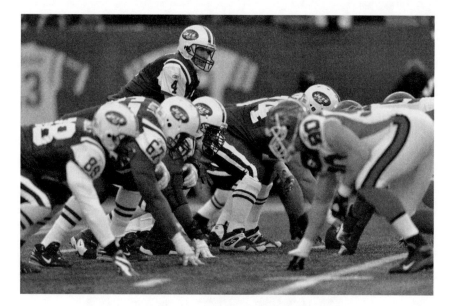

There were more than a few Jets fans who swore that what happened next was a case of divine intervention—a smidgen of justice, no doubt, for the Fake Spike and the Mud Bowl and O'Brien over Marino and Gastineau roughing Bernie Kosar in that 1986 playoff game in Cleveland and Blair Thomas and O'Donnell and two years of Kotite and Belichick bolting for New England and . . .

It was second-and-5. And Losman was rolling right, looking for fullback Corey McIntyre. Elam blitzed from the weak side, and Losman, who should have thrown the ball away, held it when McIntyre became swallowed up in traffic. Losman never heard or saw Elam steaming for him.

"I was just trying to come under control," Elam said. "I knew as long as I got there I was going to be able to make a play."

Elam only made a play that had a chance to go down in Jets lore. His strip-sack of Losman left the ball rolling free and the season rolling along with it. Bryan Thomas dived for it and missed, but it somehow bounced magically to Ellis. For a split second, as Giants Stadium did a collective double take and held its breath before recognizing that it was okay to roar, Ellis was turned the wrong way. He quickly turned back toward the goal line and barreled over offensive tackle Langston Walker. He raced down the left sideline with an 11-yard touchdown run, and it was 31–27 with 1:54 left.

"A lot of guys get in that situation and don't come up with it, or the other team falls on it," Ellis said. "I was trying to focus on getting the ball in my hands and after that I was just trying to make a play. It saved the game. I don't know about the season yet."

How could anyone know? Favre had thrown two more interceptions. He was 5-of-13 for 58 yards in the second half. He was showing alarming signs of slippage.

"That play Shaun and Abe made, when you look back, who knows, that may be one of those plays that catapults us into something great," he said.

Tannenbaum dreamed the same dream. "I thought, 'You know what? Maybe this is one of those years where the ball's bouncing our way,'" he said.

There would soon be whispers that the play call might catapult Jauron from a contract extension to the unemployment line (it didn't) after Revis and Rhodes iced the game with interceptions.

"It's fairly excusable in the situation if it works, and when it doesn't work, it's on my shoulders," Jauron said.

The back page of the Monday tabloids: POT LUCK.

The 9–5 Jets, Patriots, and Dolphins remained locked in a three-way tie. The Patriots routed the Raiders in Oakland, and Pennington, who had finished with 11 straight completions against the Bills and started with six straight to break Marino's franchise record (16), threw a pair of touchdown passes in a 14–9 victory over the 49ers.

The Jets controlled their own destiny. Beat Seattle in Seattle and Pennington and the Dolphins in the regular-season finale at Giants Stadium and welcome to the Second Season. Branch Rickey said that sometimes it is better to be lucky than good, and Mangini wasn't offering apologies for being lucky.

"It's not like the BCS," he said. "We don't get voted down for style points."

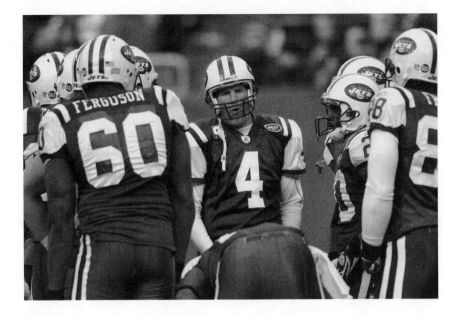

The Jets were clearly staggering, and the pressure built on Mangini when an NFL-high seven Jets—Jones, Faneca, Mangold, Jenkins, Revis, Washington . . . and Favre—were voted to the AFC Pro Bowl team. Benigno, filling in for Mike Francesa on this day, went into his vintage apoplectic mode when he learned that Favre was chosen as a backup. "A joke," he called it.

Miami Herald columnist Greg Cote felt that Pennington had been jobbed: "Pennington has a better passer rating, 95.1 to 86.5. Pennington has a better TD-pick differential, +8 to +4. Pennington has more yards, 3,218 to 3,052. Pennington has a better yards per attempt mark, 7.8 to 6.8. Both men's teams are 9–5, but Favre inherited a 4–12 team and Pennington took over a 1–15 team. Yet Favre makes the Pro Bowl!? That's a habit pick borne of his popularity, the romance of his comeback and his team's bigger market. It is unjust. Matter of fact, it's stinkin' lame."

Agreed. Not to mention that Favre also had a superior supporting cast.

From Armando Salguero's blog in the *Miami Herald*: "At 4 p.m. on Tuesday when the Pro Bowl rosters were announced, Sparano called Pennington to console him somewhat and express his feeling

that Pennington should have made the team. Pennington answered the phone and invited Sparano to speak to him personally. He was in the film room preparing for KC. It was a day off for players but Pennington was in the film room at 4 p.m. That's work ethic, folks."

Favre's quarterback ratings against the Broncos (60.9), 49ers (60.8), and Bills (61.4) marked the worst healthy three-game stretch he'd had since the end of the 2002 season. Outgoing president Bush had been greeted by a pair of errant flying shoes at a Baghdad press conference that weekend from a disgruntled Iraqi journalist, and the *New York Post*'s Brian Costello wrote, "The Iraqi shoe tosser showed more accuracy Sunday than Favre." Alarmingly, Favre had completed only 12-of-47 (26 percent) deep passes that traveled 21 or more yards, with five touchdowns and eight interceptions.

LAST STAND

At Seattle • Miami

If ever Mangini needed to solve the West Coast problem, it was now. On the three previous cross-country trips, the Jets had left on Friday. Mangini and Tannenbaum looked into leaving Saturday this time, but the high volume of holiday traffic prevented Delta from accommodating them. Mangini moved practice back on Thursday and Friday so the players could get a little extra sleep.

Favre was fading so visibly that some wondered whether his shoulder might be affecting his quarterback rating. "The good one or bad one?" he said, and chuckled. "It feels okay. I haven't kept up with the passer rating, nor can you figure it out, but it has nothing to do with my shoulder."

He was lying, of course. It had everything to do with his shoulder.

In truth, he had felt a nagging discomfort as far back as training camp. Little by little, his arm withered, and betrayed him at inopportune times.

"I wouldn't feel it tear, but it just got a little bit more fatigued," Favre said on the day he retired. "There were times at practice

223

I would throw, and I threw almost every day at practice. There were very few days I took off, but I would throw. I didn't have the velocity all the time. I started noticing that more passes were wobbly or whatever. I think I started kind of altering my throwing motion, and that was from the first game on, you know, I didn't think about it much early in the season. But as it progressed later in the year, I noticed I would ice every so often, which was rare for me. I never iced in training camp. So just little subtle hints like that, to the point where almost every throw I felt it."

The media persisted in the useless exercise of asking Favre about his future—whether the ending to the season would have a bearing on his decision.

"Who would've thought that I'd be sitting here answering that question in front of you?" he began. "If you would have asked me that last year before the [NFC] Championship game, I would've said you need to quit drinking." He smiled. "Here I am. Who knows? I think that's pretty positive that we don't know what's going to happen. To predict or to assume is wrong. My sole focus is to try to beat the Seattle Seahawks. I know that's going to be difficult. I know what's possibly ahead for us, but I have no idea what's possibly ahead for me."

What was immediately ahead of him was the head coach who had nurtured him and molded him into a Super Bowl quarterback. Except this time Holmgren, in his last home game as coach of the Seahawks, was scheming against him, trying to wreck his season.

"I can honestly say that I would not be here today if it were not for Mike Holmgren," Favre said. "He and I worked to get here a long time ago, but the things that he taught me really hit me a little bit later, how much of a perfectionist that he was and how hard he was on me. That's the way that I study and prepare today. To him, everything had to be perfect in order to win. He put me in a position to succeed. He allowed me to play, or use my abilities the best way possible, to not only catapult me but to help our team win. He was an unbelievable playcaller. He was a great motivator."

Favre hadn't been getting much help from his supporting cast. The Jets had slipped to sixth in rushing defense and the biggest reason was the wearing down of their biggest player. "I wish I could be Superman for everybody and I wish that I could be one hundred percent perfect every single time I go out there," Jenkins said.

The Jets didn't look like a team ready to seize the moment, but at least the Great Escape against the Bills had kept them off the psychiatrist's couch.

"We haven't rushed out and purchased a bunch of Zoloft or anything," Mangini said.

Snow had been predicted for Seattle on Sunday, so maybe the first major snowstorm of the season that blanketed Florham Park for the Friday practice was an omen. The Jets looked like children frolicking in the snow, holding destiny in one hand and snowballs in the other. An unsuspecting Favre was victimized by a sneak attack from behind by Richardson, who dumped a shovelful of the white stuff on his helmet and shoulders. "He always gets me," Richardson said. "So I felt like I had an opportunity to get him back today."

Favre was 1–6 on the road when the temperature fell below thirty-four degrees but on this day looked primed to make it 2–6. "I told Laveranues, 'Man, he's throwing it like it's ninety degrees out here,'" Cotchery said. "He was zipping it, and every ball was a spiral. I think he's very comfortable with this weather."

It was a mirage.

And Mangini would look just as uncomfortable.

Favre and Holmgren exchanged pleasantries forty-five minutes before the game and posed for pregame photos. There were intermittent snow flurries around game time, a relative calm before the storm of giant flakes that would fall in the second half.

Favre and the Jets resembled a green-and-white snowball rolling downhill over the Seattle defense on their opening series. An improvisational Favre shovel pass to Coles got 5 yards during the 78-yard assault. Favre was 5-of-6 on the drive. But then Mangini opened himself up for an avalanche of Monday morning quarterbacking when, fourth-and-1 at the 2, he opted for a 20-yard Feely field goal.

How about running your team MVP and most inspirational player, the AFC's leading rusher (Jones), and getting seven points on the board? How about showing some nerve and sending a message to your team that you believed in your offense, and if you didn't make it, you believed in your defense to keep Seneca Wallace—Seneca Wallace!—pinned by his goal line? Why not go for the jugular and try to blow out a 3–11 team? "Why wouldn't they?" Seahawks linebacker Lofa Tatupu asked. You know No. 4 wanted to go for it, even if he refused to second-guess Mangini. "There was no sense in thinking we wouldn't be back there," he said. Part of what made Parcells and Belichick great coaches was their willingness to trust their gut, to be fearless riverboat gamblers in the big moments of big games. To gauge the pulse of their team. Mangini's lack of such instincts took the steam out of the short-lived momentum Favre & Co. had built.

"I anticipated the game being tight, and I thought at that point, being the opening drive, the important thing would be to get points," Mangini said. "I wasn't sure how much the weather would continue to worsen as we went. I really felt like it could come down to three points, so I wanted to get the points on the board at that point, figuring that we had a long time to go, but that was the important thing there."

This wasn't Friday in Florham Park anymore for Favre, who had been 9-of-10 in the first quarter. Flushed to his left, forgetting that his fatigued right arm was no longer forever young, surrendering to another brain freeze, he uncorked what looked more like a Hail Mary toward the other side of the field, off the wrong foot, into double coverage, for Cotchery. It was intercepted by Josh Wilson.

Wallace, Matt Hasselbeck's backup, handled the deteriorating conditions far better than Favre. A 2-yard touchdown pass to rookie tight end John Carlson against David Harris at the end of the first half gave the Seahawks a 7–3 lead that swelled to 10–3 late in the third quarter. The Jets again failed to mount a meaningful pass rush (no sacks) against an offensive line that consisted of five backups and was paving the way for Maurice Morris to rush for 116 yards. Jones, on what should have been a running back's field of dreams, would finish with 67 yards on 17 carries.

A grievous delay-of-game penalty nullified Feely's 45-yard field goal early in the fourth quarter. "There was no real reason for that," Mangini said. "The official had his hand on the ball, and we have to wait until he takes his hand off the ball to be able to kick it. Once that happened, it was too late. It should never happen. The decision was made with plenty of time, and we had the group out there.

"[Long-snapper] James Dearth does an excellent job of that, he is very aware of the play clock. He wasn't able to get set and snap the ball in time to execute the kick."

There would be no 50-yard field goal attempt. "When he put the ball down, it was just ten seconds left," Feely said. "You're supposed to reset the clock."

Mangini sent in Hodges to punt, even though Feely had made 13 consecutive field goals. "I felt like a fifty-yard field goal, if you miss that field goal, you're putting them in very good position," Mangini said.

But even if Feely misses the field goal, why be afraid to trust your defense against . . . Seneca Wallace? Seneca Wallace!

Favre had engineered forty-one fourth-quarter comebacks. Panic-stricken Jets fans prayed now for a forty-second. Finally, fourth-and-2 at his 20, down 10–3, 2:21 and all three time-outs left, Mangini went for it. *Now* he shows chutzpah? Another example of being scared of your defense. Against Seneca Wallace! Then, instead of a safe pass for the first down, Favre heaved one over the middle into double coverage that should have been, but wasn't, caught by Coles. "I left a lot of plays out there that I should have had," Coles said. "A lot of blame should be pointed at me. Anytime I have an opportunity to make a play to let us win, I should do that."

Favre finished 18-of-31 for 187 yards with two interceptions against the worst pass defense in the NFL. He alarmingly under-threw receivers. "If we could play like we did against New England and Tennessee every week, we'd be hard to beat," he said. "But I don't have all the answers."

He and the Jets were hiding the answers.

"There was a point in the Seattle game I threw numerous seam passes," Favre said on the day he retired. "I think all but one were to

Laveranues Coles and I underthrew, I think, every one of them. They were into tight coverage, and when I let it go the end result was not where I was wanting it to be. It had to have been a perfect throw to be completed, but I felt like I could make that throw. Not only once, but numerous times."

Favre met Holmgren on the field again when it ended. Said Holmgren, "I just wished him well and said next year when I am riding my motorcycle around, I want to come down [to Mississippi] and have a little catfish with him and just sit down in a different setting and see where he lives."

Favre and the Jets were pelted with snowballs as they headed off Qwest Field. Ellis stopped on his way to the visiting locker room to heave a giant chunk of snow into the stands. It was videotaped by a fan and shown on YouTube. The league fined Ellis $10,000.

"It was all in fun," Ellis said. "Coming off [the field], everybody was throwing snowballs, so it was kind of like a little battlefield out there, so to speak. It was all in fun just going to the locker room."

Mangini wasn't laughing. "That situation in the stadium in general was not a very safe situation for anybody involved," he said. "That doesn't justify us getting involved in it on the flip side. [Ellis] understands that. We thought that there could've been more done to prevent what was happening in terms of the safety from snowballs coming down."

The Jets had unraveled. "We had a lot of success early on and I don't think that we responded to it well," Jenkins said. "I think that success can be an adversity if it's not handled the right way, and that's what happened. Once we got into the funk it kept on going. Right now, the reality of the situation is we are painted in the corner. We have to find a way to survive and we need help or it's going to be the end of the season."

Over the last four games, Favre had thrown one touchdown pass with six interceptions, giving him a league-high nineteen. "It just didn't work today," he said. "You see players come and go all the time but didn't realize the opportunity they had. I think this team really does realize it. That's what's disappointing about this."

He told Schottenheimer and Tannenbaum about his problem. "They knew my shoulder had been bothering me," Favre said on the day he retired.

But not enough to consider sitting him for Clemens. Even in his diminished state, Favre still gave the Jets their best chance to win. Throwing Clemens to the wolves would have been folly. "The week he went to the Miami game, I thought the ball looked like it had a lot of juice," Tannenbaum said.

The Patriots had already obliterated a shameful Cardinals team—an eventual Super Bowl team—that took one look at the driving snow and wondered if it could find a nice hot chocolate emporium instead of playing a football game at Gillette Stadium. Pennington and the Dolphins could have cowered in the minus-twelve windchill in Kansas City. Instead, Pennington completed all seven of his passes for 65 yards on the decisive 13-play, 85-yard drive that consumed eight and a half minutes in crunch time. Final: Dolphins 38, Chiefs 31. "I didn't have to say a word," Pennington said. "I could see it in the guys' eyes. We knew this is the drive; this is it. This is what we've got to do. Still, with that sense of urgency there was never a nervous moment. Everybody was calm and everybody was collected."

And here's what it all meant: Favre versus Pennington.

Favre's wing—a Jets victory—and a prayer—a loss by either the Patriots in Buffalo or the Ravens to the Jaguars—and the Jets would make the playoffs.

Or: Pennington returning to Giants Stadium to reach the playoffs at the expense of the coach and the team that had unceremoniously dumped him.

For Johnson, for Tannenbaum, for Mangini, this had to be their worst nightmare—the prospect of the weak-armed quarterback beating Favre to the playoffs with the world watching. Tannenbaum, with pressing salary cap concerns and a stunning dearth of trade partners, had made no attempt to trade Pennington; partly out of loyalty, he had freed him to cut his own deal. Never in Tannenbaum's wildest dreams could he have imagined Pennington resurrecting a 1–15 Miami franchise, even if Parcells was pulling the strings behind the scenes.

There was nothing in Favre's recent December history to suggest one last gasp from the Jets. Over the last five games of the 2005 season, he had thrown one touchdown pass with ten interceptions; over the same stretch of the 2006 season, four touchdown passes with eight interceptions; and over the same stretch of the 2007 season, six touchdown passes with seven interceptions.

One final indignity, of course, had followed the Jets off Qwest Field before the depressing flight home. "We were on the runway for quite some time [because of] the weather and de-icing and things like that," Mangini said. "It gave you extra time to watch tape."

Tannenbaum was disappointed and frustrated. "Real empty feeling, knowing that we no longer controlled our own destiny," he said.

Johnson, who never made it to Seattle because of the snow and ice storm, had watched the horror show at his apartment. "We showed no life whatsoever at that point," he would recall.

The customary conversation with Tannenbaum wasn't a pleasant one. "We were trying to figure out, trying to explain what is going on here," Johnson recalled. "I mean, how can you be Dr. Jekyll and Mr. Hyde [and] the first part of the season you're beating the Titans? The second part of the season you get a little jet lag, and you can't do anything."

Benigno's Monday rant, a WFAN.com video with eyes bulging and arms flailing, was a classic.

"I'm obviously disgusted today; it really doesn't get any worse than what we saw yesterday from this just absolutely disgusting . . . *disgusting* . . . franchise, that masquerades themselves as an NFL football team.

"I'll start with Eric Mangini; he's gotta go. Enough. In a big spot, maybe the worst-coached game I have ever seen—by *anybody*! Enough, this guy . . . he's so over his head . . . where do I begin?

"Should we start with the opening drive when he doesn't go for the first down on fourth-and-one from the two-yard line, can we start with that, and settles for the field goal? And you knew right there, the Jets were dead. Can we talk about the unconscionable . . . *unconscionable* delay-of-game penalty on Feely's forty-five-yard field goal, and *then* the decision by the brilliant head coach not to try it again! When Feely made it, it woulda been a sixty-yard field goal. He woulda easily made it from fifty.

"To the topper of all toppers in the game—with more than two minutes to go and *all* his time-outs, on a fourth-and-two from about his own twenty-yard line, and he goes for the first down instead of punting?

"With *all his time-outs and the two-minute warning?* The Jets coulda got the ball back with a time-out left! Unbelievable.

"This guy's gotta go, and he can take the freakin' Hall of Fame quarterback with him, 'cause I've had enough of him too. Let him go to Mississippi, he's done, he's finished, please Brett, go home, and go fishing for the rest of your life, because I can't take it anymore, he's been a disaster. I wanted him here, God knows; I was wrong. He's finished, done, stick the fork in him, and I don't wanna hear about any playoff scenarios—New England is not losing to Buffalo, the Ravens are not losing to the Jaguars. And let's be honest—are the Jets beatin' Miami here? C'mon, let's get real. Let's get *real*. I've had enough. Mangini has to go, his whole coaching staff too, go draft a quarterback in the draft, there's a ton of good-looking quarterbacks comin' out. Maybe the Jets get lucky—look at Baltimore, they're gonna go to the playoffs with a rookie coach and a rookie quarterback. Same thing with Atlanta—they're already in the playoffs, with a rookie coach and a rookie quarterback. I've had enough of this guy. Mangini must go. He's *totally* in over his head. Anything bad I ever said about Herman Edwards—I thought Herman Edwards was terrible—it's not even close. As bad as Herman was, he got my team to the playoffs three times . . . they didn't choke in three times trying to get to the playoffs when he was coaching the team, and even his lousy Chief team that's lost twenty-two of their last twenty-four at least is continuing to play competitive football as they did yesterday even though they wound up losing that game to the Miami Dolphins.

"I don't know what else to say about the Jets—I'm disgusted, I'm beaten up, I'm tired. This franchise has given me nothing but pain for

forty years. . . . I hate this team. I hate them. I *hate them*! And I can't
stand Eric Mangini. Eric, go have another hamburger, please."

Favre's Wednesday press conference began at 10:30 a.m. It wasn't
long before reporters were furiously blogging the news that Favre
believed his arm wasn't right.

"I'm sure if we MRI'd enough, we'd probably find something," he
said and smiled. "During the course of the year, there were numerous
times where I had been asked about my shoulder. It had been hit a
couple times. I don't know. . . . Just knowing my body, there may be
something, but there's no test yet to reveal anything. . . . I think it will
reveal one way or another if there is something wrong. I don't want
to make a big deal of it. I don't want to make excuses because I feel
like I can make every throw."

But why make it public now? Was Favre simply being honest?
Was he trying to dupe the Dolphins? Was he crying for help from his
teammates, hoping they would rally around him and raise the level of
their play? Was he indeed making excuses? "He was in pain," James
Ihedigbo said.

Schottenheimer never heard Favre complain much about his arm.
"Occasionally he'd say, 'Yeah, it's a little bit sore,'" Schottenheimer
said. "It would stiffen up on him. A few times he'd ask Eric if we
could go in the indoor facility. It was easier for him to stay loose."

And it was easier to play if he could save his arm. During the Jets'
closed practices toward the end, Clemens did the lion's share of the
throwing: Favre mostly handed off. Asked how often Favre would
throw, Woody said: "On any given day it was very minimal. I would
say during team periods, he threw about three, maybe four passes."

Asked how long this went on for, Woody said, "Probably about
four to five weeks."

According to Clemens: "I was probably getting maybe thirty percent of the reps." Although Clemens allowed that it could have been
more. "If he'd gotten hurt on a Sunday, I'd take all the reps on a
Wednesday."

Stuckey's recollection: an even split, with Favre executing newly
installed pass plays.

The sight of Favre standing idly by the huddle prompted this barb from defensive players: "Hey, Brett, are you gonna practice today?"

But if you were looking for Favre's name on the injury report, you were out of luck.

During the press conference, Favre waxed nostalgic and sounded very much like a man about to play his last game should there be no wild-card playoff berth. Of course, you never etch anything in stone with Favre, because he might be even more mercurial than Parcells, who changed his mind every five minutes.

"It's been a great career," Favre said. "This year was a gamble, I guess you could say a risk, whatever you want to call it. I can honestly say I'm thankful I was given the opportunity here. It's been a lot of fun. It's been good and bad at times as far as our season has gone, but I'm glad I came. I made the right decision. Hopefully we win this football game and see what happens. I'm sure a lot of people are not saying good things about us, but it's been fun fighting with these guys. Whatever happens after this, happens."

For the umpteenth time, the media wanted to know what he expected to happen. "There's still one game left," Favre said. "Do I see myself playing here next year? I didn't see myself playing here this time last year. There are some things that the team probably needs to think about as far as next year's concerned and some things that I need to think about and we need to discuss amongst ourselves. It's way premature to think about that when we have the Dolphins coming in. I have no idea. I know some things need to fall into place for us to make it. Most importantly, we need to win this football game. We obviously have struggled here lately. They brought me in here to lead this team and win football games, and that's what I'm trying to do. I don't want to focus on what's going to happen next year. This very well could be my last game. I'm aware of that.

"I'd like to make it a memorable one."

The overtime interception by Webster in the NFC Championship game had no bearing on his decision to retire and then unretire. "Believe me, for a kid from Southern Mississippi who wanted to dress out in a pro football uniform and dreamed of playing for the Saints, it's been a pretty good run," Favre said. "Whether I walk away today, three years ago, I can't look back and say, 'Boy, that's one thing I wanted to do.' It's been outstanding. So one play, one season is not going to make a difference."

He planned to sit down with Tannenbaum and Mangini when the 2008 season ended and promised there would be no repeat of the will-he-or-won't-he dog-and-pony show. Mangini had been asked at his press conference minutes earlier whether he wanted Favre back, and he said, "Yes." Now, what else would you expect him to say? And who even knew whether Mangini would be coaching Favre if he did come back? "Mike has said to me numerous times, 'Whenever the season is over, take a little time. We'll talk about it,'" Favre said. "Unless I just go in there today and say, 'That's it,' which is not going to happen. I don't want to go through what happened last year, for me and for everyone else. Physically that has something to do with it, as well. I played every game since '92. That's not to say that some things don't bother me. That will play a part in this decision, as well."

Either way, when it came time for him to leave, he would not leave as Regret Favre, playoffs or no playoffs. "I'm disappointed, as everyone else in this building is disappointed," Favre said. "The opportunities that were presented to us, we couldn't have asked for a better opportunity. I'm disappointed because we didn't capitalize on that, as our fans are, and as everyone else is."

But imagine the disappointment—outrage—if the Patriots or Ravens were to lose and Pennington were to outduel Favre. "I don't think I need to justify anything," Favre said. "I don't think Chad needs to, as well. . . . He's worthy of everything that's being said about him. . . . It goes without saying the type of leader he has been for them and for this team. I haven't found one person in this building that has said one thing negative about Chad Pennington. It's not about me and Chad Pennington, although that is what basically plays out most of the time, especially when we're playing against them, the fact that they're where they are and we have kind of fallen to where we are.

"The only thing I can say is I'm glad I got an opportunity here. I hope from a leadership standpoint I'm everything and then some that they wanted me to be. I can assure you the Dolphins will say the same thing [about Pennington]. Both teams are obviously better than they were last year. That's not because of Brett Favre and it's not because of Chad Pennington, but I do think we've helped out some. . . . I don't feel like I have to justify anything, nor does he."

Or perhaps Favre was again trying to convince himself that he was something other than a faded thirty-nine-year-old has-been with his own agenda. As Favre's arm withered and was sabotaging the Jets' season, there were grumblings from more than a few players, who perceived a double standard from Mangini when it came to Favre. He never, for instance, chewed him out in a team meeting.

"When there was a time to have him in his office the way you have anybody else in the office, he put him on the line like anybody else," said Mangini ally Teddy Atlas. "Accountability is very important to Eric. Favre would be held to the same things as anyone else when they had to be dealt with by the coach."

Asked whether some Jets grumbled about a double standard, Clemens said, "Before Brett was here it was a very strict environment. There were policies put in place and you abided by them and that was the end of it. You sign Brett, the Man, the Myth, the Legend, the atmosphere changes and the way things are run to a certain degree. That probably hurt guys' pride more than anything . . . you're talking about three or four guys."

Pennington's Wednesday press conference began at 2:10 p.m. in Davie, Florida. The Dolphins, inundated with New York media requests, had made a shrewd organizational decision to limit Pennington to this one session.

"As only fate would have it, this is how sports always works out, so this situation doesn't surprise me," Pennington said. "I pretty much banked on it. It's a good thing. I'm excited about it; the whole team is excited about having the chance to be able to have one shot into the playoffs. That's what you work so hard for the whole season, to get to this point to have an opportunity to play an extra game."

It is always about the team with Pennington, and he was not about to fuel the fire with any talk of personal redemption or vindication, even if the Jets had moved mountain and earth for Favre, even if

Favre had beaten him on Opening Day, even if Favre had gotten the Pro Bowl berth that Pennington deserved.

"As far as the emotional part of that, that happened the first game and I'm glad that it did happen in the first game so now it's strictly business, trying to win a football game," Pennington said. "It just so happens we're playing my former team. Will there be some emotions? Sure, you're going back to the Meadowlands where you played eight years. I just don't think it will be to the magnitude that it was in the season opener when the situation was so fresh and so new. Now we're seventeen weeks into it, it's a little bit different now. We have two really good football teams vying for a playoff spot and it's going to be an exciting game."

His roller-coaster days in New York had hardened him, taught him how to keep his eyes on the prize and block out the peripheral factors and how to subjugate embedded emotions or motivations that can sabotage most mortals.

"You've got to think about it, you've got to assess the situation," Pennington said. "You've got to realize and hopefully lean upon your past experiences that you may have had. That's why I think the first game has helped me because there were a lot of emotions in that game. . . . We have a saying, 'Keep your eyes on the front of the rim,' and if you're able to do that, that blocks out all of the distractions. That takes away all of the little things, all of the emotions. In front of the rim is different for each individual in that huddle. For me it's different than the left tackle because our assignments are different. By focusing on those little things, that blocks out all of the bigger distractions and really simplifies the game. In the quarterback room we talk about, in the clutch, you rely on your fundamentals. When you think about your fundamentals in the clutch, all of that other stuff kind of dissipates and goes away and that's what it boils down to."

No one had thought Pennington could come back from two rotator cuff surgeries; Pennington did. No one had thought the Dolphins could be playing for the division title in the regular-season finale; Pennington did.

"If you don't have those expectations for yourself as an individual, especially as a quarterback, you don't believe you can help change a team, help a team and lead a team to victory, you really don't have business being behind a center," he said.

If Favre was the Iron Man, then Pennington was the Irony Man; it was quite possible that he suddenly controlled the fates of both Favre and Mangini.

"This could be my final game too," Pennington said. "We never know. You're always one play away from hanging the cleats up. I never think about that. We've all been around long enough to know that with Brett, you never think that either. That's just part of the business; not knowing what your fate is. That's why we're all scrapping around here and that's why the veterans, you've got to really talk to the younger guys about, 'Hey, this stuff does not happen all of the time and when you have an opportunity, you really have to seize that opportunity. This is not an everyday occurrence. This isn't something where just because you had a successful season this year, you'll have a successful season next year.' The opportunity is now and it's a nice opportunity to have and you really want to take advantage of it."

Favre won his Super Bowl after Pennington had been redshirted after his freshman season at Marshall. The two had clearly developed a mutual admiration society. "I've been a fan of Brett because he has so much fun playing the game and it shows," Pennington said. "When he plays, he plays with a passion, he plays with a fire, he plays a lot of time like you were kids in the backyard; just having fun, and you have a responsibility, but you don't let that responsibility weigh you down so much that you can't enjoy it. He enjoys the opportunity, he enjoys the game. At this level, sometimes that's hard to do. He's been able to do that his whole career and I think that's what's refreshing about him because he still brings that to the game."

Jets fans who never got the chance to say good-bye to Pennington would now be getting the chance to say hello again. The ones who shamefully booed him on Opening Day 2007 when he went down with his ankle injury didn't figure to be as kind.

"I think that's one of the things for a younger player to understand is that when you play a game your whole life and it's one for all, all for one, fans are for you, even the local writers in your hometown are for you regardless of how you play," Pennington said. "When you get to this level, they're really not for you. It's all about what's in the 'now.' If the 'now' is not good enough or not successful, it is a difficult situation. That's something as a professional you have to learn, and that's part of being a pro; learning how to compartmentalize that and put aside and focus on the job at hand. It's difficult as a young player to deal with. I think you not only learn a lot about yourself in that situation, people learn a lot about you and how you handle a situation like that and how you change. You can't control if people around you have changed, but you can control whether or not you stay the same. That's most important and I think that's at the end of the day what people respect about you."

Of course he had communicated with some of his former teammates during the course of the season. "A bunch of different guys texting here and there," he said. "A phone call here and there."

Coles and Pennington had spoken the previous night. "When you play each other that week, there's not as much as there is when you're not playing each other because it's easier to talk and discuss and things like that," Pennington said. "When you're playing each other and you're the enemies of each other, it's a little bit different to have a civilized conversation."

Then there was Sparano, who had had every bit the rookie season Mangini had in 2006 with Pennington. Sparano had one unmistakable advantage over Mangini as the game drew near: he had Parcells and wise old offensive coordinator Henning as invaluable resources.

"I think that Bill knows me well enough that at this point, he probably needs to leave me alone," Sparano said. "He knows where my mind is. I have picked his brain on one particular issue right now this week just from a personnel standpoint as you're getting ready to go into this. That's a good problem to have; having him there to be able to bounce something off of. Even Dan Henning; I go around and around with Dan a little bit with some of those things because these guys have been in these situations before. I'd be a fool and not doing my job if I didn't do that."

• • •

Mangini's even-keeled, stoic nature, which had come under fire given that the team had seemed virtually devoid of emotion down the stretch, was keeping him grounded in the face of back-page tabloid headlines challenging him to beat the Dolphins to keep his job. I wrote one of those columns and it wasn't particularly easy to do—I liked Mangini and days earlier I had received a Christmas card with a color picture of him, his wife, Julie, and his three young sons. Talk radio, led by Benigno's hysterical rants, was raging about him.

"I don't really have talk radio in my office, but nothing against talk radio or anything like that; I listen to NPR," Mangini said. "Is that talk radio?" He smiled. "But that's usually at night, and a little different topic. The fans are passionate and I respect that. I understand that and I appreciate that. I've been on both sides of that passion. Well, really three sides of that passion: playing on the opposing sideline, feeling that energy and understanding the criticism from the other side and the passion for the team. I get it. I understand it. I appreciate it. We're going to keep moving forward and try to win the next game."

But until that next game arrived, Mangini was going to have to answer a torrent of questions about the resurrected quarterback he didn't want, the faded quarterback he had, and the job he might not have after this next game.

He expressed his happiness for Pennington and his family for his success. "You know that anytime you release a good player, you have a good chance of playing against him," he said.

But, again, never in their wildest imaginations did the Jets envision a scenario where Pennington would have the 1–15 team he inherited needing only this last victory at Giants Stadium in the regular-season finale to win the division crown.

"When we made the move, Brett was one piece in the puzzle," Mangini said. "Brett wasn't going to win games on his own and he wasn't going to lose games on his own. He was one part of the things that we were doing. We thought it was a good opportunity when we had the opportunity to get him. That hasn't changed. It's still one part of what we do each week. It's a very important part, but it's one part."

Poppycock, of course. The one part only necessitated dramatically altering the offense at the eleventh hour, and expectations from without and from within. It wasn't only the playoffs that were on the line; so was the decision to ditch Pennington for Favre.

"If you want to look at it in a very narrow context, then that could be the context that you analyze it in," Mangini said. "I've never been a part of a team where one player defines the success or failure."

Mangini must have forgotten what Namath had done once for the Jets, what Montana did for the 49ers, what Elway did for the Broncos, what Brady did for his Patriots, what Favre did once for the Packers and was brought in to do for the 2008 Jets. And yet, when asked about the Pennington-Favre showdown, he said, "They aren't in a cage match on Sunday."

It was ironic that the Jets were playing a Dolphins outfit built by Parcells, who always railed against quarterbacks who make mistakes that cause their team to lose.

Said Mangini, "There are some throws [at Seattle] that he definitely could've hit better, but there were some throws that were easily catchable and we didn't come up with the catch. You catch a few of those and things look dramatically different. There were plenty of those balls, too."

Apologini. The tape never lies. Favre looked like a shot quarterback. "Anytime you're not doing well on third down, the amount of opportunities decreases," Mangini said. "We haven't been very effective in that situation. The amount of drives lessens, the time of possession lessens, the opportunity to keep throwing the ball lessens. It's been constrictive the last four games as well."

Mangini didn't know it, but he was making excuses for a coach-killer.

He didn't detect any change in his relationship with Tannenbaum. "Mike and I talk about the opponent and our team," he said. "In terms of our relationship, it's the same that it's always been."

He said he hadn't addressed his job security with the owner, nor would he. "That's not what we ever talk about. We talk about the game, the team, the things that we're doing. That's what we focus on. That's what I focus on."

Ominously, however, Johnson had passed on several media requests to give Mangini a vote of confidence. So Mangini appeared to have no inkling when they asked him whether he would lobby for Favre to return in 2009 that he might not be returning to coach him.

"I'll definitely work on it, but it's still something that's a very personal decision," Mangini said. "We'll definitely have a long conversation about it. I'd love to hear his thoughts, I'll definitely share mine, and we'll make a decision at that point." A better question might have been: did Favre want Mangini back?

On the day after Christmas, Mangini downplayed Favre's own concern about his shoulder. "At this time of year he has historically been sore," he said. "That's not uncommon. That happens with a lot of players at this point in the year. You have different things that are nagging. As you get older it may nag a little bit longer."

Why no MRI to find out what was bothering him? One: the Jets weren't about to chase a playoff berth with Clemens or Ratliff. Two: Favre wasn't about to have his Iron Man streak come to a crushing end, not here, not now. "This isn't anything that we're trying to avoid," Mangini said.

Tannenbaum: "I knew he had some pain in there. Watching him in practice, you could clearly see he had a lot of velocity on the ball. It wasn't to the point where it was affecting his performance."

Game day brought with it a report from Glazer that Favre did not enjoy playing for Mangini: "In Green Bay, Favre earned the right to be treated differently. With the Jets he's treated like everyone else. He gets called to the principal's office and is grilled by Mangini for the decisions he's making in games. On Wednesdays and Thursdays, the players are quizzed about their upcoming opponent and Favre feels it's homework they don't need. I don't think he enjoys it that much. I don't think he's happy playing for Mangini."

"I don't think that's true at all," Tannenbaum said. "I think Brett and Eric had a really good relationship, and I think Eric showed remarkable flexibility dealing with a Hall of Fame quarterback that's coming into a program."

Asked if he felt Favre did not enjoy playing for Mangini, Woody said, "If he didn't, he did a good job of covering it up." None of them looked happy playing for Mangini in Seattle, and now Pennington versus Favre would decide his immediate future. I borrow from my *New York Post* Q&A with Cotchery:

Q: What is Favre like in the huddle?

A: Very relaxed . . . you may get a joke every now and then.

Q: What was Chad Pennington like in the huddle?

A: Chad was relaxed in the huddle also, but you didn't get as many jokes. With Chad, he would make sure everyone's on the same page.

Q: How often does Brett joke in the huddle?

A: It's not like a comedy show out there . . . he knows when to joke and when not to joke.

This was clearly no time for Favre to joke. He and Pennington embraced briefly at midfield for the coin toss.

The Dolphins were booed when they entered the stadium, but Pennington was received warmly by his former fans. "It was a great reaction," he said. "I had eight great years here, and Jets fans are passionate and very loyal and I think they respect people who try to do things right. It was a good reception."

Favre tried a bomb for Coles on the first series and overthrew him.

Pennington started at his 4-yard line on his first possession and if he had glanced up and over to his right, he would have seen Fireman Ed leading the J-E-T-S JETS JETS JETS chant that had once belonged to him.

On the Jets' second possession, from midfield, Washington motioned out of the backfield toward the left sideline, leaving Favre

with an empty formation. Favre looked for Washington, isolated against cornerback Andre Goodman, pump-faked . . . and Goodman intercepted the overthrow. He didn't bite on a double move.

The Jets dodged a bullet when Ricky Williams, alone ahead of Bowens, dropped what would have been a 40-yard touchdown pass from Pennington off a fleaflicker out of the wildcat formation the Dolphins had implemented with stunning success most of the season.

Pennington had it third-and-17 at midfield when a roar went up because the scoreboard, for the first time, showed the score of the Ravens game; the Jaguars had taken a 7–3 lead near the end of the scoreless first quarter.

Favre had his big chance early in the second quarter when Jason Trusnik recovered a Pennington fumble forced by a Bryan Thomas sack at the Miami 49. On third-and-13, he found Cotchery over the middle, for 24 yards. A third-and-9 shovel pass to Washington got the 9 yards. Finally, Favre threw underneath for Coles and the former running back did the rest. Favre thrust his arms skyward and jumped into the air and hugged anyone and everyone in sight following the 13-yard touchdown. It stayed 6–0 because holder Hodges fumbled the point-after touchdown snap.

After Barton dropped a gimme interception, Pennington unleashed his efficiency and resourcefulness on the Jets defense. He escaped a third-and-5 rush at his 45 and, falling backward and throwing left, found Fasano for 8 yards. Moments later, he lofted one of his feathery touch passes over Elam in the left corner of the end zone to Ginn for a 27-yard touchdown with 2:18 left before halftime.

The Ravens, meanwhile, had regained control—only fans with BlackBerrys and iPods knew, because the scoreboard operators had their instructions—an organizational decision—to post only the good news—as Ed Reed intercepted David Garrard to preserve a 17–7 lead.

Then Favre threw the type of pass that always drove Parcells mad.

Favre pumped left and bootlegged right, looked for Jones, and found rookie defensive end Philip Merling instead. He made a fruitless diving attempt to tackle Merling at the 13 and came up holding his right hand. Merling's 25-yard touchdown romp made it Dolphins 14, Jets 6. Boos rained down on Favre as he rotated his sore shoulder on the sideline.

The Dolphins' defensive scheme called for Merling to pick up the running back when Favre rolled out looking for the screen. Merling had looked back just in time. "I didn't see the release," he said. "I just had to bring it in."

Gunslinger Favre, 21 interceptions in his holster now, was booed as he walked back into his huddle. His quarterback rating at the half was 37.1. The Patriots had beaten the Bills 13–0, and the Ravens, eventual 27–7 winners, were now pummeling the Jaguars, so another Wait Till Next Year was thirty minutes away for the Jets, no matter how their game turned out.

"Winning ten games is a successful NFL season; let's go win ten games," Tannenbaum thought.

Mangini later said he had no idea what was unfolding in Baltimore. Some of his players did. "I pretty much figured it out when they showed the score in the first quarter and we didn't see it again for the rest of the game," Baker said. "It wasn't too hard to figure out."

Fireman Ed, as much as he tried, could not fire up the fans once the Ravens began throttling the Jaguars. "Nobody was into it in the second half," he said. "They knew Baltimore was gonna win. Everybody was on BlackBerrys. They knew [the Jets] had no shot."

The Jets got a gift early in the third quarter when John Denney sailed his snap over the head of punter Brandon Fields, setting up Favre at the Miami 28. Favre hit Cotchery on third-and-14 for 15 yards, and Washington zigged and zagged his way for a 10-yard touchdown

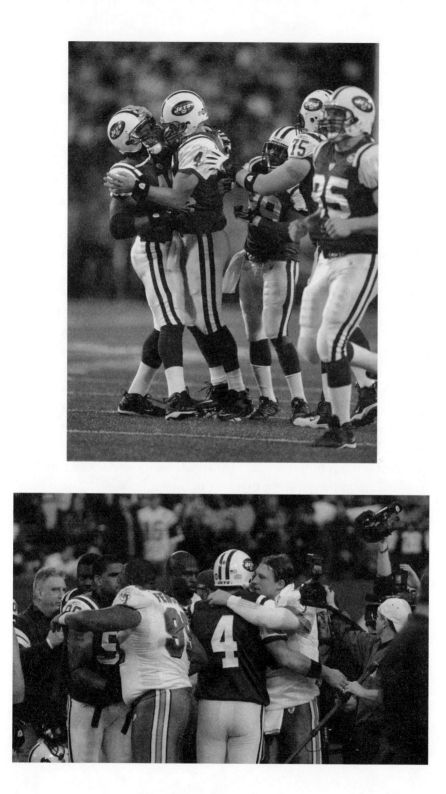

that gave the Jets a 15–14 lead. Mangini's decision to go for two this early in the third quarter was the wrong one, but it brought the right result for a change when Cotchery caught a low bullet from Favre in the end zone.

Pennington gritted his teeth and went to work. He had Ginn open deep down the field off a fleaflicker and underthrew him, but he was Destiny's Quarterback, nothing and no one was going to stop him. Ginn came back for the ball and caught it for a 44-yard gain in front of Rhodes and Law at the Jets' 36. Pennington threw another honey over Dwight Lowery to Fasano in the right corner of the end zone for the 20-yard touchdown that gave the Dolphins a 21–17 lead.

On the third interception, Favre saw the Dolphins weren't set and threw a quick dart to where he thought Coles would be and over Stuckey's outstretched hands. Coles, lined up on the left side, never ran his route, and Favre threw the ball right to Goodman, who was expecting a pump fake.

"Our defense wasn't set up, and I think he saw us scrambling around out of position and he was trying to get the ball off," Goodman said. "I wasn't sure what he was doing, but I was ready to go when I saw the ball come out of his hands."

Interception number 22. "[Favre's] real unorthodox, but he wouldn't be in the position that he's in now if he wasn't that type of risk-taker," Goodman said. "When you get your opportunity you have to take advantage of it, and make him pay for his mistakes."

For all those years, the reward from Favre had been worth the risk.

But no more.

"I don't know what he was doing," cornerback Will Allen said. "He was just tossing the ball up."

There was no magic left in Favre's arm, and now Pennington, ahead 24–17, faced fourth-and-1 at the Jets' 40 with 2:30 left. It was time to stick a knife in the Great Favre Gambit, time to stick a knife in the Mangini Era. And what better way to kill those two birds than with one stone-cold killer named Pennington?

The quarterback sneak gained 2 yards. Pennington (22-of-30, 200 yards, 2 TDs) signaled first down with his left hand.

First-and-playoffs for him and the Dolphins. Fourth-and-season for Favre and the Jets.

"I wanted that one. I really wanted that one," Pennington said. "Coach gave me the ball and I was glad I could get it done."

The rewards with Pennington were greater at the end of the day and at the end of the season because of the virtual absence of risk. "In big games like this, you have to be patient," he said. "You have to make the plays when they're there and avoid the disasters."

Touché.

Even his old pal Coles saluted him. "I am proud of him," Coles said. "I am happy for him. The people in New York booed him, bashed him, and doubted him when he was here."

The final pass of Favre's 2008 season was fittingly an illegal forward pass. He threw short to Washington, who lateraled to Favre, who suffered one last indignity when he was belted to the ground before throwing a second forward pass incomplete to Cotchery. On the final play, Favre stood on the sideline as Brad Smith replaced him for a futile Stanford band lateralthon.

Now it was time for what would be the gunslinger's final walk across the field. Sometimes Winley would walk with him after the game, sometimes Gilmore would. This time it was Winley. "He made his way over to Chad," Winley said. The two quarterbacks passing in the night shook hands. "Chad did the interview with CBS," Winley said. Favre was the one they all wanted on Opening Day. Not now. Favre jogged off the field, followed by a herd of photographers and flashing cameras. He had finished with a league-high twenty-two interceptions, nine of them over the last five games—two more than Pennington had thrown the entire season. Winley congratulated Pennington and they hugged. "You deserved it," Winley said. "Thank you," Pennington said.

Fireman Ed took one last long look at Favre. He didn't expect him to return to his team. "As much as everybody blames Favre, I don't," Fireman Ed said. "It was Mangini." He left Giants Stadium expecting Mangini to be back in 2009. "I didn't think our owner had the balls to fire him. I thought it was a wasted year. They have enough talent on that team that they arguably coulda got to the championship game. Absolutely. Why not?"

• • •

Pennington (19 TDs, 7 INTs), conducting interviews and soaking in what was arguably the most exhilarating athletic moment of his life, was the last player off the field, to chants of "MVP, MVP." He threw his hat into the stands. Then he pumped his right fist in the air as he jogged into the tunnel that took him to his joyous teammates in the visiting locker room.

But first Will Allen met him outside, hugged him, and said, "CP, come and get your hat, baby!" His AFC East champions hat, of course.

Pennington had set team records with his completion percentage of 67.4 and quarterback rating of 97.4. More important to him, the Dolphins had become only the second team in NFL history—the 1999 Colts were the first—to achieve a ten-game turnaround in one season. Pennington was kneeling in front of Sparano in the locker room now as the coach reminded the Dolphins of their "why not us?" mantra. Sparano held the game ball in his right hand. "This ball's gonna go right here to this quarterback," he announced, and bent down to hand it to Pennington, tousling the smiling quarterback's blond hair as teammates cheered.

"I told you, man. He was our savior," linebacker Joey Porter said. "They talk about everybody else being the MVP and just overlooking him. They overlooked him in the Pro Bowl too. But if you look at what this guy did, he changed this whole team. Look at today. He totally outplayed Brett Favre. He did it all year."

Nose tackle Jason Ferguson, an ex-Jet, poured salt on his old club's wound. "You cut a guy and we pick him up and he beats you in a championship game—you better believe they're thinking about that," he said.

Pennington acted as if he had been there before, and he had. "It's always a sweet feeling to be a champion," he said. "That's what we are: AFC East champions. It's a great feeling. This organization has been unbelievable. They accepted me from the get-go. This has been an unbelievable ride."

The high road, remember, is the one Pennington always takes. "It's not a revenge factor," he said. "This week, being the seventeenth week, it was strictly focused on winning the championship, knowing that we controlled our own destiny. It just so happened that it had to come through New York. That's the only way fate would have it."

He was last seen embracing his wife, Robin, and walking to the bus lovingly and triumphantly with her.

Tannenbaum would send Pennington a text congratulating him. "He was very appreciative of my text," Tannenbaum reported.

Down the corridor, Favre was grilled about the sorry ending to the season, and maybe his career. "The hardest part is the finality of it, especially when you expect to go on," he said. "It was a tough pill to swallow, but I had a blast working with these guys. It was a lot of fun. It's disappointing where we are now, but I wouldn't trade it for anything."

He offered no excuses. Sort of. "Down the stretch, it wasn't good enough," he said. "I have no excuses. I would love to sit here and tell you that it was this and it was that, but I'm not going to do that. Bottom line is it wasn't good enough. I'm sure everyone is going to say he's old, washed up and gray. Maybe they're right. If I was an expert then I wouldn't have struggled down the stretch. The only thing I know is, do I feel completely healthy? No. Did I start the season completely healthy? Probably not. In my mind, I did everything I could do and it wasn't good enough."

Favre dismissed Glazer's latest report about his alleged deteriorating relationship with Mangini. "That's news to me," he said. "I know our relationship has been a very good relationship, with all the coaches. I don't know where that would come from. I thought it was just a very good working environment with all the coaches. I have a lot of respect for them."

If there was any solace for Jets Nation it was only this—losing to the Dolphins meant Belichick and the Patriots had missed the playoffs.

David Tratner stood to Favre's left, by the entrance to the locker room, and thought, "This could be his last press conference and here I am doing it." As he passed by the visiting locker room on his way to the press box elevator, Pennington coincidentally exited. So much had happened since Pennington had hugged Speight and Tratner outside Dolphin Stadium before the opener to now. "Congratulations," Tratner said. Pennington, surrounded by well-wishers, smiled and nodded.

Clay Hampton looked for Pennington after the game in the tunnel area that led to where the visiting buses sat waiting to transport the Dolphins to the airport. "I thought I missed him; he was the very last person to go through screening to get on the bus," Hampton said.

Hampton: "Congratulations. Great year."

A beaming Pennington: "Thanks a lot. How's that little boy of yours?"

Hampton: "He's doing great."

Pennington: "Make sure you have a great holiday with him."

Hampton: "I know you've got to go. Good luck next week."

Pennington: "Thanks a lot."

Hampton couldn't help but notice a different Pennington from the one he had accompanied from Cleveland to New York. "You could tell he was really happy," Hampton said.

I hurried back up to the press box to write the following column for Monday's *New York Post*:

> This is written somewhat reluctantly, because Eric Mangini is a good man, and a good enough coach to take the Jets to the playoffs as a rookie when Chad Pennington was Comeback Player of the Year.
>
> But not good enough to prevent a Metsian collapse that goes right in there with some of the darkest endings in Jets history, not enough to prevent Pennington and the Dolphins from clinching the division and dancing on the Jet grave with a 24–17 victory.
>
> Cangini.
>
> Out with the old, and in with the new, and Happy 1969 to you.
>
> Sing Auld Lang Syne to the coach, and sing it to the Hall of Fame quarterback too.

Bye-bye, Brett.

"I wish I could have held up my end of the bargain," Favre said.

Bill Cowher represents the kind of upgrade over Mangini that we thought Favre over Pennington was back in August.

Woody Johnson will have his new stadium for the 2010 season and if he needed Favre to sell those PSLs last summer, he needs Cowher to sell them now, given the anger and depression gripping Jet Nation today.

Johnson said he would make a decision sometime this week.

Referring to his fans, already deflated by the Patriots and Ravens winning their games, the owner said: "They deserved more."

Mangini, asked if he expects to be back, said: "I do."

If Johnson is looking for more bang for his $140 million off-season bucks, Cowher is the one and only place to start.

If Cowher is adamant about not coaching in 2009—show him the money, Woody—then a champion coach like Steve Spagnuolo needs to be interviewed, and a franchise quarterback needs to be drafted. It worked just fine for the Falcons and Ravens.

The Didn't Win Now team needs a Win Now coach like Cowher. Or, if you prefer, a Chin Now coach.

For all his recent failings, Mangini, who according to one report is 50–50 to be fired, is in the playoffs if Favre (2 TDs, 9 INTs over the last five games, 3 last night, 22 for the season) is anything more than a shell of his former self after 8–3.

Maybe today's MRI will reveal something very wrong with Favre's shoulder. "Well, it hurts in the back; it hurts down the bicep; and occasionally in my neck," Favre said. "Other than that it's fine."

Guess what: that's what happens to 39-year-old quarterbacks' arms. Even his. Even him. There didn't seem to be anything wrong with his fastball yesterday, just his accuracy. "I hope it was not a factor in some of the throws this year," Favre said.

It was the right move, making the bold move for Favre and gambling that he was forever young. "I felt like I was wanted again," Favre said.

Alas, it was the right move at the wrong time, a time when Father Time showed up at the worst possible time to intercept Favre and turned him into just another Joe who wasn't Namath.

He was off-Broadway Brett.

Great guy, great teammate, great leader.

But no longer a great quarterback.

"I'm glad I made the decision to come here and play," Favre said. "I knew the odds were against us, I knew the expectations were high; but I consider that a huge challenge."

He couldn't meet it.

Favre said his family hadn't indicated anything to him other than beating the Dolphins. "I not only let this team down, I let them down; I don't know which one's harder to face," Favre said.

Mangini doesn't get to escape The Blame Game because he couldn't motivate his team down the stretch, because the playcalling and deployment of personnel were erratic at best, because he coached scared in situations that called for nerve, because his defense couldn't mount a pass rush or defend the pass and needs a more daring, inspiring coordinator.

But when December came, Bill Belichick and Tony Sparano had the two best quarterbacks in the division.

"I'm sure everyone's gonna say, 'He's old and washed-up and gray and all that stuff, and maybe they're right,'" Favre said. "That's one of the things I guess I will assess: am I old and washed-up? Maybe so. If that's the case, then it's time for me to do something else."

Thanks for the memories.

The Monday front-page headline: DUMP 'EM.

THE FINAL GUN

Mangini's optimism about returning in 2009 may have stemmed from a belief that his bosom buddy Tannenbaum would go to bat for him if push came to shove. And when Johnson met the media minutes after the coach's press conference, it appeared that the chances of push coming to shove had grown considerably.

When asked what his "gut feeling" was regarding his decision about Mangini, Johnson said, "We're gonna look at that. I'm gonna get my guys together after this and we'll go through everything."

He was visibly upset, and how could you blame him? He had spent $140 million to overhaul the team, and then added Favre. And by Thanksgiving had the town fantasizing about a Subway Super Bowl. "It's really frustrating, really frustrating," Johnson said. "[I'm] disappointed in the season. We have a lot of talent, [and I'm] unhappy with what turned out in the end. I hate to disappoint the fans; really, I feel badly for them. They deserved more and we wanted to give them more. It just didn't happen for us."

A little more than five months later, I asked Johnson what he was thinking when the Miami game ended. "At that point," he said, "it just seemed like a total collapse. Which it was—it was a total collapse."

Did you know in the locker room that you were firing Mangini? "No, not at that point."

When did that happen? "That happened later."

When the Jets sent out the following e-mail, under cover of darkness, there was no more guessing—Mangini was being shoved:

> From: Speight, Bruce
> Subject: Monday Availability
> Sent: Dec 29, 2008 2:44 am
> 10 am—Mr. Johnson and Mike Tannenbaum for season end—Time not determined yet for Coach and players

Johnson and Tannenbaum had met in Manhattan for an hour or so after the game to decide Mangini's fate. "We let the emotion subside somewhat to make sure we were clearheaded about it," Johnson recalled. Tannenbaum, back at work early on Monday morning, telephoned Mangini. "Woody and I need to see you," Tannenbaum told him.

Mangini knew right then and there it was over. He waited for the owner and the general manager in his office. The three of them sat at a round table. "Thank you for everything," Johnson said, "but we just feel like it's time that we go in a different direction."

What did Mangini say?

"He said that he's had a lot of difficult conversations at this very table when we had to cut other players," Tannenbaum said. "He understands how hard it is to do that."

What did Tannenbaum say to his friend?

"Not much . . . I was trying to keep my composure," he said. "I just said, 'Hey, I think the world of you; you did a great job here. Sometimes, these things work out best for everybody.'"

Mangini was gracious. "He understood that it's part of the business," Tannenbaum said.

It made it easier on Tannenbaum. But only slightly. "As a human being, you feel really terrible," Tannenbaum said. "I remember [ESPN's] Peter Gammons saying something on his Hall of Fame speech when he was inducted into Cooperstown, he said, 'As a professional, you learn to tolerate everybody and deal with everybody. As a human being, you're allowed to like people as well.'"

A little more than two hours later, Johnson and Tannenbaum sat side by side at a podium in the tiny press room inside the Florham Park facility. "I don't think it was one thing," Johnson said. "It was just Mike's and my judgment that we had to go in a different direction. It's a call that we made and hopefully it's correct."

Neither offered a specific reason for why Mangini was no longer their Boy Wonder, the Next Belichick. Johnson, in fact, admitted that he had mulled a contract extension for Mangini, who had one year left on his contract, when the Jets were 8–3.

"He did a great job for us for three years and he helped lay a great foundation," Tannenbaum said. "We felt, in our judgment, we want to build on that and go in a different direction."

Now, on June 9, 2009, inside the Atlantic Health Jets Training Center, it was time for the owner to come clean. "It just looked to me like the team . . . it was not as enjoyable as it should be to be a professional athlete at the New York Jets," Johnson said.

I asked him why that was. "The head coach is responsible for setting the tone. It's a tonal thing," Johnson said. "He was a total X and O guy, brilliant person, Wesleyan graduate, very, very smart . . . took the sport very, very seriously. But from this team's standpoint, there was just something missing, and it was more or less something that you get later . . . it was a relationship with the players that they needed that wasn't there."

Mangini's relationship with the players? "It was just the way the whole football enterprise felt," Johnson said. "In other words, you can go . . . you move faster when you're confident and you're having fun than you do if you're not confident and you don't know what the hell you're doing."

So, in other words, there was no joy in Jetsville. "I just felt that there wasn't the esprit de corps . . . and nobody told me that. That's just what you could see," Johnson said.

And even if Favre and the Jets had beaten Pennington, that would not have guaranteed Mangini's return. Even with a turnaround from 4-12 to 10-6, Mangini would have had no better than a fifty-fifty chance to avoid the firing squad because Johnson had abandoned the idea that Mangini could be the Next Belichick and get him to a Super Bowl.

Mangini told the players he had let them down and released the following statement:

> I appreciate the opportunity that Woody and Mike gave me for the past three years as the head coach of the New York Jets. The organization has terrific people and I wish the Jets nothing but success. The time and effort invested by the coaches and players was tremendous and I value that beyond words.
>
> We worked hard to achieve two winning seasons out of the past three.
>
> I regret that we could not reach our goals for this year. I will always appreciate the passion and support of the fans as our focus was trying to build them a championship-caliber foundation and team.

"We were always under the impression that [Mangini] had a lot of control over everything from top to bottom," said tight end Chris Baker, a Jet from 2002 to 2008 before signing with the Patriots during the offseason. "I didn't really realize how much things were different than what they really were. I think a lot of guys were surprised."

Johnson and Tannenbaum promised a "thorough" search that would be all-encompassing. "We're going to look at each individual, whether it's a first-time coach or a veteran coach," Johnson said.

But it sure sounded as if the next coach would have Favre foisted on him for 2009. Asked if he wanted Favre back, Johnson said, "I hope so. I just think he adds a lot to the team that is positive."

But the Jets would soon be getting the idea that they had seen the last of Brett Favre.

Favre and Tannenbaum met in the general manager's office later that morning. "Brett," Tannenbaum began, "I couldn't thank you enough for what you've done. You're a better person than you are a player. I don't know what the future holds, but we are so lucky that you were a member of this organization for the time you've been here. Right now we don't want an answer, so let's not even deal with it."

"That's great," Favre said. "I just want to drive home, be like the Clampetts."

"I knew he didn't want to come back to New York," said Baker. "He's from Mississippi, he was in Green Bay . . . it's just a different atmosphere. He already has the spotlight on him, but it's like so intense here. I didn't think he would come back to the Jets. Once the Jets released him, I knew he was going to Minnesota. He wants to play Green Bay. And that's any player. Obviously I want to play the Jets. You want to play a team that says, 'Okay, well, you can't do this,' especially in his case, he played there for so long. He wants to beat them, he wants to have a chance to win. Minnesota now is built to win. And also they can be like a little anonymous in the grand scheme of things 'cause it's in Minnesota as opposed to being in New York. And also Mangini being fired and all that, it was just too much going on for him. . . . He wants to be in more of a remote setting even though Jersey's kinda remote. I just didn't feel New York was like where he wanted to be."

Before heading back to Mississippi, Favre had an MRI that Tuesday, which revealed a torn biceps tendon and some calcification in the area, but he would need only arthroscopic surgery to repair it. It was reported that he had undergone an MRI earlier in the season—it came back negative—when he complained of pain.

"We knew his arm was hurting," said Baker. "It was mid-to-late November . . . or it may have been early December. We knew it was hurt . . . we knew he had done something to his arm, 'cause we were practicing, he went to throw it, and he grabbed his arm. You could tell he was in pain. . . . I think they were trying to get the bicep tendon to tear naturally."

"I'd watch it on tape sometimes," Woody said. "He'd make a throw, then clutch his arm. I've seen it happen more than once. As the season wore on, you could just tell his arm was just slowly declining."

Over the final five weeks of the season, Favre threw forty-three times against the Broncos, thirty-one times against the 49ers, thirty times against the Bills, thirty-one times against the Seahawks, and forty times against the Dolphins. Only twice in the first eleven games (Kansas City, forty-two; San Diego, forty) had Favre thrown forty or more passes. No one clamored for Favre to sit at the time. Favre had made a career out of toughing it out through a myriad of ailments, often successfully. And Mangini and the Jets clearly didn't trust Clemens with the season on the line. And don't forget this: the owner and the GM wanted Favre back for a second season. And this: no matter what he said, Favre didn't want his streak to end.

Did the players think Favre should have been rested to let Clemens make a start? "It wasn't that. . . . It was more, 'Why have him throw the ball forty times?'" Baker said. "The last game of the year, we threw the ball forty times. Why? It was a close game. It's not like you're coming from behind or anything like that. We have a running game. That was more the frustration. Like 'let's lean on the running game'. . . 'cause all the interceptions he was throwing, he was trying to throw the ball forty yards down the field. And it's like, rely on your running game and go from there . . . let him throw the ball fifteen, twenty times and we can win like that. . . . I just think they should have managed him better. That was a lot of guys' thinking, especially myself. We had a good enough running game, we had a good enough offensive line—let him make the short throws like we were doing before and run the ball."

The owner, for his part, swore he never noticed even a subtle difference in Favre's fastball during practices. When Favre threw. "It was coming in same as it always was," Johnson said.

Asked five months after the season whether he thought Favre should have been sat down, if only for one week, Johnson was adamant that he defers to the head coach on such matters. "If the quarterback is part of the problem, you've gotta look at options," Johnson said. "I don't know if we ever had a moment where we were saying, 'Pull this quarterback.' I never had that conversation."

Even though Favre's fastball was on a strict pitch count in practice, his teammates clung to the romantic notion of the old gunslinger warming to the Sunday gunfight at the Not-So-Okay Corral. "We felt like he was always capable of making that play," Woody said.

Down in Miami, Sparano announced after practice in front of the team that Pennington had won his second Comeback Player of the Year award. The first time he won it was 2006, when he took a rookie head coach named Eric Mangini to the playoffs. "I think it's a reflection upon this organization and upon my teammates, I really do," Pennington said. "This could've easily been an awkward situation with a new guy coming in the day of the first preseason game. It could've been an awkward situation, it could've been a situation where there could've been sides chosen, things like that. These guys in this locker room, they wanted no part of that. They just wanted whoever to come in and help them win. It's been a blessing; I've been blessed to have great teammates, to have great coaches, and to be in a good situation. I'm just really thankful for it."

Pennington is not one to say these things because they are politically correct. He says them because he means them. "It's a special time for me, especially when you've gone through a lot of different challenges, physically and mentally and emotionally," he said. "To be rewarded like that, that's why I want it to be a team award because without my guys in the locker room, it just doesn't happen. It's been a great situation for me."

In classic Pennington style, when asked his secret for winning the award twice, he joked, "Get hurt the following year and then come back."

The collapse ignited an unsavory open season on Favre. Jones was interviewed by host Angie Martinez on New York's Hot 97 FM radio station right before New Year's.

"We're a team and we win together . . . but at the same time, you can't turn the ball over and expect to win," Jones said.

"The other day, the three interceptions really hurt us. I mean, that's just reality. If I were to sit here and say, 'Oh, man, it's okay,' that's not reality. . . . . I don't like it, I know everybody else on the team doesn't like it.

"If somebody is not playing well, they need to come out of the game.

"You're jeopardizing the whole team because you're having a bad day. To me, that's not fair to everybody else. You're not the only one on the team. So when you get to the wire and somebody is just giving the game up, I mean, it's just not [fair]."

Newsday quoted an anonymous Jet who described Favre as a "distant" teammate who often spent his downtime in Florham Park in his own private office. "There was a lot of resentment in the room about him," Deep Jet said. "He never socialized with us, never went to dinner with anyone."

These complaints came on the heels of a get-with-the-program edict from Rhodes the day Mangini was axed. "If he's dedicated and he wants to come back and do this, and do it the right way . . . and be here when we're here in training camp and the minicamps and working out with us . . . then I'm fine with it," Rhodes said. "But don't come back if it's going to be halfhearted or he doesn't want to put the time in with us."

And there was this anonymous quote in the *Newark Star-Ledger*, from a player asked about the offense's crippling struggles: "It's the quarterback throwing the ball all over the place. And he didn't suffer any repercussions. He kept doing it. People said Eric called him out in meetings. I didn't see it. Eric treated him like he was Brett Favre. A lot of guys didn't like it."

Some guys understood. "Think about it: Brett's older than Mangini," Woody said. "That's a hard situation to manage right there. What can you say to Brett Favre really? The guy's one of the most recognizable athletes in the world. It's hard for a head coach, especially a young head coach." Mangini never chewed out Favre in team meetings; he instead tried to walk the tightrope of making everyone, including the Hall of Fame quarterback, accountable.

"Eric always made a point [that] nobody is above the team," Woody said. "He always pointed plays out—whether it was Brett, myself, Alan [Faneca]—plays we could have done better."

Did Mangini treat Favre differently? "I think a little bit, but with Eric, he changed a lot, he won a lot of guys over this past year by showing more of a human side . . . he treated him a little bit different, but he was older than Eric," Baker said. "That wouldn't bother me only because he's on a different level, he's accomplished a lot of things that most of the guys in the locker room hadn't accomplished and things like that. And it wasn't blatant, like, 'Okay, well, Brett, you don't have to practice, you don't have to do this, or you can come late to meetings.' It wasn't something like that, but he's on a different plane than most of the people in the locker room, so some things like that you can understand, you can live with it, it's not a big deal."

Baker added: "I know guys were mad about the way he played down the stretch. . . . He's on a different playing field. You have to understand, like, if you're the Washington Wizards and they bring Michael Jordan in, well, guess what? He's gonna have some perks that maybe you don't have."

The club recoiled in horror when Jones's hatchet job on Favre was plastered on the back page of the *New York Daily News*. Jones appeared the next day on ESPN2's *First Take* and backpedaled furiously.

"I've got the utmost respect for Brett," he said. "He's one of the best quarterbacks of all time. He's a great teammate, you know, he brought a lot to our team this year. I didn't go up there [to] participate in Brett Favre questions. So when she asked me the question about the interceptions, I answered it as far as how I felt from the game, the Miami game."

"I have not seen the comments," Favre told longtime pal Al Jones of the *Biloxi Sun-Herald*. "To be honest, I am not worried about the comments either. Was Thomas backed into a corner or in a bad mood when he said those things? I don't know, but ripping Thomas is not my nature. The bottom line is I didn't play well in the final five games. It starts with me and it should. My expectations of myself are high and the only one that I let down was myself."

As for the criticism that he was unsociable, Favre said, "I am not going to let one or two guys ruin a career for me or the relationship I had with my teammates. If you poll my past teammates, I bet ninety percent would say they enjoyed playing with me. I am not so insecure as to let the comments bother me."

Baker concurred: "He had a good relationship with everybody. People were saying stuff like, 'Oh, well, he doesn't hang out with the guys.' I mean, he's almost forty years old—he's not gonna go to a local bar and hang out with guys. I think guys that were saying things like that, I don't know what their problem was, but I think it's selfish or whatever to try to throw him under the bus. He was older than most of the coaching staff. He's gonna live a different lifestyle. He has his family and things like that. He's set in his ways as far as practice habits and things like that. He was a good guy to everybody. He didn't make it where it was like, 'Oh, he's trying to be better than everybody else.'"

In other words, he tried to fit in. "Exactly," Baker said. "He tried to fit in. Obviously, he would need certain things. Like we go on the road, he had to have somebody with him, because he's gonna get swamped by people."

Woody took issue with the characterization of Favre as distant. "I think that's the furthest thing from the truth," Woody said. "He was always in the locker room, he was always joking with guys. Brett was always doing something silly, especially at practice. All the pictures you see of Brett on game day, whether in Green Bay or here, acting like a little kid, that's the way he was every day." Woody considered Favre a breath of fresh air. "I think the one thing he did that was invaluable was the looseness that he brought to the facility on an everyday basis," Woody said. "You can't overstate that. I think the main thing I took away from the whole Brett Favre experience was that fact of him taking the stuffiness out of the building and letting guys breathe—even coaches."

Then there was former Mike Tyson trainer Teddy Atlas, who helped Mangini pick out fight tapes to motivate his team before games and came out punching when his friend was let go. "I think Brett Favre basically is a selfish guy," Atlas said. "Brett Favre goes out there with his gray hair, his Wranglers, and gets up when he gets hit. I understand why people like that. But there's another side. He's a selfish guy."

Fireman Ed poured water on Mangini. "Look at him on the sideline—the guy's got no emotion," he said. "He chews that gum . . . he's pathetic! You get away with that when you're Belichick—you got three rings. What's this guy done?"

In Fireman Ed's opinion, Mangini ruined the Jets defense by stripping it of aggressiveness. "He makes his players think so much, like they're on the offensive end of the ball," he said. "They went out and got the guys he wanted to get. What did he do with Calvin Pace? This guy is a stud. They got him covering tight ends, they got him covering running backs! Are you kiddin' me? You gotta be kiddin' me!"

But Fireman Ed retained a blind spot for Favre. He was reminded of the quarterback's nine interceptions over the last five games. "Three or four of 'em weren't his fault. Did we lose the games because of him? I would say we lost a couple of games, not four of 'em. No way."

His ire turned back to Johnson for being out of the country when Cowher was mulling a return to the sidelines, even if it was the longest of long shots. The owner, however, wasn't interested in a high-priced coach who wasn't interested enough to wait a few days for the owner to return.

Fireman Ed was certain Favre was not washed up and wanted him back. "Do I think he was hurt? Yeah I do," he said. "I'll tell you the play he got hurt. He got hurt in the Cincinnati game. That linebacker [actually defensive end Jonathan Fanene] came up and nailed him. But he's a tough guy. He plays through it. He don't blame nobody. Did you see Coles and Cotchery get separation? I mean, come on! Those guys are second receivers, third receivers. Yeah, I'd love him back. Do I think he's comin' back? If I was him, I wouldn't come back."

Would the 2008 Jets have made the playoffs with Pennington? "We had more talent than Miami last year," Baker said. "Offensive talent, defensive talent. I'll let you be the judge of that. The thing is . . . I think Brett would have led us there if he didn't get hurt."

Pennington's four-interception nightmare in a 27–9 wild-card loss to the Ravens only reaffirmed what Fireman Ed had believed all along. "Chad showed what he is," Fireman Ed said. "Chad takes you to just where he is now and that's it. He ain't gonna take you to a world championship. We've been there, done that. Great guy. Love him. Great teammate. You know what? When he hurt his shoulder the second time, it was over. You wanna keep drives alive, you gotta make that out pass."

In Green Bay, meanwhile, McCarthy accepted blame for the Packers' 6–10 season, but in his mind the decision to turn to Rodgers was vindicated. "I think we definitely made the right move at the quarterback position," McCarthy said. "I was pleased with the productivity from the quarterback position. From an individual standpoint, I think Aaron Rodgers played at a very steady, steady level—which was a high level, based on his statistics. He's given us a baseline, a standard that we'll hold him to." That standard: 4,038 passing yards, 28 touchdowns, 13 interceptions, and the first hints of the toughness— he played on despite a sprained throwing shoulder that would not need postseason surgery—and leadership that defined the Favre Era. "I played well in stretches and I didn't play well at times," Rodgers said. Asked whether he had stepped out of Favre's shadow, he paused and said, "No." Asked if he thinks he ever will: "Not to some people. But I'll be honest, I don't worry about that stuff. You can maybe ask some of the fans. I don't know."

The Dolphins? They had a thirty-two-year-old quarterback who, through the force of his personality and charisma, had helped change the culture in Shulaville. Who finished second in the MVP voting to Peyton Manning. Who actually believed he had a chance to get to his first Super Bowl—until Ed Reed intercepted two of his passes, one of which he returned 64 yards for a touchdown.

Someone asked Pennington how he would rate his season after the Ravens disaster. "I play to win," he said. "When it ends like this, it's difficult to deal with right now."

He bled mostly for his team and teammates. "It could have easily been an awkward situation when things happened on August the eighth. . . . It's been magical; it has . . . that's why it hurts even worse, 'cause I really wanted to keep this thing going, and to really do some not good things, but great things."

Only days after the Dolphins' season ended, Pennington consented to a morning conference call with New York–area reporters he knew well. He allowed that, in his mind, the beginning of the end of his Jets days came when Mangini benched him for Clemens during that horrific 2007 season. "Regardless of who was brought in to replace me, I just felt like my time was up," Pennington said. "I'd had those feelings way before this year's training camp. I'd felt that ever since I was replaced in the 2007 season."

And how could he not have those feelings? Clemens was drafted by Tannenbaum and Mangini. If Clemens had been the goods, he would have been named the starter heading into 2008 training camp, and Favre wouldn't have been a Jet. Perhaps Pennington wouldn't have been a Jet either. "At the end of the day, the organization didn't feel that Chad Pennington could get them where they wanted to go," Pennington said.

And maybe, just maybe, Favre could, and sell some PSLs even if he couldn't. "This is a game, but it's a huge business," Pennington said. "Business decisions are made regardless of what happens within the white lines sometimes. You have to keep it in perspective to understand it."

There had been no uproar when Tannenbaum released Pennington, but it's difficult to imagine the Cutthroat Bros, Parcells and Belichick, for instance, simply rewarding a player for eight years of service without demanding assets in return. Then again, no one was knocking down Tannenbaum's door. "I was actually very grateful they allowed me to be a free agent," Pennington said. "I don't think a lot of organizations would have done that for a player."

Bottom line: if Tannenbaum, for one second, thought that Pennington could have been a threat, even in his division, he would not have been so gracious and accommodating. No one in and around the Jets believed that Pennington had another Comeback of the Year season in him. "That whole situation, I think they just got blinded by the fact, 'Let's get Brett,'" Baker said. So if you didn't think the ghosts that have been haunting the franchise since January 12, 1969, hadn't moved from Weeb Ewbank Hall and taken up residence in Florham Park, here was more evidence for you.

There were rumblings, only after Mangini was fired, that Favre had been forced upon him, but no one held a gun to his head and forced him to make that eleventh-hour recruiting pitch to Favre from Florham Park. "To me, the situation boiled down to who Coach

Mangini wanted to lead his team," Pennington said. "One thing he knew was he did not want Chad Pennington to lead his team." Sure, Mangini would have to revamp the playbook and integrate a legend, but wasn't Schottenheimer supposed to be a Boy Wonder? And hadn't Mangini just gone 4–12 with Pennington/Clemens? And he and Tannenbaum were friends—their children would frolic on the practice field after summer practices—making it inconceivable that this general manager would betray this head coach. "It was a collective effort," Pennington said.

Did Mangini want Favre? "The way they built the team last year was custom fit for Chad—strong running game, they brought in the linemen we needed to have a strong line, play action, you had a couple of good tight ends, not great receivers but good receivers. I think they built the team to make the pass work off the run," Baker said. "A ball control . . . and that's what Chad obviously does, and that's what he did in Miami. So I think he was ready for that. Bringing in Brett, you know Brett's a gunslinger and all that kind of stuff . . . knowing Eric and the type of team he wanted to build, I can imagine that wasn't his first. . . . I think he wanted to keep the guys he had and kinda just play ball control and play defense. But you wouldn't be able to tell. He embraced Brett the day he walked in, so you wouldn't be able to tell if he did or if he didn't."

While Johnson and Tannenbaum prolonged the process of interviewing candidates for the vacant head coaching job—forlorn Jets fans were becoming convinced that Kotite would yet emerge as a mystery candidate—Mangini was hired by the Browns to succeed Romeo Crennel. "I'm happy for him he has another opportunity," Pennington said. "I'm positive he'll do some really good things in Cleveland and learn from the experience he had in New York."

They made a heckuva team in 2006, the Comeback Kid and Mangenius. Then Mangini whacked Pennington, and Pennington whacked Mangini one day before Johnson and Tannenbaum did. "Nothing in this league surprises me," Pennington said. "I certainly believe it's not all of his fault, just like last year wasn't all of my fault."

Within thirty minutes of the Ravens' AFC Championship game loss to the Steelers, Jets officials were leaking word that Ravens defensive coordinator Rex Ryan was getting the job—a popular choice to Jets Nation. Ryan was introduced at a 10 a.m. press conference in the auditorium at the Jets facility on the following Wednesday.

Ryan's braggadocio—he promised to be shaking the new president's hand before the end of his first term—won over the crowd in the Jets auditorium, a crowd that included Cotchery, Revis, Harris on crutches, and Clemens. Did he want Favre back? "Brett Favre is a tremendous player," Ryan said. "I got whiplash coaching against him, watching him go up and down the field. I know the kind of talent he has and the kind of competitor he is. I think anybody would want a player like that on his team." Of course, what did you expect him to say? It's one thing for yours truly to write a column the previous day urging the rookie coach to sack Favre as his first order of business, quite another for the rookie coach to tell a Hall of Fame icon thanks but no thanks with his new owner, visions of PSL monies dancing in his head, gripped by Favrelust sitting on the dais to his left.

The Jets wanted an answer from Favre before the free agency period would begin February 27. Ryan gave Favre his space and never telephoned him. "We had a couple of conversations along the way saying that he was really having second thoughts," Tannenbaum said. R-Day—Retirement Day—arrived on the morning of February 11. Cook called Tannenbaum.

"You gotta speak to Brett right away," Cook said. "He's really in a good place with everything."

It was 8:30 a.m.

"Mike, I am done," Favre said. He thanked Tannenbaum for everything.

"Brett, we're lucky that we had you," Tannenbaum said.

Johnson told Favre the same thing in their conversation.

"The farm is always open anytime you come through," Johnson told Favre. "I understand Green Bay's your team, but know this is your team too."

The Jets talked with Favre about a formal retirement announcement. He declined. "I've already done that once," he said.

"We behaved in a way to make it a long-term relationship knowing that it could very well be a short-term relationship," Higgins said.

Favre had sent ESPN's Ed Werder a late-night e-mail revealing that he had instructed Cook to inform the Jets that he was indeed retiring. "And wanted time to have that conversation before anything was reported about it," Werder said on ESPN Radio. Werder, honoring the request, made sure the conversation had taken place; the scoop—shared with Mortensen—was posted on ESPN. com at 9:29 a.m. Werder was on *Mike & Mike* on ESPN Radio at 9:20 a.m. while Mortensen was on *SportsCenter*.

"Mike and Woody, as well as the entire organization, have been nothing short of outstanding," Favre said in the e-mail. "My teammates—Thomas and Kerry included—were a pleasure to play with. My time with the Jets was short, but I'm honored to be given that chance."

The Jets Store immediately slashed the price of its authentic Favre jersey in half, to $110.

Pundits debated whether Favre meant it this time, or was scheming to win his release from the Jets and join the Vikings to stick it to the Packers.

Favre conducted a farewell teleconference call at 6 p.m. from his Mississippi home that was aired live on ESPN News. His voice didn't crack the way it did at his weepy Green Bay farewell press conference. He sounded very much like all the other thirty-nine-year-old broken-down warhorses who were forced to confront the end of their athletic immortality.

"Physically, for the most part I feel the same, aside from the most important thing, and that's my throwing shoulder," Favre said. "Progressively, it got worse throughout the year. Other than that, I can't complain. I'm very thankful and blessed that I withstood so much for so long, and I guess it was a matter of time before something broke down and it happened to be, for a quarterback, the most important thing, and that is his throwing shoulder. Obviously, it's something that I was able to play with. I don't think I was nearly as productive as the season progressed, but that very well could be fine next year, and I'm well aware of that. Then again, it could linger and bother me throughout the year, and I just felt like it was time. I think to me, that more than anything was a wake-up call." In other words, he recognized that he could no longer be Brett Favre. "I just said, you know what, okay, I finally can't throw the ball like I once threw it and that probably more than anything is what is telling to me," he said. The Graybeard Who Cried Wolf assured skeptics—and even family and friends—that his decision was final. "It's been a wonderful career," he said. "I couldn't ask for anything more. It was worth a shot for me to go to New York. I wish I could have played better down the stretch. I didn't and it's time to leave." He said he didn't ask for his release, meaning he remained Jets property, temporarily soothing the conspiracy theorists. "It all comes down to physically how I feel," Favre reiterated. "Once again, that could change, based on arthroscopic surgery or whatever, but I'm not willing to do that, and I'm not willing to take that chance, and that more than anything is why I'm retiring."

Favre appreciated that the Jets didn't press him for a decision, the way the Packers had a year earlier, and he reciprocated by allowing them to move forward with the offseason contingency plan they had prepared for Life without Jet Favre. "I just felt like it's time for them to move on," Favre said. "Even though they didn't ask for an answer, I just felt like it was time, in fairness to them, to let them pursue what they're going to do." But what if Favre had that itch again, and were to ask for his release before the start of the 2009 season? He swore he wouldn't put the Jets in that predicament. Said Tannenbaum, "I can only take him at face value."

Those who believed he had tarnished his legacy were dead wrong. He tried to take a Little Engine That Couldn't of a franchise back to the future. He gave his all. His all, after eighteen seasons, after 269 straight starts, wasn't enough. There is no shame in that. He didn't embarrass himself. Besides, Willie Mays isn't remembered as the floundering, fortysomething Mets outfielder who wouldn't read the handwriting on the centerfield wall; he is remembered for his 1954 World Series catch on Vic Wertz and all the basket catches and stolen bases and caps flying off his head and the home runs. "I honestly believe that it was more of a positive than a negative," Favre said.

Ted Thompson? "He had his reasons, I had my reasons," Favre said. "Who is to say who is right or who is wrong? He has a plan. I'm not mad at him for that. Other people may be, but I don't know. It's a touchy situation. I know that my stay in Green Bay was unbelievable and nothing can take that away. Not one person. That organization has been outstanding to me throughout my career. It is what it is. It's unfortunate, but, at some point, it will be dealt with." When will his No. 4 be retired? "I hadn't even thought about it," Favre said. "For the teammates that I played with in Green Bay and for the fans, nothing has changed from day one. It's a shame what has unfolded throughout this whole thing. I don't know. I don't have an answer for that right now. It may be five years, it may be the first game." Regret Favre? Not a chance. "I thought the fans were great," he said. "Did I ever feel like it was home? Probably not, because of all the years I'd spent in Green Bay. But I truly, honestly enjoyed the whole experience. I say that it was everything I thought it would be and then some. I just wish we could have gone a little bit further." Where will he rank among modern-day quarterbacks in history? Top ten for sure. I'll put him at number six for now—behind Montana, Unitas, Elway, Marino, and Brady, for certain, with Peyton Manning nipping at his heels.

"I've had my share of mistakes," Favre said. "I've had my share of lucky breaks. You name it. I wouldn't trade my career for anything."

At the beginning of the next week, equipment manager Gus Granneman asked Tannenbaum if he should take Favre's nameplate down in the locker room.

"Absolutely," Tannenbaum said.

It wasn't long before Cook was asking for Favre's release, the first sign that Favre was getting ready to reserve the right to change his mind again. "Let's see how this spring goes," Tannenbaum told Cook.

Was Tannenbaum surprised or disappointed? "Any player, I would think, would want their options open," he said.

Regret Favre? Not Fireman Ed. "Honestly, I'm glad we had him than never had him," he said. "I have a picture [of Favre] in my bar I'm lookin' at right now. I don't have any regrets whatsoever. The only regret I have is I wish it could work out where we had him for two or three years. If I was him, I would try to have the Jets trade me.

"I'm glad we had him. I'll be at his Hall of Fame induction."

Regret Favre? Not Tannenbaum. "He'll have an enduring legacy regardless of what happens in the future," he said.

Would he do it again?

"Absolutely," Tannenbaum said. "It's an art, not a science, building a football team, and I think if Erik Ainge or Leon Washington, or all the other young players he touched while he was here, are better pros because of what they saw in Brett, five years from now it's worth it . . . it's like what Curtis Martin did for Keyshawn Johnson in 1998, if he made Keyshawn Johnson a much better pro. Curtis Martin filled a role that had nothing to do with playing running back. And I think Brett brought a lot of those things to our organization as well."

Was Favre worth it? Yes he was. He cost the Jets a third-round draft choice. The gambit failed, but I can't fault the Jets for daring to be great.

It's just that in the NFL, life doesn't begin at almost forty.

At 6:34 p.m., precisely when Favre was concluding the call—seemingly his Last Call—Tratner sent out the following release:

> Brett Favre Placed on Reserve/Retired List
> **Feb. 11, 2009**—The New York Jets have placed QB Brett Favre on the Reserve/Retired list. The announcement was made by Jets General Manager Mike Tannenbaum.
> **J-E-T-S.**

Tannenbaum had one last trick up his sleeve. Stealing the show at the 2009 NFL Draft, Tannenbaum, with help from none other than Mangini, orchestrated a blockbuster trade that netted him his new franchise quarterback, USC's charismatic Mark Sanchez. Mangini agreed to give Tannenbaum the fifth overall pick of the draft in exchange for Tannenbaum's seventeenth pick, a second-round choice, and three players—Brett Ratliff, Abram Elam, and Kenyon Coleman.

Two days later, Sanchez was cheered as he threw out the first pitch before a Mets game against the Marlins at brand-spanking-new Citi Field. Three days later, Sanchez' new No. 6 jersey went on sale in Manhattan.

The drafting of Sanchez made everybody happy: the Jets were able to release Favre that night and clear his $13 million from the 2009 books, and Favre was granted his freedom to flirt with the Vikings.

"Nobody I've ever seen—especially a thirty-nine-year-old—had as much fun playing the game of football as Brett Favre," Clemens said.

Index